REFERENCE BOOKS
IN INTERNATIONAL EDUCATION
VOL. 26

RUSSIAN EDUCATION

GARLAND REFERENCE LIBRARY
OF SOCIAL SCIENCE
VOL. 906

RUSSIAN EDUCATION

Tradition and Transition

Brian Holmes
Gerald H. Read
Natalya Voskresenskaya

GARLAND PUBLISHING, INC.
New York & London / 1995

Library of Congress Cataloging-in-Publication Data

Holmes, Brian.
Russian education : tradition and transition /Brian Holmes, Gerald H. Read, and Natalya Voskresenskaya
p. cm. — (Garland reference library of social science ; vol. 906. Reference books in international education ; vol. 26)
Includes bibliographical references and index.
ISBN 0-8153-1169-9 (alk. paper)
1. Education and state—Soviet Union. 2. Education—Russia. I. Read, Gerald H. II. Voskresenskaya, Natalya. III. Title. IV. Series: Garland reference library of social science ; v. 906. V. Series: Garland reference library of social science. Reference books in international education ; vol. 26.
LC116.S68H65 1995
370'.947—dc20 94-8442
CIP

Printed on acid-free, 250-year-life paper
Manufactured in the United States of America

In memory of our colleague Brian Holmes

Contents

Series Editor's Foreword

This series of scholarly works in comparative and international education has grown well beyond the initial conception of a collection of reference books. Although retaining its original purpose of providing a resource to scholars, students, and a variety of other professionals who need to understand the role played by education in various societies or regions of the world, it also strives to provide up-to-date information on a wide variety of selected educational issues, problems, and experiments within an international context.

Contributors to this series are well-known scholars who have devoted their professional lives to the study of their specialization. Without exception these men and women possess an intimate understanding of the subject of their research and writing. Without exception they have not only studied their subject in dusty archives, but they have also lived and travelled widely in their quest for knowledge. In short, they are "experts" in the best sense of that often overused word.

In our increasingly interdependent world, it is now widely understood that it is a matter of survival that we not only understand better what makes other societies tick, but that we also make a serious effort to understand how others, be they Japanese, German, or Chilean, attempt to solve the same kinds of educational problems that we face in North America. As the late George Z.F. Bereday wrote: "[E]ducation is a mirror held against the face of a people. Nations may put on blustering shows of strength to conceal public weakness, erect grand façades to conceal shabby backyards, and profess peace while secretly arming for conquest, but how they take care of their children tells unerringly who they are" (*Comparative Methods in Education*, New York: Holt, Rinehart & Winston, 1964, p. 5).

Perhaps equally important, however, is the valuable perspective that studying another education system (or its problems) provides us in understanding our own system (or its problems). To step outside of our own limited experience and our commonly held assumptions about schools and learning in order to look back at our system in contrast to another places it in a very different light. To learn, for example, how the Soviet Union or Belgium handles the education of a multilingual society; how the French provide for the funding of public education; or how the Japanese control admissions into their universities enables us to understand that there are alternatives to our own familiar way of doing things. Not that we can often "borrow" directly from other societies; indeed, educational arrangements are inevitably a reflection of deeply rooted political, economic, and cultural factors that are unique to a society. But a conscious recognition that there are other ways of doing things can serve to open our minds and provoke our imaginations in ways that can result in new approaches that we would not have otherwise considered.

Since this series is intended to be a useful research tool, the editor and contributors welcome suggestions for future volumes as well as ways in which this series can be improved.

Edward R. Beauchamp
University of Hawaii

Preface

The development and imposition of communism in Russia in 1917 and its systematic pursuit for the next seventy years marked one of the biggest aberrations of the twentieth century. The dynamics that were set in motion affected a great many societies throughout the world and resulted in substantial and fundamental economic, political, cultural, and educational transformations. Soviet educators, in their commitment to mold the minds of Soviet youth, regarded organized education with a seriousness that far surpassed that of the leaders of the free societies. As this book shows, before any basic systemic and revolutionary transformations could be achieved in Soviet education in the 1980s, communism in its central doctrines, purposes, and practices had to be repudiated. As Gorbachev painfully learned, this meant nothing less than the repudiation of Marx, Engels, Lenin, and Marxism-Leninism.

This book is a record of one of the great achievements of the Soviet Union—its mass educational system. It is written in the belief that the lessons learned from the Communist Party's commitment to educate all Soviet youth are still important today, to the citizens of both Russia and other nations. It presents an assessment of the Soviet educational ideals and aspirations, school reforms, and the pedagogical system which, for the most part, in those days received the support of the populace. Although the Soviet system depended on power, patronage, fear, and intrigue for ensuring compliance, it also functioned through the willingness of the masses to contribute years of their lives in the unrelenting toil of carrying out the many tasks that had to be performed in a modern society. The communist ideal was accepted and believed by many Soviets even after it was revealed to be just a myth. The myth came crashing to earth in 1991 as a result of many intricate forces and personalities, not the least being Mikhail Gorbachev's declaration of "*perestroika* and *glasnost*"

Russian Education: Tradition and Transition is a book that examines and analyzes the basic features of Soviet and Russian education as well as details of some of the special aspects of its institutions and processes through the eyes of three persons uniquely fitted for this analysis. The contributors are two outsiders and one insider, each from a different country and with totally different contributions to the book.

Brian Holmes is an English educator best known for his penetrating and sometimes skeptical analyses of the philosophical, social, political, and economic interactions within the education space and the consequences that follow implementation of reforms. He was the foremost comparative educator of his age. As professor and chair of Comparative Education at the University of London, he authored and edited more than fifty books, reports, and articles and served as thesis adviser to some one hundred doctoral candidates from all over the world. Brian was fully engaged in writing, analyzing, and editing the manuscript for *Russian Education: Tradition and Transition* at the time of his death in July 1993.

Gerald Howard Read is the second important contributor to this volume. His interest and expertise were recognized in the 1950s by the Fund for the Advancement of Education of the Ford Foundation, which named him codirector, with William W. Brickman, of a team of distinguished American scholars to observe and analyze the strengths and weaknesses of the Soviet educational system. The two-month seminar in the Soviet Union resulted in the publication of *The Changing Soviet School* by George Z. F. Bereday, William W. Brickman, and Gerald Read. This report warned the American public that Soviet education of the masses was one of the great and inescapable realities of the contemporary epoch, one which free people could ignore at their peril.

This was a time when the United States feared communism, believed that the Soviet system was gaining ground in international rivalry, and thought that lessons might be learned from establishing contacts with Soviet educators. Although dissatisfied with their own system of education, American critics and would-be reformers had failed to rigorously examine the realities of institutional schooling, higher education, and lifelong educational processes of the modern world.

Over a period of three decades, 1958–1988, Gerald's seminars to the Soviet Union were sponsored by Phi Delta Kappa, Kappa Delta Pi, Pi Lambda Theta, Delta Kappa Gamma, the Comparative and International Education Society, the Association for Supervision and Curriculum Development, the National Council for the Social Studies, and many universities. On the Soviet side, the seminars were arranged by the USSR Institute of Theory and History of Pedagogy, the USSR Academy of Pedagogical Sciences, and the USSR Trade Union of Education and Scientific Workers. In recognition of Read's many years of building bridges of professional contacts and understanding between Soviet and American educators, the Russian Institute of Theory and History of Education and International Research in Education awarded him, in 1992, the title of Honorary Professor. And, in 1993, the Russian Academy of Education named him Honorary Academician. As Emeritus Endowed Professor of Comparative Education at Kent State University, he continues to pursue an active career.

Natalya Voskresenkaya is the third distinguished author. She experienced the rigors of Soviet education just as the Stalin era was ending. Although raised to be a dedicated Bolshevik, she refused to join the party and suffered, as a result, a derailed career path. She was for many years a researcher at the USSR Academy of Pedagogical Sciences with the special task of analyzing educational criticisms and reform movements in the United States and the United Kingdom. A distinguished linguist and voracious reader of professional books and journals, she has served as interpreter and professional guide to many important scholars inside and outside Russia. It was in this capacity that she met Holmes and Read and thereafter their professional paths frequently crossed. She is a senior research scholar of comparative education at the Russian Academy of Education. When *Russian Education: Tradition and Transition* grew beyond a glint in the eyes of Holmes and Read, they sought a Russian colleague who possessed professional depth and had the confidence to challenge the assessments made by the two outsiders. They also wanted someone who would be able to maintain an objective distance from the official communist rhetoric that was spun by the Soviet scholars. Voskresenskaya was chosen as the best candidate and she was asked to join the two outsiders.

The strong personalities and differing theoretical approaches of the three authors made the task slower than was originally planned. The respective contributions of the three authors can be summarized as follows. Read became the organizer of the project and accumulator of data; Holmes was the conceptualist, evaluator, priority assigner, and writer of many of the draft chapters; and Voskresenskaya was the source of many of the inside stories, tracer of accounts to their roots, and final critic.

It is an honor to introduce this important book. I know, respect, and admire all the authors for their respective contributions to this volume and in a host of other ways. I have known Brian Holmes as a distinguished scholar, perceptive analyst, and generous friend since my studies at the University of London, beginning in 1963. I was a member of Brian's seminar to the USSR in 1968. I have seen his organizational genius in various international gatherings since then, having served with him as a conference organizer.

I have known Gerald Read increasingly well for the same period of time, for he was a frequent visitor and seminar lecturer during my student days at the University of London. I admired his successful seminars to the USSR and envied his ability to establish contacts with leading Soviet educators. His determination to keep politics and education in their correct perspectives made him welcome in many politically forbidden societies, where his initiatives led to rapprochement and recognition of an excluded people. In the long run, his influence has been for understanding and trust. These ideals led Gerald Read, together with William W. Brickman, to found the Comparative Education Society in 1956. These ideals still form his *leitmotif*.

Natalya Voskresenskaya has been my acquaintance and my friend for a very much shorter time. We are collaborating on an internationally funded project of curriculum reform and textbook writing—that of writing a Russian textbook for democratic civic education. She contributed a chapter for each of my editing tasks: *Education and Cultural Perspectives: New Perspectives* (Garland 1992); a review of *Education and Human Rights* for the Comparative and International Education Society's conference in Kingston, Jamaica, in 1993; and a forthcoming assessment of *Education and Human Rights* for the International Bureau of Education. In each of these projects she has defended Russian traditions and ideals while criticizing their shortcomings. Her perspective is international, her expertise is exceptional, and her future is certain to be brighter than her past, which was subject to troublesome constraints.

Douglas Ray, Ph. D.
Professor of Education
The University of Western Ontario
London, Canada

Chronological Guide

November 7	1917	The Party of Bolsheviks proclaimed a dictatorship of the Proletariat and imposed an absolute rule over the former Russian Empire.
November 9	1917	A State Commissariat for Education was established. Lenin assigned to all educational and cultural institutions the task of transforming the course of Russian history, molding the New Soviet Man, and achieving a classless society of universal brotherhood and equality.
November 22	1917	Anatoly Lunacharsky was appointed Commissar of Education.
February 5	1918	A decree was issued by the Council of the People's Commissars mandating the separation of church from state and school from church.
March 23	1918	Lenin founded the State Academic Council on the People's Education with leadership roles given to Nadezda Krupskaya, Stanislav Shatsky, Pavel Blonsky, Alexei Kalashnikov, and Moisey Pistrak.

October 16	1918	The RSFSR People's Commissariat for Education issued a "Declaration" proclaiming all educational institutions from kindergarten through the university to be one common system, one uninterrupted ladder in the service of the Soviet proletariat. Marxism and the "Basic Principles of the Unified Labor School" were imposed on the teaching of all school subjects as well as the moral, cultural, and aesthetic upbringing of children in the USSR.
March 18–23	1919	The Eighth Congress of the Russian Communist Party confirmed the goal of a free, secular, and compulsory general, polytechnical, labor-unified educational system for all Soviet children until the age of seventeen. The Party set the task of transforming the school from an instrument of class domination by the bourgeoisie into an instrument for total elimination of class division of society.
March 17	1921	Lenin initiated the New Economic Policy (NEP).
April 3	1922	The Politburo elected Joseph Stalin the General Secretary of the Central Committee of the Party at its Eleventh Congress.
January 21	1924	The death of Vladimir Ilyich Ulyanov (Lenin). The struggle for power began between Stalin and Trotsky.
December 27	1927	The First Congress of Pedologists was held with physicians, psychologists, physiologists, and pedagogues committed to developing a communist science of the child and education. Trotsky was expelled from the Party and banished to the provinces.

	1928–32	At the November 24, 1918, Plenum of the Central Committee of the Party, Stalin laid out a policy of a complete socialization of industry, trade, finance, health services, and education as well as the collectivization of agriculture. Targets were announced for the First Five-Year Plan calling for a massive training program and greater respect for technicians, specialists, and experts. This set the stage for a five-year-long pedagogical debate as to the need for a new framework for Soviet pedagogical science. In 1929 Lunacharsky was dismissed from his post as the People's Commissar of Education.
August 14	1930	Education through the fourth grade was made compulsory for all Soviet children.
September 5	1931	The Central Committee of the Party issued a resolution "On the Primary and Secondary School," which criticized the progressive school curriculum and called for a return to the traditional disciplines. Albert Pinkevitch confessed to errors in judgment and publicly announced his willingness to campaign against his mistakes in advocating the pedagogical ideas of the 1920s.
August 25	1932	The Central Committee of the Party called for a revision of all courses taught in the primary and secondary schools, strengthening of school discipline, and restoration of the authority of the teacher. Anton S. Makarenko's theories on collective education, developed at the children's colonies, were officially sanctioned by the Party.

November 17	1933	The United States accorded diplomatic recognition to the Soviet Union.
	1935–1955	For two decades Stalin's totalitarianism suppressed free and creative discussion and research. Ideological functionaries of Stalin's "personality cult" issued a steady stream of political documents and resolutions that impacted on educational theory and practice.
September 3	1935	The Council of People's Commissars restored the numerical system of grading that had prevailed during czarist times: (1) very bad, (2) bad, (3) satisfactory, (4) good, (5) excellent.
July 4	1936	The Central Committee of the All-Union Communist Party issued a resolution officially banning pedology, the science of child development, and called for its ongoing criticism. The experiments conducted by pedologists on the development of mental and natural abilities and talents of children were branded pseudo-science. The following year the leadership of the People's Commissariat for Education was denounced and many leading educators were imprisoned.
Summer	1936	The Great Stalinist Constitution proclaimed the right of citizens to an education—a universal, compulsory and free education up to and including the seventh grade and a system of state stipends for students of higher education who excelled in their studies. The separation of the church from the state and school from the church was reaffirmed.
June 27	1941	Germany invaded the Soviet Union.

August 2	1943	The RSFSR People's Commissars published "Roles for Pupils," detailing behavior in and out of school, which all students had to memorize and observe.
June 21	1944	The USSR Council of Ministers instituted a system of special examinations at the end of the fourth, sixth, and tenth grades in the general education schools.
August 14	1945	The surrender of Japan brought an end to World War II. At a meeting of the All-Russian Conference of People's Commissariat for Education, V. P. Potyomkin declared Stalin to be the "Genius and Teacher of the People" and the task of the school was to "instill love of Stalin, the teacher and friend of all children."
October 8–14	1952	The Nineteenth Congress of the Party called for a transition by the year 1955 to universal ten-year secondary schooling for urban boys and girls, polytechnical education at all grade levels, and a curriculum based on scientific principles.
March 5	1953	The death of Stalin. The Politburo elected Georgy Malenkov the First Secretary of the Party's Central Committee.
March 14	1953	Nikita Khrushchev succeeded Malenkov as First Secretary of the Central Committee.
February 14–25	1956	At the Twentieth Congress of the Party, Khrushchev's speech condemning Stalin and the "Personality Cult" became the keystone in the de-Stalinization process.

October 4	1957	The successful launching of *Sputnik* was attributed to the quality of Soviet science, engineering, and education.
October 23	1957	The start of the Hungarian Revolution.
November 12	1958	The Central Committee of the Party proposed new guidelines for Soviet education "On the Strengthening of the Relationship of the School with Life and the Further Development of the System of Public Education in the Country."
December 12	1958	The USSR Supreme Soviet approved the "48 Theses for School Reform" proposed by Khrushchev.
September 15	1959	Khrushchev arrived in the United States on an official visit.
September 19	1960	At the Fifteenth United Nations General Assembly session in New York City, Khrushchev denounced Western colonialism with a temper tantrum, display of shouting, fist-pounding, and banging his shoe on a table.
June 21	1963	At the plenary meeting of the Central Committee of the Party, Khrushchev denounced all economic, Party, government, and education bodies for their irresponsible attitudes in carrying out the 1958 education reforms.
October 14	1964	The Central Committee of the Party accepted Khrushchev's request to retire as General Secretary of the Party and Premier of the USSR.
October 15	1964	The Politburo elected Leonid Brezhnev the First Secretary of the Central Committee of the Party.

November 10	1966	The Twenty-Third Party Congress annulled the Education Reform of 1958, renewed the emphasis on general education, established the USSR Ministry of Education, and upgraded the RSFSR Academy of Pedagogical Sciences to an All-Union body. A Commission of the USSR Academy of Sciences and the USSR Academy of Pedagogical Sciences was appointed to develop new curricula and syllabuses for the ten-year school.
November 7	1967	The Fiftieth Anniversary of the Bolshevik Revolution was observed.
September 8	1970	The ten-year schools were reorganized into three-year primary, five-year junior, and two-year senior sections.
June 20	1971	The Party's Central Committee issued a decree, "On Completing the Transition to Universal Secondary Education of Youth and the Further Development of the General Education School," mandating a gradual transformation of all vocational schools to secondary general-vocational-technical institutions.
September 11	1971	Khrushchev died of a heart attack.
February 24	1976	The Twenty-Fifth Congress of the Party declared that on the sixtieth anniversary of the October Revolution the USSR had reached the stage of "Developed Socialism."
October 7	1977	The New Constitution of the Union of Soviet Socialist Republics was ratified.

December 1	1977	The decree "On the Further Improvement of the Teaching and Upbringing of General Education School Pupils and Their Preparation for Labor" called for a closer unity of ideological, political, labor, moral, and aesthetic education with general, technical, scientific, and cultural schooling.
February	1981	The Twenty-Sixth Congress of the Party debated a report that critically analyzed the state of education in the USSR. It recommended greater Party supervision and guidance of Soviet educational development and the appointment of a School Reform Commission. Konstantin Chernenko was appointed Chairman of the CPSU Central Committee's School Reform Commission.
November 10	1982	The death of Leonid Brezhnev. The Politburo elected Yuri Andropov the General Secretary of the Central Committee of the Party.
June 13–14	1983	The Education Reform Commission submitted its report on the "Reform of the General School and the System of Vocational Education."
June 14–15	1983	The Central Committee of the Party held a "Plenum on Youth and Ideological Questions," which called for more refined methods of ideological education.
January 4	1984	Chernenko submitted to the Central Committee of the Party a draft of the "Fundamental Direction of General and Vocational Educational Reform."
February 10	1984	The death of Yuri Andropov.

February 13	1984	The Politburo elected Konstantin Chernenko the General Secretary of the Central Committee of the Party. Mikhail Gorbachev assumed the chairmanship of the School Reform Commission.
April 12	1984	The USSR Supreme Soviet approved the "Guidelines for the Reform of General and Vocational Schools" and called for a nationwide discussion of them.
December	1984	Sergei Shcherbakov was appointed USSR Minister of Education replacing Mikhail Prokofyev, who had served since 1966.
March 10	1985	The death of Konstantin Chernenko. The Politburo elected Mikhail Gorbachev the General Secretary of the Central Committee of the Party.
April 23	1985	At the plenary meeting of the Party, Gorbachev announced the Party's new strategy of *perestroika* and *glasnost* to accelerate the process of revolutionary change. Yegor Ligachev assumed control of the Party's ideological secretariat, which included the Department of Research and Educational Institutions.
June	1985	Gennadii Yagodin was appointed USSR Minister of Higher and Specialized Secondary Education replacing Vyscheslav Yelytin, who had held that position for thirty years.

February 27	1986	At the Twenty-Seventh Congress of the Party, Gorbachev affirmed his support for the School Reform of 1984 and called for full and complete implementation of the Leninist principle of combining instruction with productive labor and the rearing of conscientious builders of a new society.
June 27	1986	The Ostankino telecast of an interview with teacher-innovator Yevgeny Il'in set off a three-year "War of the Media" to reform Soviet education.
October 16	1986	The teacher innovators issued the "Peredelkino Manifesto" calling for a "Pedagogy of Cooperation."
March 20	1987	The Central Committee of the Party approved Yagodin's "Basic Guidelines for Restructuring Higher and Specialized Secondary Education Schools."
October 17	1987	The teacher innovators issued a second manifesto, "The Democratization of the Personality."
February 17–19	1988	The Central Committee of the Party held its plenary meeting on the "Restructuring of the Secondary and Higher Education Schools."
March 8	1988	The USSR State Committee for Public Education was established; Gennadii Yagodin was appointed as its Chairman and Vladimir Shadrikov as Deputy Chairman.
March 19	1988	The teacher innovator group issued a third manifesto, "Methodology of Renewal."

June 1	1988	The USSR State Committee for Public Instruction entered into a contract with Eduard Dneprov's VNIK (Temporary Scientific Research Group) to develop proposals for education reform based upon the recommendations of the February Plenum of the Party.
August 18	1988	VNIK's "Concept of General Secondary Education" was published, followed by that of the USSR Academy of Pedagogical Sciences.
December 20–22	1988	The All-Union Congress of Education Workers was convened to approve the goals and strategy for educational reform recommended by the Plenum of the Party.
May 29	1990	Yeltsin was elected Chairman of the RSFSR Supreme Soviet.
June–July	1990	The Extraordinary Congress of the Russian Supreme Soviet issued the "Declaration on State Sovereignty of the RSFSR." Eduard Dneprov was appointed RSFSR Minister of Education. The Russian Supreme Soviet enacted the "Law on Freedom of Religion," which extended total freedom and independence to all churches and religious associations.
December 1	1990	The USSR State Committee for Public Education issued its proposal for the "Basic Curriculum of the Eleven-year School."

June 11–12	1991	Yeltsin was elected President of the Russian Supreme Soviet. His first decree, "On Priority Measures to Promote Education," directed the Russian Minister of Education Dneprov to develop a program for the development of education and the government to guarantee financial support on nonstate educational institutions.
July 20	1991	Yeltsin issued a decree dismantling Communist Party cells in all factories, schools, government offices, and workplaces.
August 19–21	1991	The State Committee for the State of Emergency declared a "State of Emergency in the USSR." Yeltsin branded the attempted coup to overthrow the Gorbachev government illegal and placed all USSR bodies of executive power that operated in the RSFSR territory under the elected President of the RSFSR.
August 23	1991	After Yeltsin issued the decree "On Suspending the Activity of the RSFSR Communist Party," Gorbachev resigned as General Secretary of the Central Committee of the Party.
October 1	1991	The opening session of the Russian Congress of the People's Deputies was convened.
December 9	1991	Yeltsin issued Decree 58 converting the USSR Academy of Pedagogical Sciences to the Russian Academy of Education.

December 31	1991	The Commonwealth of Independent States was established. The Union of Soviet Social Republics ceased to exist. The RSFSR State Committee on Higher Education, Science and Technology was established.
April 7	1992	Yeltsin issued Decree 225 granting the Russian Academy of Education complete independence from the Russian Ministry of Education.
May 22	1992	The Russian Supreme Soviet's Committee on Science and Education under Chairman Vladimir Shorin enacted "The Law of the Russian Federation on Education."
December 4	1992	The Russian Minister of Education Dneprov resigned. Yevgeny Tkachenko was appointed Russian Minister of Education.
July 13	1993	The Russian Supreme Soviet adopted an amendment "On Making Changes in and Additions to the Law on Freedom of Religion," which prohibited religious activity on Russian territory by foreign organizations.
September 1	1993	Yeltsin issued a decree suspending Alexandr Rutskoi from the office of Vice President.
September 21	1993	Yeltsin issued a decree discontinuing the legislative functions of the RSFSR Congress of People's Deputies and the Supreme Soviet of Russia.
October 4	1993	Chairman of the Russian Supreme Soviet Ruslan Khasbulatov and Vice President Alexandr Rutskoi were placed under arrest.

December 21	1993	The 1993 Russian Constitution was ratified and deputies to the new Russian Federal Assembly were elected. Article 43 of the Russian Constitution guaranteed free pre-school, basic general, and secondary vocational education at all state and municipal educational institutions and at enterprises. Basic education (nine years) was declared compulsory.

PART ONE

Away from the Past

CHAPTER 1

Education Before Gorbachev

Had the educational debate in the USSR after 1985 not been part of a much wider political and economic revolution it might well have been seen as a further example of the disquiet expressed about education in all developed nations. Educators and politicians everywhere were facing challenges in school systems in which the aim of providing education on a lifelong basis was viewed as one of the universal human rights and seemed about to be achieved. After a long and hard struggle over some six decades, Soviet educators in the 1980s faced problems created, first, by their own success in building up a mass system of education and, second, by having done so on the basis of policies determined by an inflexible ideology.

In 1917 the Soviet authorities inherited an underdeveloped system of rural education in which locally controlled elementary schools provided a basic education in the three Rs based on the three principles of autocracy, orthodoxy, and nationalism. The academic secondary schools, both private and state, were similar to those in Western Europe and prepared members of an elite for well-established universities and technological institutions of higher learning. These schools were selective both in terms of the social position of parents, abilities of children, and national identity. Quotas were set for the admission of non-Russian children. According to N. P. Kuzin (*Education in the USSR*, Moscow: Progress Publishers, 1977, p. 16), "Prerevolutionary Russia had no system for training skilled workers." As in the rest of Europe (apart from Britain), sharp distinctions were made between schools providing a general education and institutions providing vocational training.

Throughout the vast Russian Empire the provision of elementary schools varied greatly. In the then independent Latvia, Lithuania, and Estonia (which later became Soviet republics), the proportion of children attending elementary school was far higher than in most parts of the Russian Empire. For example, on the eve of the Revolution, even in Russia, a great many of the children of school age were not attending school. The non-Russian-speaking ethnic groups were much worse off. Many of the nomadic tribesmen in the Far North did not even have their own written language. In many parts of the country much less than 10 percent of the population between the ages of nine and fifty were literate (the figures given by Kuzin were: Tajikistan, 2.3 percent; Kirghizia, 3.1 percent; and Turkmenia, 7.8 percent).

Curricula in the academic schools were similar to those in continental Europe in that they were encyclopaedic. A major difference between the Russian schools and those, for example, of France and Germany was that less emphasis was placed in the former on the classical languages—Greek and Latin—as the source of a sound general education. The study of foreign languages and mathematics was, however, prized throughout Europe. Thus in Russian academic schools a range of subjects regarded as worthy of study in universities was provided and the universities bore comparison with the older universities in Western Europe.

Throughout Europe during the early part of the twentieth century some basic aspects of educational provision were legitimized by the theory advanced by Plato in *The Republic.* Plato's theory was based on the assumption that individual differences were inherited. Clever parents seemingly begot clever children. Such children should be educated as potential "philosopher-kings." The vast majority of the population, who from birth were destined to be workers, were to be trained for an appropriate niche in the workforce and were to be content to remain in that position throughout life. This acceptance by European educators of the theory of inherited individual differences justified selection between the ages of ten and twelve into different types of second-level schools. Further selection took place at the point of entry to the universities to ensure that a potential political elite was appropriately educated.

A further purpose of education was character development, which was to be achieved by inculcating knowledge of the transcendent ideas that would give to material objects their essence. Knowledge was equated with wisdom. The wise were the natural political leaders. This emphasis on rational thought, rather than on empirical scientific investigation, in the schools of Europe owed much to the Platonic tradition. However, the restricted number of subjects regarded by the Greeks as the foundation of a sound general education was extended in the seventeenth century. Under the influence of Comenius it included all the accumulated knowledge of mankind. Hence, on the eve of the Revolution, curricula in the traditional secondary schools of Europe and Russia were made up of a large number of subjects, each treated in terms of its historical evolution.

A second theory, Marxism, was founded upon a utopian conception of human nature and society wherein each individual under communism would have the opportunity to achieve an all-sided development of his capabilities. Distinctions between different forms of labor would vanish. The union of mental and physical labor would enable individuals to unite both theory and practice in all branches of production and to free themselves from narrow and specialized labor. This concept of integrated training was the basis of polytechnism.

The Soviet theory of polytechnical education made a unique contribution to educational theory. It has never been widely debated, let alone accepted, in Western Europe and America. It was put into practice in the Soviet Union in many forms, such as productive labor, industrial and agricultural techniques, scientific laboratory work, school excursions and field trips, and the unified labor school. Hence the period of Soviet education from the Revolution until the 1930s was uniquely experimental, collectivistic, and egalitarian.

In *Capital* Marx cited Robert Owen as showing that the "germ of the education of the future is present in the factory system; this education will in the case of every child over a given age, combine productive labor with instruction and gymnastics, not only as one of the methods of adding to the efficacy of production, but as the only method of producing fully developed human beings" (Karl Marx, *Capital*, Vol. 3, London: Lawrence and Wishart, n.d., p. 614).

Plato's theory of inherited individual differences was rejected by Soviet psychologists and educationists who explained individual differences not in terms of genetically inherited abilities but rather in terms of environmental inequalities (A. V. Petrovsky, "Basic Directions in Development and Current States of Educational Psychology," *Soviet Education*, Vol. 15, No. 5–6, March–April, 1973; and L. S. Vygotsky, "Learning and Mental Development at School Age," in *Educational Psychology in the USSR*, ed. by Brian and Joan Simon, London: Routledge & Kegan Paul, 1963). In his article "The Psychophysiology of the Student-Age Population and the Assimilation of Knowledge" (in *Soviet Education*, Vol. 15, No. 5–6, March–April, 1973), B. G. Annaniev stated, "The environment, upbringing and education actively shape abilities and are not merely a prerequisite to the manifestation of some *a priori* genetic features. The role of genetic make-up only indirectly influences the development of abilities and, while solely determining innate disposition, cannot decisively influence the development of abilities" (pp. 143–144). This theory consistently justified the maintenance of a common unified school and the same curriculum for everybody because it supported the belief that equality of provision would raise members of the whole society to the same level of achievement.

A. S. Makarenko's work in the children's colonies, set up shortly after the Revolution to deal with orphans and young vagabonds, served to justify the lack of attention paid to the needs of individual children. Central to Makarenko's theory was the belief that learning is best, if not exclusively, achieved through the collective. Clearly this belief had a great bearing on the moral education of children. Their behavior was monitored by members of the group. Collectivism made for a community of spirit, but limited freedom at the expense of conformism.

The unique features of Soviet political, economic, and educational theory were grounded in scientific materialism, derived from Marx, and elaborated by Lenin. In *The Communist*

Manifesto (ed. by Samuel H. Beer, New York: Appleton-Century-Crofts, 1955) written with F. Engels, Marx described capitalism as being made up of two classes; namely, capitalists, who owned the means of production and could buy and sell labor, and workers, who could live only as long as they were able to work. Moreover, under capitalism the interests of the two classes were incompatible; conflict and, ultimately, revolution were inevitable. In a classless society there could be only one political party, a workers' party, which plays a leading role in achieving a society in which social equity, collectivism, internationalism, and common property ruled.

From the start of Soviet power in 1917, in theory and in practice economic and political policies in the USSR were unique among the nations of Europe. The early documents of the Soviet government and the Communist Party proclaimed free education on all levels for all students. There was to be no discrimination based on religion, race, sex, nationality, or social status. There were to be no private schools. Teaching could be conducted in the native language, and financial support could be given to those who studied. Marxism-Leninism theories, therefore, legitimized the distinctive educational policies designed to transform the Czarist system.

A third major societal theory that influenced education policies was based on a nineteenth-century belief in the efficacy of induction as the scientific method of inquiry. Soviet didactics and materialism shared this belief in the importance of scientific knowledge. Those who believed in induction as the method of science asserted that absolutely true, unconditionally valid general relationships about nature and society could be induced from the objective collection, classification, and juxtaposition of relevant "facts."

For the Soviet theoreticians, socialist realism had a central role to play in the way life should be lived. Scientific knowledge should inform policy and be the essential basis of communist morality. It should inform matters of taste.

At a macro level, using this method, Marx was able to prophesy the inevitable downfall of capitalism. At another level, knowledge acquired through scientific investigations justified the way in which syllabi, textbooks, and manuals about teaching methods were prepared. Another consequence of Marxist confidence in science as the cement holding a socialist society together was the status and time devoted to science in schools rather than, in the Western European tradition, to the humanism of Erasmus.

Illiteracy and Compulsory Education

The need in 1917 was to raise education in the USSR to the levels already achieved in Western Europe as Lenin was convinced that a Communist society could not be built in an illiterate country. The thrust of early Soviet policy, as in most underdeveloped countries, was therefore to eliminate illiteracy (in some parts of the country 98 percent of the population was illiterate). The Soviet government probably overstated its claim that by 1936—eighteen years after the Revolution—illiteracy had been eliminated in the Soviet Union; however, under difficult conditions marked by shortages in trained personnel and funds, the Soviets were able to significantly reduce illiteracy by mobilizing people to work among the rural population and by stepping up the efforts of the elementary schools. In comparative perspective this achievement was remarkable. It has been described by M. Zinovyev and A. Pleshakova in *How Literacy Was Wiped Out in the USSR* (Moscow: Foreign Languages Publishing House, n.d.), and by V. G. Onushkin et al. in *The Eradication of Illiteracy in the USSR* (Paris: UNESCO, 1982).

Associated with the task of eliminating illiteracy was the expansion and extension of compulsory education. This involved extending the number of years of compulsory education provided for more and more school-age children. In 1930 a law was passed making four years of elementary education compulsory; only three years later were the problems of reaching this level of compulsory education successfully resolved. Consistently, towns and cities enrolled more pupils for longer periods of time than the rural areas. Plans to achieve seven years of compulsory education in rural areas between 1938 and 1942 were thwarted by the Second World War when thousands of schools and libraries were destroyed, an untold number of teachers were killed, and millions of teenage boys and girls left school to work in wartime factories. Though by 1952 the authorities could say that seven years of compulsory schooling had been achieved, S. G. Shapovalenko (*Polytechnical Education in the USSR*, Paris: UNESCO, 1963) stated that there remained many four-year schools in rural areas.

Compulsory general education was established under the Statute of the Eight Year School in 1969. Then the call for "secondary education for all" was associated with the development of the unified ten-year complete secondary school. By the 1960s such schools had been established throughout the country. Only then did the constraints placed by ideology create problems, when high school enrollments expanded exponentially.

Curriculum Revision

Crucial to the successful performance of common or unified schools in which all teenagers are enrolled is curriculum differentiation. For example, in an effort to accommodate all youth in the American high schools, the number and variety of subjects and courses were increased from which elective credits toward graduation could be earned. Likewise, when differentiation by school type underwent modification in Western Europe, the need for curriculum differentiation in terms of individual differences became more and more apparent. Over the years, as secondary school provisions expanded in many countries, curriculum differentiation for the most part replaced differentiation by school type.

It remains to be seen whether curriculum reforms will satisfy university academics seeking to admit suitably qualified upper secondary school graduates, industrialists wanting to recruit well-educated school leavers, and those viewing education as preparing pupils more generally for "life." The curriculum needs of different identifiable groups are not the same and may not be easily reconciled.

In short, given that the Soviet authorities were from the start determined to provide education as a human right, by the

1980s they had successfully achieved their purpose by enrolling a high proportion of all Soviet youngsters in schools for ten years, beginning at the age of seven. But an ideological commitment to equality prevented policy makers from adopting pragmatically designed policies to take into account differences in the needs and abilities of individuals. Consequently, for some sixty years the general schools in the Soviet Union were, in most respects and by intention, as similar as possible throughout the country. However, the traditional status accorded to the natural sciences and mathematics, and the time devoted in the curriculum to them, made Soviet schools different from their Western European prototypes.

By 1985 Soviet educators faced the same problems that had emerged in the US after high school enrollments increased exponentially, and in Western Europe after 1945 when many governments were committed to introduce "secondary education for all" in comprehensive schools. In addition, the Soviets were confronted with problems arising from the aforementioned emphasis on the natural sciences rather than the humanities, the aim of creating the "new Soviet Man," and the elimination of subject content and interpretations that were judged to be bourgeois.

As previously pointed out, Soviet ideology prevented differentiation by school type. Almost all pupils, whatever their expectations, were required to attend the same kind of school during the period of compulsory education. This principle was continued once "secondary education for all" became a practical possibility. The difficulties many pupils faced when they were expected to complete a program of studies originally designed for a selected few were increased by the encyclopaedic curriculum inherited from Western Europe. Acceptance of this curriculum was reenforced by Lenin's assertion that a good Communist should know the entire socioeconomic historical experience of mankind. To meet examination requirements pupils were expected to learn all the facts that reflected the historical development of each subject included in their textbooks.

Only in the 1960s did the need for a fundamental reform of education become apparent. The reform was limited and circumscribed by official ideology; favorable comments on bourgeois educational models were censored. Leading members of the educational establishment were aware of worldwide educational discussions but for political reasons rejected most foreign reform policies. Since the rank and file of educators did not have access to sources outlining international trends in the reform of education, the models from which they could choose when the problems in their own country reached crisis proportions were largely limited.

The most serious educational problems were those related to the curriculum and to methods of teaching and examining. During the 1960s attempts were made to reduce the content of education without radically reconsidering the assumptions on which the curriculum was based and the achievement of pupils assessed. The basis for this curriculum reform appears to be that, from the historical development of each subject, some major academic principles could and should be selected from which pupils can deduce a host of factual data. Thus, instead of expecting pupils to memorize all the facts included in the historical development of a subject, selected general principles should be acquired.

The way in which the reform was initiated, developed, and introduced has been well described by A. Markushevich in "The Problems of the Content of School Education in the USSR" (in *Curriculum Development at the Second Level of Education*, eds., Brian Holmes and R. Ryba, London: Comparative Education Society of Europe, 1969). In his analysis, Markushevich stated that the committee of 500 scientists, drawn from the Academy of Sciences and the Academy of Pedagogical Sciences to revise the school curriculum, was established at a time when articles by scientists, writers, and teachers critical of the content of education had begun to appear in the press. The content of mathematics, the natural sciences, and the humanities was criticized because it had failed to keep pace with the current developments in science and culture. Not surprisingly, in the US and Britain, at about the same time, similar criticisms about the content of science education had given rise to reform proposals. Debates about them in all countries turned on the ability of teachers to introduce the new syllabi and the unwillingness of teachers of mathematics, to quote Markushevich, to "Sack Euclid."

As in the case of many curriculum reform proposals, the attempt to reduce the required content of education for all Soviet adolescents failed. Most classroom teachers relied completely on prescribed textbooks and were regulated by oral examinations designed to test the extent to which pupils had memorized the content of these textbooks. Added to this were the challenges presented by the explosion of knowledge, which led Soviet educators to cram into the first four years of compulsory education more than what had previously been thought possible. Research questioned the wisdom of reducing the first-level school from four to three years and suggested waiting until appropriate adjustment could be made in the syllabi of each subject.

The pre-1985 curriculum reform proposals in the Soviet Union were not unique nor necessarily radical. Neither in the USSR nor in Western Europe did educators accept pragmatic curriculum theory, which was in part designed to meet the needs of all American students rather than only those destined for a university. Neither was the American credit system accepted, which allowed for student choice from among a large number of school subjects; although Soviet reforms envisaged the introduction of a limited number of options in and after the seventh grade. In some schools, in the seventh grade two lessons a week were devoted to options; in the eighth, three lessons; and in the ninth and tenth grades, two lessons. Differentiation within the curriculum was accepted, but even in the ninth and tenth grades the time allocated to options could not exceed 20 percent of the time given to compulsory subjects (D. A. Epstein, "The Differentiation of Secondary Education," *Sovetskaya pedagogica*, No. 8., 1983, pp. 78–82).

In spite of the efforts made to effect changes in methods of teaching by publishing proposals in journals and inviting discussion, built-in constraints prevented radical change. The dependence placed by teachers on authorized textbooks, the monitoring of examinations by senior staff in schools and inspectors, and the deeply held beliefs of teachers, which activated their classroom behavior, were a few of the constraints.

Then as now, unless teachers are persuaded that change is necessary and unless they possess the skills and knowledge needed to introduce new practices, educational reform is doomed to failure.

In short, curriculum reform in the 1960s in the USSR did not succeed in accommodating the large numbers of pupils in the unified schools who had no wish to enter higher education. Instead of preparing for universities and institutes, many expected either to enter the world of work or to acquire vocational skills after the eighth grade in a vocational-technical school. An increasing number of secondary school pupils were neither motivated nor able to complete successfully a curriculum designed to meet the needs of pupils aspiring to enter an institution of higher education.

At the same time, the curriculum reforms of the 1960s did not address the problems arising from the traditional distinction between general and technical education. The solutions to these problems, enacted under the 1958 law, had not worked; and in 1964 production education was continued only in a few secondary schools where theoretical courses were closely linked to production, e.g., computer programming or laboratory chemistry, and in those where the material conditions and the competence of teaching staff made them viable. To the problems associated with providing "secondary education for all" no country has found an adequate curriculum solution. In the US, curricula designed to prepare "all American youth for life" have been criticized as sloppy, repetitious, and incapable of preparing high school students adequately for the university. The determination with which the Soviet authorities held to the principles of an undifferentiated general unified school and to a curriculum based on the notion that all the accumulated knowledge of mankind should be passed on in primary and secondary schools explains the failure of the Soviet system to adjust to a changing environment.

Polytechnical Education

Throughout the period of Soviet power, the curriculum "problem" was seen in the proposals made by Marx and other socialist educators who maintained that polytechnical education, with its close links between instruction and productive work, was the surest way to achieve the all-round development of the individual.

Of the early curriculum theories, polytechnical curriculum theory was the only one which addressed fundamental issues about the nature of general education in modern industrial societies. Polytechnical curriculum theory, like pragmatic curriculum theory, is society centered. In 1914, for example, John Dewey ("A Policy of Industrial Education," *New Republic*, 19, December, pp. 11–12) argued that a sound education in an urban industrialized society could best be provided through vocational activities of the kind undertaken by individuals in small rural American communities. In that it made experience in daily-life activities basic to a sound general education, American pragmatic curriculum theory was similar to Soviet polytechnical theory. Dewey's theory was, however, less modern because he wished to perpetuate the moral virtues of nineteenth-century frontier America in schools which would become vicarious small-town communities. Soviet polytechnical theory was based on the assumption that a sound general education could best be provided through relating labor, technological experience, and general education in a classless society.

Unfortunately, less attention has been paid to polytechnical curriculum theory by foreign observers because of its relationship to Marxist-Leninist ideology. For Americans, industrial activities in a capitalist society are based on the assumption that individuals will compete for economic success and that everyone will have a say in government. Differences in political ideology make it difficult to reconcile polytechnical and pragmatic curriculum theories. George Counts, however, impressed by his visit to the Soviet Union in the 1920s, was prepared to argue that education in the US should be used to reconstruct society (see George B. Counts, *Dare the School Build a New Social Order?* New York: National Education Association,

1932; and "The Educational Program of Soviet Russia," Washington: NEA Proceedings, 1928, pp. 593–602). In Soviet society, the means of production having been nationalized, education was geared more toward the idea that the preparation of workers was a means to the all-around development of personality.

The close link between instruction and socially useful work was written into the program of the Communist Party at the Eighth Party Congress in 1919. It was thought that P. P. Blonsky's Labor School would bring mankind's impressive technical culture within reach of pupils. While supporting his wife N. K. Krupskaya's commitment to polytechnical education, Lenin accepted that its realization in practice would take time. The attachment of labor schools to factories or collective farms institutionalized one of the different interpretations of polytechnical education. For some who favored labor schools, it meant the introduction of more vocational courses through which pupils could learn to become skilled workmen and women. The other view was that polytechnical education was a form of general education in which the fundamentals of industry and the main branches of production would be studied.

These early and different interpretations of an accepted curriculum principle continued to be discussed by Soviet educators. In 1923–24 an attempt was made to reorganize the curriculum of upper secondary school grades in order to provide a general education combined with polytechnical and vocational training. The State Academic Council in 1927 emphasized the polytechnical principle in its suggestions on how physics and chemistry should be taught. The debate reached new intensity in 1931 when attention was drawn to the fact that polytechnical instruction was being limited to training individuals for skilled jobs in the economy. With the Nineteenth Congress of the Communist Party of the Soviet Union (CPSU) in 1952, interest was renewed in polytechnical education as the basis of general education.

This led to the enactment of the 1958 law, "Strengthening the Ties of the School and Life," which had the full backing of the Central Committee of the Communist Party under Nikita Khrushchev. For some years after this law was enacted, serious attempts were made to acquaint pupils with industrial life both inside and outside the schools. These attempts were analyzed by George Bereday, William Brickman, and Gerald Read in their book *The Changing Soviet School* (Boston: Houghton Mifflin Company, 1960). Visits to Soviet schools in the early 1950s revealed how qualified teachers trained in institutes of higher education were unable to relate the principles of their academic studies to the industrial life of Soviet society. Similarly, university-bound students were unwilling to listen to the skilled workers who were brought to the schools to demonstrate industrial experiences. The law, in spite of the efforts made by the authorities, failed to achieve its purpose.

Soviet Power Structure

The failure of educators in the Soviet Union to respond to the problems associated with the introduction of "secondary education for all" and to realize in practice the principles of polytechnical education shows how well-intentioned politicians failed to change the behavior of teachers. At a time when the administrative system was designed to inhibit or control change, the result was stagnation. The constitutional position of the Communist Party justified an administrative structure in which all leading figures were members of the Party. At the national level, the Party was effectively the government. The autonomy of each republic, with the constitutional right to secede if it so wished, was in practice negligible. Policy was formulated and adopted by members of the central agencies, which over the years became stronger. For example, the Russian Academy of Pedagogical Sciences (established in 1944) became an All-Union Academy in 1966. By the same token, in addition to the All-Union Ministry of Higher Education, a second All-Union Ministry for Education at the pre-university level was created. The existence of Party committees in individual institutions enabled the Party to monitor the activities of workers in the hope that its policies would be translated into practice. Belief in the objectivity of the scientific research from which educational policies were derived legitimized the centralization of political power. In theory the administrative system in the USSR was a meritocracy. In practice it was one in which the patronage of senior members of the Communist Party determined the appointment to and promotion within the bureaucracy.

The system of administration and the ideology which informed it must be held partly responsible for the lack of reform initiatives in response to apparent problems. The system of administration was not unlike that created in France under Napoleon except that it was not run democratically. Personnel in positions of political power were not required regularly to stand for election. The close links between the Party organizations and the agencies of government ensured that members of the Party were responsible for the formulation and adoption of policy. The members of Party committees in local authorities and individual institutions were able to prevent deviations from Party government policy through their collective activities.

Yet in education the ability of political leaders to introduce practical reform in accordance with Party ideology was frequently stonewalled by the conservatism of teachers. Consequently, during the seventy years of Party power, only two major innovations were introduced into what was essentially a traditional academic education: the unified labor school and political indoctrination. These policies were legitimized by the overwhelming concern of the Soviet authorities to ensure equality of provision throughout the country. The lack of financial and material resources as well as the inadequately prepared teachers largely contributed to the failure of the radical reform which sought to combine polytechnical with general education.

Changes designed to strengthen the power of the Party and persuade individuals that it had a monopoly on truth appeared to be successful. Positive changes included the great emphasis placed in the curriculum on a knowledge of Marxist-Leninist ideology based on dialectical materialism. On the other hand, the political power of the Communist Party prevented bourgeois interpretations of the socioeconomic history of mankind. Religious teaching was proscribed. What was taught and how it was taught was controlled not only by inspectors but through the strict supervision, preparation, and distribution of textbooks and by examinations which tested the content of the textbooks.

Even at the level of research undertaken in universities and in the institutes of the Academy of Pedagogical Sciences, favorable comments on bourgeois institutions and practices were deleted by senior examiners. To be sure, enlightened classroom teachers used selected nonideological materials imported from abroad to teach some of their subjects, particularly English and the sciences.

A Time for Change

In 1985 every aspect of the Soviet system of education was in need of reform in terms of the contradictions inherent in the system. Confidence of the Soviet authorities in their system had been boosted from time to time by foreign assessments that were frequently politically motivated to secure reform in their own systems. During the first two decades of Soviet power, some American and Western European visitors enthusiastically and uncritically praised Soviet achievements. Prior to 1939 foreign commentators were usually impressed by the social experiment which was taking place and by what they were allowed to see. Some were ideologically committed to the regime's Marxist philosophy and liked what they saw. In the 1950s, Nicholas DeWitt, using the impressive statistical evidence provided in *Soviet Professional Manpower*: *Its Education, Training and Supply* (Washington: National Science Foundation, 1955), claimed that the superior quality of Soviet schools had made it possible for the Soviet authorities to beat the Americans in the space race by launching Sputnik ahead of them. The favorable comments made by Urie Bronfenbrenner in *Two Worlds of Childhood, USA and USSR*, (London: George Allen and Unwin, 1971) about Soviet schools also influenced American opinion. Visits by American and English educators to many Soviet schools during the 1960s and 1970s confirmed that there was much to be admired in what appeared from their perspective to be rather old fashioned and pedantic.

After 1958, on the other hand, account should be taken of the intense political rivalry between the two countries in assessing American reports on Soviet education. This rivalry directed the attention of foreign observers towards the Party-politicized aspects of the system rather than to an assessment of it in educational terms. While Americans were praising Soviet educational achievements, Nikita Khrushchev was demanding a sweeping reform of his country's educational system (N. S. Khrushchev, "Regarding the Strengthening of Ties Between School and Life," *Sovetskaya pedagogika*, October 1958, pp. 1–8).

> Our general education suffers from the fact that we took too much from the pre-revolutionary gymnasium whose object it was to give the graduate a definite fund of abstract knowledge sufficient for the receipt of a diploma unrelated to production. We are striving to put all our youth, millions of girls and boys through secondary school. The ten year school does not accomplish the task of preparing people for life; it prepares them only admission to the universities. Such a concept of the aim of the secondary school is not correct.

In terms of international discussions and trends, the Soviet system in 1985 was informed by unacceptable aims; it was administered undemocratically; its emphasis on the natural sciences had been at the expense of the humanities; teaching (designed to promote equality of achievement at the expense of individuality) had failed to recognize individual needs and had neglected to cater to them. Not surprisingly the slogans adopted by the reformers in the 1980s were democratization, individualization, humanization, differentiation, and decentralization. Doubtless the accounts of Soviet developments prior to 1985 failed to reveal many of the internal conflicts which took place between 1917 and 1985. Pedology was in vogue for a short time. But in the Gorky Colony (1920–1938) and the Dzerzhinsky Commune (1928–1935), Makarenko was a stern critic of pedology and the psychometric testing associated with it. Pavlov was out of favor for some time, until rehabilitated in 1950 when the gulf between Soviet psychology and Soviet physiology was bridged. The different policy interpretations placed on polytechnical education have been mentioned. Until recently little has been known of the reputation enjoyed among her contemporaries by Krupskaya, wife of Lenin and spokesperson of polytechnical education. In view of the documents that are now available, it is evident that she was criticized by her colleagues more than was publicly known.

Glasnost made it possible for scholars to consult documents from the history of Soviet education that were previously unavailable. It will be interesting to see what new light they throw on the history of Soviet education. There is no doubt that *glasnost* also allowed teachers to express the frustrations they had experienced in a system informed by the doctrine of education as a human right but run in the belief that educational policies were based on absolute truths discovered by the followers of Marx and Lenin. Under *perestroika* educational reform was debated less fiercely than political and economic reform, but changes were set in motion that will persist regardless of the results of political and economic transformations.

CHAPTER 2

Politics of a Changing Educational System

Addressing the Twenty-seventh Congress of the Communist Party held in Moscow (February 27 to March 6, 1986), General Secretary Gorbachev asserted the country had lost its momentum. Economic growth was slowing down; the quality of products was poor; industry was inefficient; raw materials were hard to get and expensive; wage leveling had become widespread; and the failure to apply advanced technology to production had widened the gap between production in the USSR and other advanced countries. In short, inertia was leading to economic stagnation (Mikhail Gorbachev, *Perestroika*, London: Fontana/Collins, 1987). Gorbachev laid the blame for this condition upon the Party.

One reason for this state of affairs was political. In his speech to the Twenty-Seventh Party Congress he warned, "For a number of years the deeds and actions of the Party and Government bodies lagged behind the needs of the times and of life . . ." (Mikhail Gorbachev, *Selected Speeches and Articles*, Moscow: Progress Publishers, 1987, p. 11). The alleviation of food shortages, investment in computers, introduction of energy-saving technologies, and the reequipment of industry were identified as urgent. The solution to these and other economic problems lay in the reformation of management by restricting the role of the more powerful central agencies to formulating the goals of balanced economic development while reducing their interference in the day-to-day activities of local factories. Gorbachev proposed that the economy should be based on genuine cost accounting, self-support and self-financing, and the creation of effective incentives. To achieve these goals the all-round democratization of management should ensure control from below and accountability. He warned that economic reform would take time and that success would depend on "a readjustment of thinking, a rejection of old stereotypes of thought and actions, and a clear understanding of the new tasks" (ibid., p. 386).

Implicitly, however, he emphasized the need to prepare young people for an economy which had still to be created; but, apart from mentioning the need to combine education with productive work, he made no suggestion about the role schools should play in the creation of new ways of thinking or in the development of a new psychology.

Gorbachev considered that the "works of Lenin and his ideals of socialism" should remain an "inexhaustible source of dialectical creative thought, theoretical wealth, and political sagacity." He pointed to Lenin's faith in democracy as the basis for furthering the democratization of society, promotion of self-government, and acceleration of society's development (ibid., p. 407). The development of self-government was the key. To this end, proposals were made to heighten the activities of the established agencies—the soviets, the trade unions, the Komsomol, the work collectives, and bodies through which the people exercised control. It was the concentration of power in the hands of the Party and the absence of accountability, democratization, and decentralization to which the reformers objected.

Powerful central ministries and bureaucracies do not necessarily mean that a system of government is undemocratic. For example, national agencies and government officials in France possess considerable power. A major difference between the French and Soviet systems of government lies in the identification in the latter of only one political party. In principle, according to Article 126 of the 1936 Soviet Constitution, citizens had the right to form political parties. It was claimed that this was not necessary since all active and politically conscious citizens in the ranks of the working class, working peasants, and working intelligentsia voluntarily had united in the Communist Party of the Soviet Union, which was the vanguard of the working people (*Constitution* [*Fundamental Law*] *of the Union of*

Soviet Socialist Republics, Moscow: Foreign Languages Publishing House, 1936, p. 103). Effectively no opposition parties were permitted.

The Vanguard of the Working People

Indeed, the position of the Communist Party was strengthened in the *1977 Constitution* by the provision of Chapter 1, Article 6: "The leading and guiding force of Soviet Society and the nucleus of its political system, of all state organizations and public organizations, is the Communist Party of the Soviet Union. The CPSU exists for the people and serves the people." Under this article, the tasks of the Party were to determine the "general perspectives of the development of society and the course of home and foreign policy of the USSR" (1977 *Constitution,* Moscow: Progress Publishing, p. 10).

This article legitimized a situation that had been established early in the period of Soviet power and strengthened under a succession of general secretaries of the Communist Party. It effectively made the Party, as part of the political system, the most powerful organ of state power. Though a distinction was made between Party and government, the Party through the influence of its members, and particularly through the power its general secretary wielded, was effectively the government. Under the Constitution's definition of democratic centralism (Article 3 of the 1977 Constitution) all agencies of state authority were accountable to the people, but the lower bodies were under an obligation to observe the decisions of higher ones. According to the Constitution, democratic "centralism combined central leadership with local initiative and creative activity and with the responsibility of each state body and official for the work entrusted to them" (ibid., p. 9). In practice, central leadership of the Soviet government was monopolized by members of the Party.

Gorbachev maintained that the success of the Party depended on the careful selection of its members, self-criticism, and the dismissal of unworthy officials. Only in 1989 did the CPSU Committee on Party Development and Cadres Policy

(*Report on the USSR*, Vol. 1, No. 223, October 23, 1989, pp. 25–26) announce that major reforms would be made in the way Soviet officials were appointed. One change required local secretaries to be elected directly by their constituents rather than indirectly through other committees (*Tass*, October 14, 1989). The process was designed to break the monopoly of power exercised by self-perpetuating cliques within the Party.

A. Yemelyanov, a People's Deputy of Russia, commented in *Moscow News* (No. 39, 1989, p. 3), "At present criticizing different departments and highly placed officials is becoming fashionable," but he asked why so many questions were still off bounds. He went on to state that press coverage was so limited that there remained a big gap between the discussions going on in various bodies and reports in the press. At the same time, Yemelyanov was quite clear that the Party organs should no longer "determine and decide everything and, at the same time, not be responsible for anything" (ibid.).

Three doctors of philosophy—A. Guseinov, V. Mexhuyev, and V. Tolstykh—wrote that the *apparat* as Party functionaries believed they could pass judgement on all major issues of policy. Such functionaries, according to the authors, lacked professional competence. The moral ailments undermining the reputation of the Party could only be cured by fundamental changes in "both inner-Party life and the Party's place in society" (*Moscow News*, No. 5, 1990, p. 5). The authors were convinced that the power of the Party leaders "must not extend beyond the confines of the Party."

In a particularly critical article in *Moscow News* (No. 9, 1990, p. 6), a writer defined the *nomenklatura* as the most important posts in the Party and government. Candidates for these posts should be discussed, recommended, and approved in advance by a relevant Party committee. Persons appointed to the *nomenklatura* were members for life and could be dismissed only with the committee's approval. The author wrote: "The most important political issue of the day is to dismantle the system of the *nomenklatura*. . . . There should be direct elections by secret ballot of Party committees and Party officials of all ranks, with all Communists of the given organization electing their secretaries of district, city or regional committees from several candidates, each with his or her own program." Since the *nomenklatura* effectively ran the country, its members had everything to lose and would fight hard to retain their power by any means.

Disunity within the Party was soon apparent. V. Sogrin, editor of the *Journal of Social Sciences*, for example, claimed in *Soviet Weekly* (March 22, 1990, p. 15) that the Communist Party was already divided into three groups of orthodox, reformers, and liquidationists. The orthodox drew support from groups which demanded Russian state sovereignty and an "independent Russian Communist Party" within the USSR as a means of holding onto power. The historian Yuri Afanasiev led the liquidationist clique whose members leaned heavily on Western political experience and advocated total private property. They charged the Communist Party with impotency and worked to get rid of the Leninist features, which rejected universal values, the rule of law, and political pluralism. They favored passing all state power to elected governments at all levels. Even more liberal were the policies put forth by the reformers (Elizabeth Teague, *Report on the USSR*, Vol. 18, May 14, pp. 1–4), which also reflected Western political concepts and experience. The Democratic Platform of reformists within the Communist Party wanted the CPSU to abandon its allegiance to democratic centralism, transfer power from the Party *apparat* to democratically elected Soviets, abolish the *nomenklatura* system of personnel appointments, and disband Party organizations in factories, enterprises, schools, and universities.

One thing was clear. A substantial body of opinion wanted to remove from the Party its monopolistic power. Pressure mounted for an amendment to Article 6 of the 1977 Constitution which legitimized the Party's power. Already in August 1989, V. V. Kusin expressed the widely held view (*Report on the USSR*, Vol. 1, No. 32, August 11, 1989, pp. 13–16) that the Supreme Soviet was enacting more radical measures than those envisaged by the Party and that the Interregional Group was advocating the abolition of Article 6. Somewhat later, Dashevich in *Moscow News* (Nos. 8 and 9, 1990, p. 3) questioned the Party's monopoly on ideas and its Marxist-Leninist world outlook. In autumn 1989, after vigorous debates by deputies in the USSR's People's

Congress, the leading role of the Party was renounced in an amendment to Article 6. The passing of this constitutional amendment did not, however, immediately destroy the power of the Party and its ability to play a decisive role in all decisions relating to life in the Soviet Union.

One of the consequences of this constitutional change was reported by L. Karpinsky ("The Falling of Idols or a Crisis of Morals?" *Moscow News*, Nos. 5 and 6, 1990, p. 2). He claimed that hundreds of thousands of members had left the Party and a growing number of Communist reformers were in favor of a Democratic Platform in the CPSU. They rejected totalitarianism and bureaucratic socialism, while supporting pluralism in the economy, politics, and ideology.

Gorbachev summed up his views on these issues in an address to the plenary session of the CPSU Central Committee in February 1990. As reported in *Tass*, the general secretary said that the Party should compete for power "strictly within the framework of the democratic process." The *apparat* should be responsible to the rank and file of members. The Central Committee should be reduced from 447 to 200 full-time members, and under revised Party rules, should be systematically renewed at Party Conferences held between full-scale Party Congresses. And the Party was to "continue to see to it that deputies are elected among the worthiest people who are capable of running state affairs" (Gorbachev, *Selected Speeches*, op. cit., p. 410). Further, the task of mobilizing all the factors of socioeconomic development could be undertaken only by the Party. On the other hand, if it was to perform this task successfully, the Party had to renounce its posture of infallibility and a fresh look had to be taken at all the activities of the Party.

Gorbachev recognized that weaknesses and failures of some Party members had justifiably aroused indignation. He agreed that there was "no such thing as the Communists' vanguard role in general; it is expressed in practical deeds" (ibid., p. 438). The problems which had piled up over the years could only be eliminated through collective decision making instead of through the issuance of instructions by an individual in a position of authority. Unworthy Party officials were to be dismissed; care was to be taken to select worthy individuals for membership in the Party.

As late as 1990 there was no evidence that an effective multi-party political system would emerge in the Soviet Union. Though in many ways discredited, the Communist Party remained the most powerful political organization in spite of *perestroika's* call for change. The Party was in turmoil. Yuri Skubko, a founding member of the Democratic Union, in an interview with Michael McFaul (*Report on the USSR*, Vol. 2, No. 30, July 27, 1990, pp. 11–14) concluded that the Democratic Union could not work within any institutionalized structure of the Communist Party. In one last effort to achieve executive power outside the Communist Party, Gorbachev allowed himself to be chosen president of the USSR by the Congress of People's Deputies.

Education Debates

Overcoming stagnation in the education sector was not one of Gorbachev's priorities during the early years of *perestroika*. It is hardly surprising, therefore, that overt criticisms of education and reform proposals took some time to emerge within the Party organization. In a speech as late as October 1987, Gorbachev (Mikhail Gorbachev, "The Shining Hour of Mankind," *New Times*, No. 45, 1987, p. 11) confessed: "We see that the educational system has in many respects fallen short of today's requirements. The quality of education in schools, colleges, and universities and of training of workers and professionals does not fully meet the needs of the day."

This lament had been voiced repeatedly during the years of the Brezhnev leadership. With the death of Leonid Brezhnev on November 10, 1982, the aging Yuri Andropov became secretary general of the Party for only fifteen months. As the former head of the KGB, he was fully aware of widespread corruption and cynicism as well as the impact that Western "rock and roll" culture was having on the ideological upbringing of Soviet youth. Equally serious, the skilled-manpower needs of the country were not being met in a stagnating economy. Due to the low prestige of the vocational schools, thousands of empty places existed in vocational-technical training programs and the number was growing each year. At the same time, the upper grades of the general education schools were not differentiated to cater to the diverse needs, interests, and talents of adolescents. These problems and other issues were discussed at a June 13–14, 1983, Party Plenum. Aging Konstantin Chernenko, a long-time protégé of Brezhnev and the Politburo member in charge of ideology, was appointed to chair a commission to reform the Soviet education system.

On January 4, 1984, Chairman Chernenko released a draft proposal of the "Fundamental Directions of General and Vocational School Reform." While a nationwide discussion of the proposed reform was taking place, Andropov died, and on March 15 Chernenko was named general secretary of the Party. Traditionally, the second secretary of the Party held the "ideology portfolio" of the Central Committee, but Chernenko believed ideological work was his main area of competence. So Chernenko broke precedent and held onto the leadership role in the Politburo's Department of Propaganda, Ideology, and Education. But the task of guiding the education-reform proposal through the Council of Ministers and the Supreme Soviet was delegated to Second Secretary Mikhail Gorbachev. He then assumed the chairmanship of the Education Commission. Other than being responsible for this procedural task, Gorbachev made no substantive contribution to the provisions of the reform.

The primary goal of the 1984 reform was to route two-thirds of the senior-level students away from the senior stage of the general education school and into the newly created vocational-technical general education schools where they would acquire a qualification in a skilled occupation. The other one-third of the students would continue with the general cycle in which they could choose one of the in-depth profiles in mathematics-physics, biology-chemistry, humanities, or social sciences. In short, the reform measures assigned to the schools the task of reviving respect for labor and accelerating the scientific and technological progress of the Soviet economy as mandated by the June 1983 Plenum of the Party. But they failed to address the problems caused by the widespread use of authoritarian methods of teaching in the Soviet classrooms, the excessive number of required subjects, the great stress put upon memorization of content, and the alienation of Soviet youth.

When Chernenko died on March 11, 1985, Gorbachev became secretary general of the Party. *Perestroika* and *glasnost* proclaimed the means of revolutionizing the Party and the USSR from their many years of stagnation. Gorbachev delegated the "ideology portfolio" to the conservative Second Secretary Yegor Ligachev, which placed him in oversight of education, science, and culture. Although Ligachev had at his disposal the levers of Party power, he was never successful in getting the education establishment to implement the 1984 education reform that called for directing the majority of Soviet youth to vocational-technical general education schools.

In 1985 Gorbachev did retire seventy-eight-year-old Vyacheslav Yelyutin from the post of USSR Minister of Higher and Specialized Secondary Education, which he had held for thirty years. A very competent and scholarly replacement for Yelutin was found in fifty-eight-year-old Gennadii Yagodin, director of the Mendeleev Institute of Chemical Technology. Highly regarded by students and professors, he was on record as demanding drastic changes in the engineering-education programs and the expansion of research facilities in the graduate departments of higher education institutions. Within a year, Yagodin had secured approval of the "Basic Guidelines for Restructuring Higher and Specialized Secondary Education."

Two years later Gorbachev relieved Mikhail Prokofyev of his post as USSR Minister of Education which he had held for eighteen years. Unfortunately, his successor, Sergei Shcherbakov, was a Party *apparatchik* who had served as head of the Department of Education and Science Institutions of the Central Committee that had drafted the 1984 education reform. Teachers and principals had little confidence in his ability to provide the leadership so sorely needed to bring about radical change in the educational system. The leadership of the Party failed to call for a real *perestroika* in general and vocational education. Instead it confirmed its faith in the goals set by the 1984 reform while at the same time declaring, in the spirit of *perestroika*, that the individual and all his requirements, needs, and problems were to become the central focus of the Party.

Perestroika, Glasnost, and Education

In this set of circumstances, it was no great surprise that the calm on the education front came to an end and a three-year "War of the Media" began in late 1986. The Party and the education bureaucracy had failed to initiate a plan for radical education reform in the spirit of *perestroika*. This indifference to the menacing problems facing teachers day in and day out in the classroom prompted two former teachers to provide the leadership in mobilizing those educators who were willing to respond to Gorbachev's call "to activate the human factor." Vladimir Matveyev, a former elementary school teacher, had been appointed editor of the teachers' newspaper *Uchitel'skaya gazeta* in 1985. Simon Soloveichik, a former teacher of literature, was a freelance journalist for two of the liberal periodicals, *Moscow News* and *New Times*. For the next three years these two journalists gave extensive publicity to criticisms of prevailing methods of teaching, suggested alternative experimental approaches that emphasized the child rather than teacher-centered teaching methods, and expressed the need to humanize, psychologize, and democratize the Soviet schools. Seven teacher-innovators issued the "Peredelkino Manifesto" in October 1986, which called upon the teachers to rise up and carry into every Soviet classroom the "Pedagogy of Cooperation." Developed by Professor I. P. Ivanov at the Frunze District Pioneer Home in Leningrad during the "Khrushchev thaw," this concept was revived and popularized by Simon Soloveichik.

The "teacher-innovators" claimed to be able to successfully teach all children in the general school with its uniform and compulsory curriculum. They boasted of their 100 percent grade promotion rates and the high grades earned by their pupils. Drawing upon the pre-Stalin "Pedology" movement and the psychological research of Vygotsky, they issued another manifesto in October 1987: "Democratization of the Personality."

Five months later still another manifesto proclaimed the "Methodology of Renewal."

In 1987 the "Battle of the Teachers" got underway with informal discussions at the "grass roots" level sponsored by the "Eureka" clubs. Their battle cry was the "Pedagogy of Cooperation." These clubs sponsored in-service institutes and conferences for classroom teachers, which led to the founding of a "Creative Union of Teachers" whose members joined the media in ridiculing the useless and irrelevant research activities undertaken by the fifteen research institutes of the USSR Academy of Pedagogical Sciences. Although they did not succeed in abolishing the "Academy of Stagnation," they hounded M. I. Kondakov, its president, into retiring in June 1987.

The attacks by the reformers escalated throughout 1987–88 with sweeping demands for immediate and radical reforms. These actions raised the hopes and expectations of those who were in the vanguard of the "New Education Left." It appeared they had the support of Gorbachev. In a speech to the Komsomols on April 16, 1987, the general secretary directly laid the blame for "wheelspinning" of the school reform movement on the deplorable state of the Soviet educational sciences. Two months later he issued a call for a "more humane socialism and democratization of society."

Hoping to stem the escalating attacks, Minister of Education Sergei Shcherbakov announced that an All-Union Congress of Teachers would be convened in July 1987 in celebration of the 70th Anniversary of the October Revolution. When the membership of the organizing committee was announced, it included not "a single teacher, not a single director of any school, not a single professor." This enraged the "Education Radicals." So vicious were the ensuing media attacks on the Ministry and the bureaucracy of the education establishment that the convening of the Congress was delayed until January 1988. When the attacks continued, the Congress was once again delayed until December 1988.

Looking back upon those three years, Politburo member Ligachev reveals that a power struggle was waged in the ranks of the Party leadership as to how to deal with the growing insurgency and issues in the education sector (Yegor Ligachev,

Inside Gorbachev's Kremlin, New York: Pantheon Books, 1993, pp. 95–96, 284–290). Two leading liberals, Boris Yeltsin and Alexandr Yakovlev, were members of the CPSU top leadership. Yeltsin's "Populist Radicalism," was perceived by conservatives to be more threatening than Yakovlev's liberalism. This permitted the Yakovlev faction of the Party *apparat* to use its power to protect the "left wing" journalists in return for keeping their attacks within civil bounds. Ligachev explains how this happened (ibid., pp. 95–96).

> A few months after the April 1985 plenum, Yakovlev was selected a secretary of the Central Committee and took charge of ideological matters. I supervised them as a Politburo member, but soon an unspoken division of duties took shape. I dealt with questions of culture, science and education, while Yakovlev concentrated on work with the mass media. It is hard to recall a Politburo meeting at which media questions did not appear.

Ligachev then described how Yakovlev was the man who determined ideological policy in the Central Committee and by "running the radical press tried to manipulate public opinion" (ibid., p. 112). Ligachev became increasingly disturbed by this policy of "distortion and slander of Soviet history in the radical press" (ibid., p 284). After Yeltsin was banished from his leadership role in the Party, the rancor between Yakovlev and Ligachev escalated.

In the Spring of 1987, the Ministry of Education under the leadership of Shcherbakov and Shadrikov and the Ministry of Higher and Secondary Specialized Education under Yagodin agreed the time had come to rein in the militants of the "Education Left" and to initiate their own school reform in the spirit of *perestroika*. Gorbachev also agreed (*New Times*, op. cit., p. 11).

> We see that the educational system has in many respects fallen short of today's requirements. . . . We must surge ahead in earnest and bring changes in this sphere too. This is the way the Party approaches the reform of secondary education and vocational training, and the reorganization of higher education. The CPSU Central Committee has

> decided to examine the topical issues of education at one of its Plenary meetings.

Ligachev is much more specific relative to the Politburo's decision to hold a February Plenum on Education (op. cit., pp. 288–90).

> The decision was made at the Politburo to hold a Central Committee Plenum devoted to Problems of Public Education. . . . We made a thorough study of the situation in the schools and institutions of higher learning, looking at what had been actually achieved in this area after the 1984 Central Committee Plenum and what had remained only on paper. Obviously the processes of democratization were changing the very approaches to child rearing, education and training. . . .

Ligachev revealed in his memoirs that one of the most aggravating bones of contention was Yakovlev's unwillingness to accept what Ligachev called "a measured dialectical approach to evaluating the historical retrospectus." Ligachev condemned the destructive action of the radical press in carelessly slandering the past (ibid., p. 288–290).

> Gorbachev had suggested I give a report at the Plenum. . . . It was clear to me that . . . it was essential to include in the report the "Problem of the slander of history." It was directly and immediately related to the upbringing of the younger generations. . . . Certain people in our country are trying to discredit the entire path of the building of socialism in the USSR, to present it as a chain of nothing but errors, to disguise the nation's feat of heroism which created a powerful socialist state, with the facts of unfounded persecution.

From the spring of 1987 through December 1988, Yagodin and Shadrikov orchestrated a step-by-step education reform strategy.

1. To take emergency action to reduce the increasing number of school dropouts and to lessen the growing alienation of students.

2. To hold a pre-Plenum conference in August to determine the most pressing short- and long-term problems.
3. To convene a special Central Committee Plenum in February 1988 which would explore alternative solutions to the problems and resolutions of the issues.
4. To appoint a temporary scientific research group (VNIK) with the mission of developing a concept of general education in keeping with the "New Thinking and Renewed Socialism."
5. To convene a Congress of Teachers and present to it the recommendations and permit the delegates to take definitive action.
6. To encourage the republics and local districts to implement the recommendations approved by the Congress.

Although Yagodin assumed overall control of the entire reform process, Shadrikov was assigned the leading role in keeping the reform process on track. In July 1987 Shadrikov announced an emergency program for the 1987–88 school year. The number of compulsory subjects per week for each student in the post-primary grades would be reduced from twenty-two to fifteen, supplemented by electives to meet the interests of students. He hoped that this might alleviate the alienation of many students and lower the number of dropouts. In an effort to challenge the academically gifted, in-depth profiles were to be offered in mathematics-physics, biology-chemistry, social sciences, and humanities and in the primary grades, in foreign languages for two or three lessons a week.

Yagodin convened a series of conferences in August 1987 to identify the educational problems and issues confronting Soviet teachers, students, administrators, parents, and community leaders. Those involved agreed that the problems were much more menacing and serious than the Party and bureaucrats had publicly admitted. Actually the pedagogical problems were similar to those found in many developed countries where the explosions of population, expectations, aspirations, and knowledge raised questions about what knowledge was of most worth, to whom it should be provided, and how it should be transmitted. Over the next six months the pedagogical debates for the most part focused on six issues.

1. The demands on the part of the republics for decentralization to permit the development of their own educational policies and programs.
2. The position to be given the native languages in the curriculum and the emphasis to be devoted to the geography and history of the national republics and people.
3. The low level of academic achievement of all Soviet students in mathematics and the sciences and the shortcomings of students in the Asian republics due to the practice of using children to pick cotton during the school year.
4. The growing gap in educational quality between the urban and rural schools
5. The one-sided and distorted interpretation imposed by Marxism-Leninism on historical facts and the educational process.
6. The need to democratize and humanize the content of education and the methods of teaching children.

Some of these issues had their origins in the emergence of the Soviet Empire, in which peoples claiming allegiance to innumerable different nationalities were brought together into a superstate, held together by the Communist Party, and inculcated with feelings of solidarity between comrade workers. Throughout the whole period of Soviet power, the need for unity was central. Particularly during Brezhnev's regime, the need was felt to achieve this unity by creating through education a New Soviet Man who would be internationally-minded and whose loyalty would be not only to his ethnicity, religion, or traditional national group, but also to the Soviet state.

The special Party Plenum on "Restructuring of the Secondary and Higher Schools" was convened in February 1988 (*Uchitel'skaya gazeta*, February 23, 1988, pp. 1–2). Ligachev led off with an address challenging those present to propose reforms that would bring about the building of an educational system worthy of socialism. However, no ready-made formulas nor detailed blueprints on how best to reform the system were forthcoming from the Plenum. Instead a plea was issued for the education authorities to create those conditions in the education establishment that would bring about the release of creative and innovative forces for reform.

1. To confront the problems created by a uniform all-union centrally planned and centrally directed bureaucratic system of education and face up to the need for decentralization and diversity.
2. To democratize the authoritarian system of state education by creating public education councils, and boards of education and giving more power to the Soviets.
3. To remove the fences between the Ministry of Higher Education, the Ministry of Education, and the Committee for Vocational-Technical Education by establishing a USSR State Committee for Public Education.
4. To drastically reorganize and grant autonomy to the USSR Academy of Pedagogical Sciences (APS).
5. To explore the problems in the teaching of history and the social sciences and the need for a commitment to the truth.
6. To accommodate multinational interests through bilingualism and "parental choice."
7. To restore the prestige of vocational-technical education by stressing the post-secondary stage.
8. To recover quality education by extending the number and types of in-depth profiles in subject matter areas.
9. To meet the needs of students through greater diversity in curricula, methods, school types, methods of finance, and administration.
10. To enhance the professional qualifications of teachers by radical changes in teacher education.
11. To cancel all past administrative orders and to issue the barest minimum in the future.

This Plenum report represented a landmark in Soviet educational history in its departure from all earlier Party

Plenums which issued detailed orders to the *apparat*, administrators, and teachers in every remote village. The recommended policies of decentralization, democratization, and more public participation in decision making were aimed at greatly reducing the authority and controls of centralized and authoritarian Party and government bodies. Unfortunately, as late as December 1990, Ivan Frolov, a Politburo member and editor of *Pravda*, admitted that the Leningrad First Secretary Boris Gidaspov, for example, "had more power" in Leningrad than did the chairman of the city soviet. Gorbachev lost no time in establishing the USSR State Committee for Public Education and naming Gennadii Yagodin as the chairman with Shadrikov as his deputy. The USSR State Committee then entered into a contract with VNIK, a Temporary Scientific Research Group, under the leadership of Eduard Dneprov, to develop a new and broadly conceived concept of general education. This action served to bring many of the "Education Left" into an alliance with the State Committee, which ultimately brought an end to the "War of the Media."

The USSR State Committee proceeded to organize and change the name from the Congress of Teachers to the Congress of Education Workers to reflect the true mix of delegates representing teachers, administrators, and university instructors. Preliminary conferences with elected delegates were assembled locally to review and react to the resolutions and recommendations of the February 1988 Party Plenum. At one of the conferences held in August, for example, Shadrikov presented a proposal that the school system be organized into three distinct and separate stages of primary, basic, and secondary education ("New Humanism Called for in School Reform," *Soviet Weekly*, September 3, 1988, p. 6).

1. The primary stage would begin at either six or seven years of age, depending on the physical and mental maturity of the child. Commissions would advise as to whether the child should pursue the common curriculum for three, four, or five years.
2. The basic five-year stage of general education would allow students to elect 20 to 30 percent of their academic subjects. Impaired-learning pupils would be given

supplementary remedial class work and other subjects outside the set syllabus.

3. In the secondary stage, only one-third of the subjects would be compulsory. Students would elect academic profile areas according to their interests and abilities. Also, schools would be encouraged to develop profile areas of a specialized character other than academic. Schools would be permitted to select their own students.

The State Committee recommended that the newly reorganized general education schools adopt three goals when organizing class and school activities.

1. To maximize the development of the child's abilities.
2. To further the humanization of education.
3. To democratize the entire educational enterprise by having the teachers, parents, and students take a greater role in policy making and governance.

With the convening of the Congress of Education, Yagodin assumed a firm and commanding leadership role to forestall any maneuver on the part of the conservative teachers and administrators to derail the acceptance of what they charged were extremely radical reform proposals. The reform strategy was designed to take into consideration the resolutions and recommendations of the February 1988 Party Plenum, the recommendations of the many locally held teacher conferences, the documents produced by VNIK, and the final actions taken by the delegates to the Congress of Education Workers. The leadership of the Congress managed to secure an agreement upon (1) what were the most critical and pressing problems in general education that called for immediate action, (2) a modern concept of education in terms of the long-run needs of society and the individual, and (3) long-term goals which, if achieved, would resolve most of the major problems and issues in general education. Yagodin and Shadrikov were hopeful that, if fully implemented, such a strategy would bring together teachers, parents, students, community leaders, and school administrators to set priorities, undertake educational experimentation, and bring about school reform measures to meet the needs of local communities ("Yagodin Discusses Soviet School Reforms," *Soviet Life*, October 1988, p. 14).

Shadrikov understood that such wide-ranging educational reforms, if they were to succeed, would require a change in the attitudes not only of teachers but of administrators, students, and parents. The restructuring of an educational system would necessitate the formulation, adoption, and, above all, the implementation of a whole range of principles and policies by local authorities. Critics of Soviet education asserted that in the USSR the majority of persons responsible for implementing policy never had any substantive input into its formulation. Prior to and even in the early years of *perestroika*, few teachers assisted in the formulation of policies designed to inform the work of schools throughout the country. The teachers' newspaper, *Uchitel'skaya gazeta*, had played an important role, as acknowledged by Yagodin in his speech to the Congress of Education Workers, in transforming debates about educational reform which had focused on the inadequacies of the *ad hoc* reforms of 1984, into debates dealing with political, economic, and nationality issues as they related to education.

In widening the debate about education, *Uchitel'skaya gazeta* performed a very useful service. In the absence of any in-depth analysis by Gorbachev of the specific defects of the Soviet educational system, it fell to Matveyev, Soloveichik, and the innovators who met as a group to unleash a climate of critical opinion that led to wide-reaching criticism of teaching methods, teacher behavior in the classroom, administrative restrictions, and research undertakings of the APS. In an article in *Uchitel'skaya gazeta* (July 15, 1989), Yagodin wrote, "A humane school and an authoritarian one are incompatible."

The communist system, which imposed "planning from above," was blamed in the article "A Reader Is Thinking" (*Uchitel'skaya gazeta*, No. 24, June 16, 1990, p. 3) for the lack of reform. According to Dneprov, an outspoken critic of the educational establishment who was later appointed Russian Soviet Federated Socialist Republic (RSFSR) Minister of Education in July 1990, the Communist Party's department of science and educational institutions was holding up the reform of education (E. D. Dneprov, "It Is Difficult to Live at the Margins," *Pravda*,

March 20, 1990, p. 3). In his "Temporary Position Paper on Schools" in 1989, Dneprov claimed that the administrative layer between innovations coming from above and from the "grass roots" was still inhibiting change. The supporters of the command system, he wrote, were fighting for survival. He also said that what the schools needed was economic freedom, freedom of self-government, and freedom to use creative potential—proposals which were in line with the economic and political analysis made by Gorbachev in his address to the Twenty-Seventh Party Congress.

Non-Russian Education

Freedom of self-government and *glasnost* made it possible for national minorities to reveal the shortcomings in the education of the children of non-Russian parents. By law parents had the right to have their children educated in their mother tongue. Textbooks were published and the teaching conducted in fifty-four languages. However, a series of policies, adopted by the Party and government prior to *perestroika* and supported to some extent by non-Russian parents, had reduced the ethnic schools in the USSR to a desperate state ("National Language Relationships in the USSR: State and Prospects," Moscow: 1989, p. 105, 157; and "Problems of the National School in the USSR: A History and Contemporary View," *VNIK Shkola*, Moscow: 1989, p 34). This so-called Russification policy was regarded by many education reformers as unacceptable.

Proposals to reverse the trend by insisting on the introduction of native languages in schools were, of course, supported by political movements in the republics to make their own national languages the official state languages. Under *perestroika*, calls were issued for changes in language policies. Questions such as when, how much, and to whom national languages should be taught were raised. However, there seemed to be a measure of agreement among participants in the debate that, although Russian should be accepted in schools as the language of interethnic communication, national languages, histories, and cultures of the republics should be emphasized. In the article "Greedy Ones Pay Twice" (*Uchitel'skaya gazeta*, May 4, 1990, p. 2), I. Kolesnykova summarized the situation by stating that many peoples did not know their ethnic language, history and literature. National traditions, customs and handicrafts were being lost forever and modern curricula and textbooks frequently neglected national problems. Many reformers placed the reversal of these trends high on their agenda.

The trend away from historical nationalism was reflected in the emphasis prior to *perestroika* on Soviet culture authoritatively defined by the Communist Party. For example, in the teaching of social studies great emphasis was given to Marxist-Leninism, the evolution of the Communist Party, and the history of the Soviet Union in prescribed syllabi but very little information was given on the history of the republic in which a school was situated. Proposals were made to remedy this perceived deficiency (the republican element) in the revised curricula ("State Committee: Preschool and General Secondary Education," No. 1, 1990).

Rural Education

Teachers in rural areas came in for special criticism. In an article "Are We Sowing Knowledge Among the People?" (*Izvestia*, September 18, 1987, p. 3), I. Ovchinnikova asked what kind of respect pupils could have for their teacher when they saw that the teacher knew no more than they would know had they read the same pages in the school textbook. In particular, "Today's rural teacher supplements her earnings by slopping hogs, doing construction work, and selling vegetables in the market." On the other hand, a representative of the public education journal *Narodnoe obrazovanie* claimed in January 1991 that while rural conditions were frequently primitive and rural schools lacked the resources available to urban schools, it was interesting that there were more men teachers in rural than urban schools and many of these teachers were often active innovators. It seems unlikely that in such a large country, in which there are so many rural schools, valid generalizations can be made about such teachers and schools. Yet according to Yagodin, in his speech to the Nineteenth Party Conference ("Address at the Nineteenth All-Union Party Conference," *Pravda*, July 2, 1988, pp. 2–23), the physical facilities in schools were generally deplorable. He reported, "Half the country's schools do not have central heating, running water, or sewers. One-fourth of the children attend school in two shifts, some of them in three shifts. Some 1.5 million children do not have the opportunity to attend kindergartens."

Prelude to Two Concepts of General Education

One of the tasks assigned to VNIK was to formulate a new concept of education for discussion at the All-Union Congress of Education Workers. The building on Smolensky Boulevard that housed VNIK became a center for creative and critical educationists. Their aim was to conduct educational research which would render practical help to the schools. An assumption accepted by members of the group was that all-round education of individual children was inconceivable without cooperation between teacher and pupil and between school and parents within a pedagogy freed of authoritarianism and compulsion (V. Zhmakina, "The First Dimension of the VNIK," *Soviet Women*, No. 10, 1989, pp. 18–19). Criticism was leveled at the research undertaken by the Institutes of the Academy of Pedagogical Sciences (APS) because it failed to meet these requirements. According to Academician Arthur Petrovsky, through inertia most academicians "had stubbornly rejected the vast experiences of Soviet educationists I. Zankov, V. Davydov, and Sh. A. Amonashvili and the creative quest and findings of innovator teachers" (ibid.). Nor did the APS researchers have much impact in reducing the content of the encyclopaedic curriculum that placed undue pressure on all but the most able students. Yet all students had to take the same courses and were expected to meet the same standards of achievement in all subjects. Students were not given an opportunity to decide on which of the required subjects they would like to concentrate their studies. Within a subject all students had to study the syllabus in great detail and at a pace determined by state standards. Constant testing (students were awarded marks for all answers in a classroom lesson) and regular examinations were closely linked with syllabi. All of this placed students under great and constant pressure to meet curriculum requirements and the demands of teachers who assumed that the same method of teaching was appropriate for all students regardless of their interests and abilities. The uniformity of approach was reenforced by a single authorized textbook for each subject in the curriculum. Students who failed in one or more subjects were compelled to repeat the entire year. As more and more students entered the upper grades of the secondary school, the number of students required to remain for at least another year in the same class increased enormously. To avoid this, some teachers gave satisfactory marks to students whose work was below the required standard.

In recognition of this state of affairs, the State Committee issued Regulation 540 in 1989 (G. Yagodin, "So What Education Do We Have?" *Uchitel'skaya gazeta*, November 23, 1989), which allowed students with up to three failing marks to proceed to the next grade. The regulation created much discussion among teachers and in some cases outright defiance. In an article published in *Uchitel'skaya gazeta* (No. 29, July 14, 1990) by a group of teacher-deputies of the USSR Congress and members of the Supreme Soviet Committee for Science, Education, and Culture and Upbringing, the opinion was expressed that Regulation 540 gave the green light to the promotion of failing students to the next grade. In doing so, the authors argued, the State Committee had committed itself to reducing the criteria against which knowledge was measured and "undermining the prestige of knowledge in general."

Yagodin pointed out to the critics who blamed the State Committee for Regulation 540 and for the unsatisfactory state of the schools that Regulation 540 was only temporary. In fact, the Order was withdrawn in late 1990. Yagodin still maintained that the schools were failing to meet the interests and aspirations of students and that this was the main cause of student failure. He quoted the results of sociological research which showed, for example, that only 9 percent of students in the upper classes of secondary schools displayed any interest in learning. Only 30 percent wanted to become really qualified members of the workforce. Twenty percent were convinced that in order to acquire vocational skills, it was not necessary to work hard at school. Fifteen percent of students were sure that they were wasting their time at school. Not surprisingly, the research showed that some 18 percent made no effort to learn at school; 63 percent learned from time to time; and only 19 percent worked systematically and reached the required standards. Parenthetically, it is worth noting this last percentage (19 percent) is not vastly different from the percentage of students who, traditionally, were selected in Western European countries for admission to academic secondary schools in which the emphasis was on the preparation of students for university entrance examinations.

In another article ("It Is Necessary to Fight for Success," *Uchitel'skaya gazeta*, July 15, 1989, p. 2), Yagodin pointed to the circumstances which prompted the State Committee to introduce social promotion through Regulation 540. His first point was that the regulation would prevent teachers from getting rid of difficult students through their freedom to allocate examination marks. He then went on to point out that underachieving students were often disadvantaged children who had not been taken proper care of in their early childhood. Many had been chased away from school and abused. Some 300,000 students had left schools every year without having completed their secondary education. A link had been shown between the rise in juvenile delinquency (which doubled in some parts of the country within a year) and problems at home and school. Yagodin concluded that the highest delinquency rate was among those who neither attended school nor worked. Under these circumstances the State Committee had no option but to introduce Regulation 540. This report highlights the extent to which, in attempting to promote equality, the Soviet schools had alienated a very high proportion of school-age students and that the resulting dropouts had contributed to juvenile delinquency.

Many critics claimed that the schools also contributed to the ill health of their students. Frequent reference was made in the literature to the number of children suffering from some kind of disease—according to some estimates, 80 percent of school-age children in the Moscow area were in this position. In the case of preschools, overcrowding had been detrimental to the health of children and to their spiritual and moral development (B. Gershunsky, *Prospects for the Development of Continuous Education*, Moscow: USSR Academy of Pedagogical Sciences, 1990). In one typical Moscow kindergarten, the playing area for 30 children was no more than six square meters. Instead of accommodating 50 children in reasonable comfort, the kindergarten looked after 153 ("Everything Is Calm in the Council of Ministers," *Uchitel'skaya gazeta*, No. 19, May 12, 1990, p. 5). According to the data of psychiatrists, among preschool children a great many children were neurotically disturbed. "By grade 5, half of all boys and one-third of girls displayed neurotic tendencies" ("Life Does Not Go On," *Pravda*, May 30, No. 150, 1989, p. 3). Overcrowding contributed to decreased attendance because children often fell ill. Gershunsky (op. cit.) reported that "150 million workdays were lost in the Russian Federation alone due to looking after sick children at home, which was equivalent to the exclusion from production of some 650,000 workers." Many children also suffered from stress. A very large number of suicides among school-age children were reported each year. While it would be unwise to blame the schools for all the physical and mental ills among children, there is no doubt that stress was created by an overloaded curriculum and rigid methods of teaching.

Many teachers were convinced that putting more pressure on students would bring success. The chairman of the State Committee rejected this notion and consequently placed himself clearly among the critics of the old system in which the power of teachers to coerce students was accepted. He acknowledged, however, that such teachers did not necessarily not love children or care about them, but had simply been brought up in a system informed by an antiquated set of values.

An analysis made by V. Shadrikov, first deputy chairman of the USSR State Committee on Public Education, placed these views in perspective. In an article ("Return to the Child," *Uchitel'skaya gazeta*, No. 22, June 2, 1990), he identified the roots of the contemporary educational crisis. "The causes (of the present crisis) go back to classical education theories, mainly of the *encyclopaedists*, who in teaching knowledge gave teachers the role of enlighteners and students the role of listeners." This philosophy created an education in which subject-object relationships dominated and, according to Shadrikov, was now simply called the authoritarian theory of education. He might have added in this context that the curriculum theory of the *encyclopaedists* legitimized the overloaded curriculum about which critics complained.

Shadrikov maintained that as soon as teaching the foundations of science became the main aim of the school, life left educational institutions. The scientific rationalization of knowledge inhibited the child's fantasy, and replaced freedom of thought. Parenthetically, he wrote, without denying the role of science, it was necessary to enrich the child's curriculum by introducing holistic ideas about the world, fantasy, and emotions and by not disregarding irrational explanations of phenomena that science could not explain. Shadrikov stated that since the acquisition of a certain body of knowledge and skills became the main aim of education instead of the child's development, pedagogical theory ceased to take any interest in personality and an educational process that disregarded the natural needs of the child became dominant. The demand "Study everything that will be of use in life!" could not stimulate children. The demand "Do as you are told!" was another feature of an authoritarian theory of education that eventually alienated students. Shadrikov did not blame bad teachers nor the impersonal nature of this or that course of study; he blamed the system of education formed over the decades of Soviet rule.

Most systems of education are the product of theories and practices formed over many years. Many of the authoritarian practices Soviet critics rejected are still found in many modern systems of education. What distinguished Soviet education was that overt and public debate about changes was constrained by a political ideology that maintained that irrefutable scientific knowledge of social processes, including education, could be acquired. Shadrikov's article questioned a basic assumption undergirding the Soviet Union's system of education.

Two Concepts of General Education

In social reform it is rare that a full analysis of problems is completed before solutions to vaguely perceived problems are advanced. More often than not new policies are formulated and even formally adopted before precise ways of implementing them have been worked out. The reform of education under *perestroika* in the Soviet Union revealed some features of the general problems. The same general problems that were identified under *perestroika* had been tackled in many democratic industrialized societies. In those countries the prevailing authoritarianism in pedagogy and school administration and the overloaded curriculum were identified as major problems. In the USSR there was general agreement among most of the formulators of policy, though not among all teachers, that these were serious defects in the system of mass education that had evolved since 1917. There was much less agreement on how they could be solved.

Among the many documents prepared by members of VNIK, including new syllabi and the principles designed to inform them, was a concept of education published in *Uchitel'skaya gazeta* on August 19, 1988, and accepted by the State Committee. Two days later a lengthier document on the same subject was published by the Academy of Pedagogical Sciences.

The VNIK concept of education was adopted by the Congress of Education Workers in December 1988 and subsequently formed the basis of the State Committee's policies. The VNIK document maintained that revolutionary and comprehensive changes were needed if the system of education was to be restructured. It said: "There is only one way out of the present situation, namely, radical revolutionary renovation of school policies and the school itself" (*USSR State Committee for Public Education, VNIK* "Draft Concept of General Secondary Education," *USSR State Committee for Public Education, VNIK,* Moscow, 1988, p. 3). The Academy's document was not as radical as that of VNIK; it also mentioned that the existing system of education was not adequate to the new social and economic times, but it advocated change at a slower pace.

Both VNIK and the Academy agreed that the existing system of education needed to be democratized and made more humane. The Academy added three other necessities: individualization, differentiation, and the integration of schools with society. Both wanted to establish a system of continuous education in which schools would play a significant part. In subsequent chapters these various proposals and their applications will be discussed.

The VNIK concept was not without critics. In an article in *Communist* (V. Pirozkov, "Lenin's Decrees on the School and the *Perestroika* of Education," 17/133, November 1988, pp. 69–71), Pirozkov complained that the principles of cooperation and the activity approach did not offer any practical suggestions as to teaching methods and classroom management. Educators were advised to win the respect of learners, gain their confidence, and thus help them realize their genuine aims and understand the reasons for their failure or success. But he asked: What to do next? Teachers needed clear-cut and intelligible guidance to help them restructure schools. The VNIK concept did not answer the question: How should educators act? Other unanswered questions were: With what language should school graduates leave school? How should the school curriculum reflect the demands of technological progress? What should the core curriculum look like? Is it possible to say how many years a child should remain in school without knowing the fundamental theories of human development? Although further vocational training and lifelong education imposed many practical tasks on the system, these tasks were not made explicit in the VNIK concept.

Indeed, such proposals as those made by VNIK and the APS have to be translated into policy statements. As debate in the Soviet Union became more open, the aims of education were more freely discussed. Policies designed to humanize education, democratize the administrative system, finance the schools, determine the various school types and how they should be articulated, differentiate curricula, and decide how teachers should be trained and educated were subjects of active discussion. These debates are examined in subsequent chapters.

The difficulties of reforming such a system were noted by a number of critics. While several leading figures warned that reform would necessarily take time, some radicals became impatient. At a meeting at Kent State University, Ohio, on November 18, 1989, Dr. Nikolai Nikandrov, a leading figure in the Academy of Pedagogical Sciences, said that some educators were very optimistic and thought that *perestroika* would bring about many positive changes. Others were optimistic but still had some reservations. Still others were cautious and noncommittal, waiting to see how things developed. Probably the majority of educators were pessimistic and resistant to change. An example of the range of opinions regarding reform was provided at the Congress of Education Workers in December 1988, where many changes were proposed and discussed, but only a few finally found expression in the resolutions put to the Congress. In the debates at the Congress, some participants pushed hard to secure change, others were militantly opposed, but most remained silent.

There can be no doubt that Gorbachev's address at the Twenty-seventh Congress signalled a breakdown in the overt agreement which had characterized Soviet statements about education for many years. The failures of the Khrushchev reforms and the curriculum reform proposals in the 1970s and the 1984 reform suggested that there was strong resistance to change from above, resistance which was very effective in spite of the political influence of the Communist Party leadership at every level of education and in every institution.

Research sponsored by the USSR State Committee in 1989 revealed that more than 30 percent of school teachers believed that *perestroika* had achieved some positive results and that Soviet educators were not a homogeneous mass endorsing any one particular position or experiment. Obviously one-dimensional viewpoints were a thing of the past. Many of the teachers perceived *perestroika* as a fast-moving revolutionary process, not a gradual forward movement. At the same time, the strength of conservative forces who wanted "Everything to stay as it was!" had to be recognized. This was the point of view taken by half of all educators, mostly secondary school teachers. The moderates accounted for almost a fourth of all school and college teachers (A. Ovsyannykov, "A Fleeting Picture: The Sphere of Education Viewed by a Sociologist," *Pravda*, No. 15, 1989, p. 3). In 1991, less systematically collected data suggested that these differences in attitudes to educational change still existed. However, it was not easy to identify educator members of the Party who were for or against reform. Many had left the Party; others had remained but still supported reform.

Dneprov was one of the major critics of the pace of reform. He pointed out that while his "Position Paper" on schools had been adopted by the State Committee, the old statutes adopted by the Council of Ministers in 1970 had not been repealed. These statutes gave conservatives a pretext for sabotaging the new document; so that in many local areas it was simply not applied. The alliance between the State Committee and the Ministry of Finance, according to Dneprov, did not function, and local financial authorities ignored the provisions of his "Position Paper." In an article in *Uchitel'skaya gazeta*, "A Reader Is Thinking" (No. 24, June 9, 1990, p. 10), it was claimed that central funding was playing a negative role by denying schools the economic freedom reformers regarded as necessary. As a result, schools remained totally dependent on different educational authorities with bureaucratic control over their economic resources. Obviously the authoritarian style of regulating school activities was firmly established and would not be easily changed. A majority of respondents to the *Uchitel'skaya gazeta* article pointed out that school administrators did not tolerate a variety of opinions and adhered to old methods of leadership. The conclusion reached was that a major obstacle to the renewal of schools remained in the bureaucratic attitudes of the Party *apparatchiks* and state bureaucrats. Together, it was held, they would "kill the teachers in us." Most worrying for Dneprov was the fact that many teachers were being alienated from *perestroika* and were no longer supporting the teachers' movement. Within the ranks of the educational aristocracy, there were those with a nostalgia for the less troubled times of the past. Pressure from the Party *apparat* had increased. Elections to administrative positions in schools were less well supported. As a result, administrative power was concentrated in the hands of many incompetent people, some of whom were former Party functionaries prepared to boycott *perestroika*. Such administrators often acted in an arbitrary fashion and "cultivated at schools eyewash, careerism and servility" (ibid.). At the same time, those educators who were looking for clarity and certainty tried to convince the leadership that rank-and-file teachers were not prepared to change until clarity and certainty had been achieved. Sentiments such as these, according to an article by Dneprov in *Pravda* ("It Is Difficult to Live at the Margins," *Pravda*, 20, March 1990), reflected a new type of conservatism. Yagodin identified (in *Uchitel'skaya gazeta*, No. 24, July 16, 1989, p. 2) some of the academician deputies of the People's Congress who were resisting proposals made at the Congress of Education Workers. He wrote that while there was no question of returning to the past, he was prepared to meet these deputies on the "shore of the democratic and newly developing school."

The danger of identifying and labelling protagonists in the debate as conservative Communists and radical-lapsed Communists was illustrated by Dneprov's support for one of the new leaders of the ideological department of the Party's Central Committee, V. Ryabov, who considered that the "all-round democratization of the schooling and upbringing process, of the whole life of educational institutions, is an enormous and to my mind the most influential factor in the *perestroika* of education" (Dneprov, *Pravda*, op. cit.). It would be an oversimplification of a very complex political situation, therefore, to say that Dneprov, with a power base inside the Russian Federation, represented in 1991 the radicals and that most members of the Academy of Pedagogical Sciences were the conservatives, with the leading members of the State Committee mediating between the two factions. In fact, both sides were committed to reform. Both sides included among their members persons who had remained members of the Communist Party and those who had resigned from the Party. Among classroom teachers and directors of schools, many were strongly in favor of reform and active in introducing changes in their schools. Soviet observers suggested, on the other hand, that a formidable proportion of the teaching force was opposed to radical change. Under these circumstances it is well to examine the reform proposals on their own merits

CHAPTER 3

Theories and Objectives of Soviet Education

There was a world crisis of confidence in education during the 1980s. In the US, in 1983, a report—*A Nation at Risk*—by a panel of scholars appointed by the president repeated many of the criticisms that had been made of American education and progressive educators during the 1950s. Standards in learning achievement in American schools were low. High-school curricula were, for the most part, a mishmash of low-level, unrelated subjects, and basic intellectual skills were neglected.

The 1988 Education Reform Act in England and Wales, passed by a Conservative government against the strong opposition of the Labor Party and members of the educational establishment, was designed to level up standards of achievement. In fact it set the stage for a redistribution of power within the educational system.

In Japan the aim of Prime Minister Nakasone's *ad hoc* Council for the Reform of Education was to reform for the third time in 100 years the whole system of education. The council's report was critical of the power exercised by the Ministry of Education; it deplored the intense competition which informed the system from the point of entry to kindergartens through the primary, junior high, and senior high schools to admission to universities. It pointed to the need in Japan for schools to make a contribution to the internationalization of citizens in view of the country's new role in world affairs.

Debates in the Soviet Union should, therefore, be viewed within the framework of a crisis that had its origin in euphoric movements in education that had gained momentum after World War II in the Western World. Throughout the world, education was beginning to be embraced as a human right as proclaimed in the United Nations Universal Declaration on Human Rights in 1948. The declaration had been adopted without dissent by the General Assembly. The USSR and some other nations abstained, but there was a long-standing commitment in the Soviet Constitution to this principle (*Human Rights: A Compilation of International Instruments of the UN*, New York: United Nations, 1973, pp. 1–3).

Somewhat earlier, the founders of UNESCO, meeting in London in 1945–6, claimed that universal education, and particularly literacy, would raise standards of living, guarantee world peace, and ensure the establishment of democratic governments. The opening sentence in UNESCO's charter stated, "That since wars begin in the minds of men, it is in the minds of men that peace can be guaranteed." This sentiment ran contrary to the Marxian assertion that conflict arises as a result of the economic exploitation of workers and their relationship to the owners of the means of production. The reluctance of Soviet representatives to accept the assertion on which UNESCO's charter was based may explain why the Soviet Union delayed joining UNESCO for many years.

Governments in most countries accepted that education should be provided as a right. Attempts were made to extend provision to all school-age children and young adults regardless of race, language, religious belief, place of residence, and social class. Most governments also proposed to increase the period of compulsory attendance. A succession of literacy campaigns in many Third World countries, frequently supported by UNESCO, was designed to provide everybody with the skills that previously had been possessed only by a favored minority. These policies were justified simply in the light of normative assertions of what ought to be the case. Such statements were accepted or rejected on their own merits. There was no requirement that they should be justified in terms of personal and societal outcomes. Only later were governments forced to justify their expenditures for education.

Many teachers accepted the role ascribed to them by UNESCO as architects of a new world order. For example, they hoped that by changing the structure of schooling, particularly at the second stage, class differences could be modified. They were prepared to agree that investment in education would lead to economic growth and that manpower needs would be met. These arguments, by pointing to the societal benefits, made it possible for governments to justify the high cost of providing an education for all.

The subsequent failure of schools to raise standards of living everywhere, to guarantee peace, and to ensure the victory of democracy gave politicians and members of the public an opportunity to criticize teachers. The critics' major complaint was that the schools had failed to reduce violent crime, drug addiction, divorce, and the breakup of families.

Soon after World War II it became clear that, after education had been made available in most industrialized societies to all youth as a human right, these nineteenth-century European systems had not been modified sufficiently to cope with the demands of the twentieth century. The theories which legitimized practice in the past had been challenged; but neither in Western Europe nor in the former USSR had radically different theories been formulated from which new successful practices could be devised.

The dilemma was faced at the end of the last century in the US when, as a result of the efforts of the pragmatists to create a new rationale for American industrial life, educational innovations accommodated the demand for education as a human right, ensuring the survival of a humane political democracy. One of the architects of this progressive movement, John Dewey, while appreciating that modern industrial societies made rural communities problematic, nevertheless wished to perpetuate in urban schools the values of nineteenth-century frontier communities.

In other industrialized countries, for the most part, *ad hoc* reforms were imposed onto systems designed to educate a carefully selected elite of potential leaders and to train the majority of young people for productive work in industry and commerce. The formulation of a new philosophy in which the aims of education could be logically placed received less attention than it deserved.

Soviet reformers in the late 1980s were dissatisfied not only with education but with the economic and political system. Like American pragmatists, in their own way they were searching for a new rationale. They questioned many of the theories inherited from Marx and Lenin but were by no means agreed on what should replace them; and many were not willing to accept capitalism as a satisfactory alternative.

Soviet schools had failed to develop the New Soviet Man. Traditional Soviet theory asserted that education could contribute to the reconstruction of society only after the means of production had been wrested from the capitalists and taken into public ownership. After this had been achieved by a revolution, education could and would help to bring about the socialist millennium. The creation of a New Soviet Man would facilitate this process. Policies were designed to inculcate in young people a commitment to socialism and to build a socialist society as outlined in *The Communist Manifesto*. Then in the late 1980s *glasnost* revealed that the policies relentlessly pursued since the October 1917 Revolution had not worked.

Soviet achievements in providing education as a human right had created their own problems. Despite the chaotic conditions immediately after the October Revolution and the devastation of the Second World War, the expansion of education had been remarkable. The worldwide explosion of educational aspirations after 1945 had been anticipated by many years in the Soviet Union. But the situation was complicated by the growth of the population and the explosion of knowledge which followed World War II. Soviet educators had to accommodate more and more students into a traditional school structure. More and more knowledge, particularly scientific knowledge, was incorporated into curricula.

Although the problems faced by Soviet educators were similar to those faced by educators everywhere after 1945—especially in the US, Britain, France, and Japan—the foundations of the socioeconomic and political systems in these countries were never seriously questioned. In none of these countries, however, were educational debate and proposed reforms viewed within a revolutionary context. In the Soviet Union, educational reform proposals should be viewed in the context of proposals to radically change the political, economic, and administrative system that had been built up since the Communist Party came into power. Problems in education were to some degree systemic ones.

Education as a Human Right

Education as a human right has had a distinguished history in the Soviet Union. Indeed Y. Anisimov wrote in an article, "Splinters of the Empire" (*Moscow News*, No. 51, 1989, p. 10), that "[t]he Declaration of the Rights of the Peoples of Russia and other acts of the October Revolution proclaimed the destruction of the prison of the peoples—the Russian Empire—and the formation on its ruins of a new state based on equal rights for all." He also mentioned the equal right to education. This was never publicly denied by Soviet authorities. In the 1936 Constitution" Chapter X, "Fundamental Rights and Duties of Citizens" (*Constitution, Fundamental Law of the Union of Soviet Socialist Republics*, Moscow: Foreign Languages Publishing House, 1962, p. 99), Article 121 stated: "Citizens of the USSR have the right to education." It went on to say how this right was to be ensured through the "extensive development of general education, vocational-technical general education, vocational-technical education, and specialized secondary and higher education that established close ties between the educational institution, real life, and production activities." In the Constitution adopted at the Seventh (Special) Session of the Supreme Soviet of the USSR, Ninth Convocation, on October 7, 1977 (*Constitution* [*Fundamental Law*] *of the Union of Soviet Socialist Republics*, Moscow: Novosti Press Agency Publishing House, 1988, p. 19), under "Citizenship of the USSR, Equality of Citizens' Rights," Article 34 stated that citizens in the USSR were equal before the law and their rights were guaranteed in "all fields of economic, political, social and cultural life." In Article 45, basic rights were identified under the heading "The Basic Rights, Freedoms, and Duties of Citizens of the USSR" (p. 25).

> Citizens of the USSR have the right to education. This right is ensured by free provision of all forms of education, by the institution of universal, compulsory, secondary education and broad development of vocational, specialized secondary, and higher education, in which instruction is oriented toward practical activity and production; by the development of extramural, correspondence and evening courses; by the provision of state scholarships and grants and privileges for students; by the free issue of school textbooks; by the opportunity to attend a school where teaching is in the native language; and by the provision of facilities for self-education.

In none of the debates about education under *perestroika* was there any suggestion that education should not be regarded as a basic human right. Indeed, in the concepts of education of both the Academy of Pedagogical Sciences (APS) and VNIK (see chapter 2) the extension of education as a human right was proposed by advocating a system of continuous education. However, doubts were cast under economic restructuring as to whether the constitutionally guaranteed right to work (Article 40, 1977 Constitution) could be maintained. The right of citizens to profess or not to profess a religion was more controversial. Article 52 of the Constitution stated:

> Citizens in the USSR are guaranteed freedom of conscience, that is, the right to profess or not to profess any religion and to conduct religious worship or atheistic propaganda. Incitement of hostility or hatred on religious grounds is prohibited. In the USSR, the church is separated from the state, and the school from the church.

In the US and in France the church is separated from the state and, although church-run schools are permitted, those who run them cannot, as in England, receive public money to finance them. Children attending parochial schools in the US may receive some support as individuals for services such as busing. Catholic schools in France may enter into a contract with the secular authorities so as to receive financial help to pay teachers in short supply, e.g., of mathematics and physics, attractive salaries. Nevertheless, in neither country are obstacles placed in the way of individuals to worship as they think fit. Religion is not regarded, as Marx asserted, as the "opiate of the masses."

Perestroika brought many changes in Soviet church-state relations. Bibles became more available. Some religious schools were opened. In particular, the demands of Muslims in the Central Asian republics to allow schools to teach Moslem values were heard in a number of their Supreme Soviets and in the press. An editorial in *Soviet Muslims Brief* (Vol. 66, No. 4, November–December 1990) claimed that education was the most controversial issue in the Law on Freedom of Conscience and Religious Organizations passed on October 1, 1990. Prior to the October Revolution, the editorial claimed, Muslims were free to learn about their religion. But under *perestroika*, the article claimed, the state was still wedded to secular education and would not take responsibility for religious education which lacked funding, facilities, and premises. Although after 1989 there was a slow growth in the number of mosques, and two new Muslim schools were opened in Bukhara and Tashkent, the All-Union legislation on religious organizations made no provision for re-creating the former educational system for Muslims. Diehard atheists opposed any change under *perestroika*, but constitutional protection gradually became more honored as more and more citizens claimed the right to worship and receive an education in accordance with their traditional beliefs.

Equality of Education

Under the banner proclaiming education as a human right, equality of provision received more overt attention in the Soviet Union than in countries where the ambiguities associated with the slogans liberty (freedom) and equality have evolved since the French Revolution. The Soviet authorities had paid less attention to freedom of choice and were thus able to singlemindedly adopt policies designed to provide equality of educational provision.

In 1977 the USSR Minister of Education, Mikhail Prokofyev, stated that regardless of where a boy or girl lived, whether in a city or a remote village, he or she should have an equal chance to benefit from a secondary school or institution of higher learning. To make sure children from different linguistic groups had equal opportunities, lessons were conducted in fifty-four of the different languages spoken in the country. Special school provision was made for children who were mentally retarded or physically handicapped. In principle, only those children suffering from severe brain damage were considered unable to complete secondary education.

Aims, Objectives, and Theories of Education

The ways in which the Constitution guaranteed an education were widely debated under *perestroika* (see chapter 2). The resolution of such debates depends in most societies on agreement about the aims, objectives, and theories of education. In open societies objectives which have already been formulated can be freely accepted or rejected. In this case the evolution of educational systems can be viewed as a series of occasions when accepted objectives are challenged and alternatives are proposed. The fact that new aims are not universally accepted or indeed internalized by some of the educators accepting them accounts for the uneven change. Child-, society-, and knowledge-centered aims can be identified and made compatible in most systems of education.

Historically, teachers have accepted their task to be the transmission from one generation to the next of the accumulated wisdom of mankind. The Brahmins passed on knowledge of the *Vedas*; Moslem teachers, knowledge of the *Koran*; the scholar officials of China, knowledge of the Confucian classics; Jewish teachers, knowledge of the *Talmud*; Christians, teachings of the *Bible*; and the secular teachers of Europe, knowledge of the Greek and Latin classics. Whatever child- and society-centered aims are accepted, teachers in most countries have seen the transmission of worthwhile knowledge as their objective. The constituents of worthwhile knowledge determine what is taught. Child- and society-centered aims determine how it is taught and to whom. Today differences among all three aims is one way to differentiate one national system from another. The fact that before the 1917 Revolution Russian educators accepted traditional academic aims and theories places current debates in the former Soviet Union in context.

Prior to 1985, discussion in the USSR about the child-, society- , and knowledge-centered aims of education was limited and confined to scholars working in the universities, teacher training institutions, and research institutes of the Academy of Pedagogical Sciences. Insofar as child- and society-centered aims were profoundly influenced by Marxist-Leninist political ideology, the hoped for outcomes of education were distinctly different from those envisaged in Western Europe and the US. The interpretation of worthwhile knowledge in the Soviet Union also differed from that in Western Europe but was similar in some respects to that of the American pragmatists. The officially proclaimed objective of Soviet education, the all-round development of an individual, was widely and heatedly debated among Soviet educators as to its meaning and how to apply it in the teaching process.

Within the context of a coherent Soviet philosophy of education shaped by the authority of the Communist Party, the most widely proclaimed aims of Soviet education were easily identified. However, the failure of the Khrushchev reforms indicated that not all of them, particularly the poly-technicalization of the curriculum, were understood well enough for them to be put into practice. Debates since 1985 suggest that not all of them were accepted, much less internalized, by teachers.

Theories of Child Development

In the Russian language a distinction is drawn between education (*obrazovanie*) and upbringing (*vospitanie*). *Vospitanie* concentrates on the all-round and moral development of children and is frequently achieved through extracurricular activities. *Obrazovanie* has as its aim the inculcation of worthwhile knowledge that will benefit society. If a distinction can be made, *vospitanie* is informed by child- and society-centered aims; *obrazovanie* by knowledge- and society-centered aims. In Soviet theory the schools sought to forge links between *vospitanie* and *obrazovanie* or between child-, society-, and knowledge-centered aims. Child-centered aims, namely, the all-round intellectual, moral, aesthetic, and physical upbringing of children was frequently mentioned by Soviet educators and the wife of Lenin, N. K. Krupskaya. In her book *On Education* (Moscow: Foreign Languages Publishing House, 1957, pp. 119–120), Krupskaya wrote:

> The Soviet system of education aims at developing every child's ability, activity, consciousness, personality, and individuality. . . . We are for the all-round development of our children . . . [W]e want to make them strong physically and morally, teach them to be collectivists and not individualists. . . . [T]he collective does not destroy a child's personality, and it improves the quality and content of education.

Reformers in the 1980s, such as G. Yagodin, V. Shadrikov, and others, were in favor of child-centered aims, but they disagreed with Krupskaya's view that children should necessarily be taught "to be collectivists and not individualists." Indeed *glasnost* literature was replete with criticisms of the failure of Soviet education to pay enough attention to the development of a child's personality. Prior to 1985 the official view was that schools had a common purpose, namely, to train active builders of a communist society. For example, as USSR Minister of Higher Education, V. Yelyutin (*Higher Education in the USSR,* London: Soviet Press, p. 41) wrote in 1959:

> The role of Soviet education is to assist in the building up of a communist society; in shaping the materialist world outlook of the students; equipping them with a good grounding in the different fields of knowledge; and preparing them for socially useful work.

To assist in the further development of a socialist, and eventually a communist, society the bourgeois nature of man had to be changed. Thus during the period when the Communist Party reigned supreme, the child-centered purpose of education was to create a New Soviet Man. This aim was emphasized during L. I. Brezhnev's reign as general secretary of the Party. In his report to the Twenty-fifth Party Congress in 1976, he commented on the success of the Party's work in developing individuals with a psychology and morality fundamentally different from individuals educated in capitalist societies (*Soviet Union*, Moscow: Progress, 1977, p. 459). He said:

> Soviet Man is a man, who having won his freedom, has been able to defend it in the most trying battles. A man who has been building the future unsparing of his energy and making every sacrifice. A man who, having gone through all trials has himself changed beyond recognition, combining ideological conviction and tremendous vital energy, culture and knowledge and the ability to use them. This is the man who, while an ardent patriot, has been and will remain a consistent internationalist.

Unfortunately, in this quotation Brezhnev did not spell out precisely those characteristics of the New Soviet Man which distinguished him from individuals who contributed to political and economic success in nonsocialist countries. On the other hand, a well-known historian of education, R. Vendrovskaya, claimed in *Uchitel'skaya gazeta* (No. 30, July 21, 1990) that during the 1920s the task of bringing up a new man "was accomplished, a generation of enthusiastic [C]ommunists had been cultivated." Later on, however, as more people became disillusioned with their material conditions, it was more difficult to inculcate utopian communist ideals in the rising generation.

Not surprisingly neither Brezhnev's aim nor that of his predecessors was fulfilled in the long run. Evidence submitted to the USSR State Committee for Public Education and to VNIK indicated the extent to which youth had been alienated from society. In many articles the growth of violence, crime, and antisocial behavior among youth was described. An article in *Soviet Weekly* (September 9, 1990, p. 6) reported, for example, that one in four crimes in Moscow was committed by a teenager. Large numbers of students had little or no interest in an education designed to make them new socialist men and women.

Traditional Soviet pedagogical theory held that upbringing, "like any other phenomenon of reality, proceeded in accordance with definite objective laws" (I. Monoszon "The Establishment and Development of Soviet Pedagogy," *Soviet*

Education, January 1989, Vol. 31, No. 1, p. 23). Marxism-Leninism asserted that "laws exist objectively, which is to say independently of people's consciousness" (ibid., p. 24). An understanding of such laws made it possible to assert that the "upbringing process represented the continuous transformation of external influences on the individual's internal processes and thus the shaping of his personality" (G. L. Shchukina, *Theory and Methods of Communist Upbringing in School,* Moscow: Novostí Press, 1974, p. 30).

In the immediate postrevolutionary period vigorous debates about educational theory were encouraged. For example, during the 1920s and early 1930s, pedology was in vogue and provoked heated discussions. Pedology, the science of children, originated in the late nineteenth century. One of the main tenets of pedologists was that "a child must be studied comprehensively by the joint efforts of psychologists, physiologists, doctors and teachers." Important educational psychologists such as L. S. Vygotsky, P. Blonsky, and L. V. Zankov were "nurtured on pedology," which resulted in the wide use of psychological tests throughout the country. In 1927 the People's Commissariat for Public Education, in fact, banned the excessive use of tests legitimized by some pedologists.

Pedology came under attack when, according to Felix Fradkin in *A Search in Pedagogics* (Moscow: Progress Publishers, 1990, p. 203), it came into conflict with the Stalinist viewpoint on the fundamental problems of personality development. "In striving to create the new individual, they (Stalinists) discarded inheritance as a factor in the formation of personality." For Stalinists, only "a transformed environment" could positively affect people. As a result of the determined attack on pedologists, "Many of them died of shock, some were arrested, and still others subsequently worked as psychologists and pedagogues" (ibid., p. 206).

By the mid-1930s the shift in priorities resulted in a decree, published on July 4, 1936, but never revoked, in which pedology was condemned as anti-Marxist, reactionary, bourgeois, and counterrevolutionary because its fundamental law maintained that the fate of a child was determined by biological and social factors, heredity, and a constant environment. Academician

Petrovsky protested that pedology never made such claims. In any case, Blonsky and Vygotsky were disgraced.

Fradkin concluded that "[f]or over half a century, the fundamental questions on the interlinks between the school and the environment, on the correlation between spontaneous and specially organized educational influences, and on ideological and sociopsychological factors in forming a child's personality disappeared from the field of vision of pedagogics" (ibid., p 209). He maintained that "the results of destroying the science of personality development in children are apparent today" (ibid.). On the other hand he failed to mention that in the 1960s and 1970s Ravich and Sherba's team conducted research on the biological factors in child development and dominant characteristics of school-age children.

Under *perestroika* the works of pedologists along with those of other disgraced psychologists were once again debated. Theories of child development competed for support. Some views were based on traditional Soviet pedagogical theories of personality and others on the influences of the development of children. The interaction between these two sets of factors was discussed in the USSR (see I. Monoszon, "The Establishment and Development of Soviet Pedagogy," *Soviet Education*, January 1989, Vol. 31, No. 1, pp. 24–26) as it was by Western European and American psychologists. Clearly there were in the 1980s many psychologists in the USSR who still accepted the basic premise of the Marxist-Leninist theory of man, namely, that a person was the "aggregate of social relations" and that "objective laws determined a person's full all-round development." When these theories came under criticism, the aim of creating a New Soviet Man was questioned. Much more attention was given thereafter to the need for an educational system which would simply develop the innate all-round potential of individual pupils.

General Education Aims

The new educational aims formulated by reformers still had not been officially accepted when the USSR report to UNESCO/IBE

(International Bureau of Education) in Geneva (*Public Education in the USSR (1986–88) and Its Development*, Moscow: 1988) was prepared. It stated: "The aim of public education in the USSR . . . is to bring up well-educated, creative minded, harmoniously developed citizens, possessing a stock of knowledge, to raise them as convinced fighters for communism by teaching Marxist-Leninist ideas, to cultivate an uncompromising attitude to bourgeois ideology and morals and foster love for their socialist Motherland and pride for being its citizens . . . and to stimulate their active involvement in running the affairs of society and state" (p. 51).

Few documents revealed more succinctly the extent to which the climate of opinion in education had changed in what was then the Soviet Union than the 1990 report prepared for UNESCO/IBE *(The Development of Public Education in the USSR: Structure and Basic Indices and Educational Reforms in the 1980s*, Moscow: 1990), which stated that the aim of the system was to provide "for both the general and also the occupational and specialist education and training of its citizens" (p. 43). There was no mention of fighting for communism, and even though the section in which the resolutions passed at the Twenty-eighth CPSU Congress in 1990 were listed, a caveat was entered: "However, one should not regard this or other CPSU documents as a direct instruction from the government, as it would have been in the past. Today it merely represents one point of view concerning educational reform" (ibid., p. 47).

Among the goals listed in *Pravda* (June 14, 1990), the humanist purpose of public education and its importance in restoring the economic, political, moral, and intellectual health of Soviet society was confirmed. Continuous education was seen as an integral part of life, which would effectively retrain people in accordance with the structural shifts in the economy and the dynamic changes in the application of labor. Reformed education was to provide a really free choice of occupation through a variety of schools and colleges and different methods of instruction. The structure and content of education in higher and specialized secondary education were to be adapted to the long-term needs of society and the development of the republics and regions. The moral and physical upbringing of children at all stages of education was to be restructured in accordance with the democratization and humanization of society. Education was to be democratized, the autonomy of educational institutions extended, and international cooperation developed. Both secondary and higher education were to pay more attention to the arts and humanities and develop closer links with national and world cultures. The prestige, living standards, and working conditions and the salaries of teachers were to be raised.

The UNESCO/IBE report outlined the variety of views and experiments that were in sharp contrast to the former official pedagogical science. Under the individual's rights and liberties the previous emphasis on equality, while not rejected, was replaced by a recognition of specific educational needs. Instead of being merely a preparation for life and work, education was regarded as an independent stage in life. The strict hierarchy of relations between teachers and pupils and between educational institutions and their superior administrative bodies was rejected in favor of wider democratization, more open relationships between teacher and student, and the self-management of educational institutions. Educational institutions were to be integrated into the life of local communities. The proposal for a continuous and dynamic system of education open to innovative changes was in sharp contrast to the old dogmatic views of education.

The UNESCO/IBE report reflected the caution of the officials who prepared it at a period when most of the proposals for reform were still under debate. It provided a framework, however, for the creation of a humane, democratic system of continuous education in the USSR. Especially important were the proposals that individual needs and interests of children should receive greater attention.

Child-centered Aims and Objectives

Most all of the reformers saw the need for a shift to child-centered aims. For example, in the manifesto of the innovative teachers the central place of the child and the development of the pupil's creativity was stressed. This theme was taken up by the

Academy and VNIK documents and by representatives of the State Committee on Public Education.

For example, in the speech of Yagodin, as chairman of the State Committee on Public Education, to the USSR Congress of Education Workers (December 20, 1988) and in an article by Shadrikov, first deputy chairman, in *Uchitel'skaya gazeta* (No. 20, May 19, 1990, p. 8) on the crisis of the school and the philosophy of education, stress was laid on child-centered aims. The Academy document referred in its stated aims to the need to lay the foundations of "an intellectual, highly moral personality with a Marxist-Leninist outlook." VNIK's document spoke about revealing the creative capacities of individuals and forming a communist outlook but implied that education should be not only a preparation for life but life itself. In this latter respect it anticipated the contrast made in the IBE report between the old pedagogical view of education as a preparation for life and work and the new concept that asserted "that education is an independent stage of life which must not be sacrificed to the future by depriving the coming generation of its childhood and youth" (UNESCO/IBE Report, op. cit., p. 52).

Yagodin, having stated that the Twenty-seventh Congress of the CPSU "placed the individual and all his requirements, needs, and problems as the central figure of every plan and concern," asked, "What is socialist humanism if not the realization of the potentials of every individual and the development of the individual's spiritual wealth?" (*USSR Congress of Education Workers*, December 20, 1988, Moscow, p. 3). He went on to say that the aim of the secondary school was to "instil the basics of a materialist world outlook and universal moral norms" (ibid., p. 5). All three views implied that the aim of education was to prepare young socialists, that is to say people with a materialist world outlook. In general, however, while saying that in education the "requirements of society" should be combined with the "maximum development of the capabilities of every student," Yagodin did not mention the requirements of either a socialist or communist society. Shadrikov complained that when the acquisition of knowledge and the needs of society, not the child's development, had become the main aims of education, interest in the educational theory of personality had ceased.

Finally, in the draft legislation on "Public Education of the USSR and Union Republics," published in *Uchitel'skaya gazeta* (No. 15, April 1990, p. 9), the main aim of education was stated to be the "various sided development of personality and the intellectual and physical abilities of every Soviet man." The document spoke of the highest values of a humane, democratic, socialist society and, in the section under objectives, about "universal human values." The inculcation of universal human values was, indeed, an implicit aim of the reformed system of education.

The child-centered aims as expressed in these official Soviet documents and in the articles by influential officials were very similar to those agreed on by inference in the official recommendations prepared for the UNESCO/IBE conferences in Geneva. They differed, of course, in that the universal human values which should be acquired in the USSR were implicitly appropriate to the kind of society for which children were to be prepared. Significantly, almost all Soviet reformers retreated from the view that children should be brought up as "convinced fighters for communism." They did refer, however, to "a materialist world outlook," "communist outlook," and a "Marxist-Leninist outlook." The humanization of aims placing children at the center of the educational process left open the question of whether or not appropriate values could be located within a humane, democratic form of socialism. The reform of socialism was debated by politicians and economists as well as educationists.

A. Tsipko, a well-known Soviet philosopher who expressed progressive views about changing Soviet society, appeared to take a very conservative position in this respect. Certainly he called into question Gorbachev's concern that the attitudes of Soviet men and women would have to be transformed if they were to meet the challenge of a technological society. Tsipko (A. Tsipko, "Man Cannot Change His Nature," *Soviet Education*, Vol. 32, No. 3, March 1990, pp. 7–29) suggested that it was unnecessary and even impossible for man to change his nature—an aim of Soviet education for many years. Tsipko asserted that attempts to develop production while thwarting initiatives from below had proved to be in vain and that a "mystical faith in the miraculous possibilities of technology and machines" (ibid., p. 24) had resulted in an "underestimation of the complexity and value of peasant culture and the spiritual richness of the peasant as a type of individual" (ibid., p. 8). For him, the human factor was more important than the introduction of more and more machines. Tsipko stated that "[m]an is truly a free and creative being" (ibid., p. 10). The fact that "people are different by nature" (ibid., p. 12) and that there "are limits to which an individual can be educated" (ibid.) suggested that it was neither desirable nor possible to create a new man through education. On the contrary, the restoration of humanistic values meant for Tsipko that "we must think about guarantees based on a world outlook for the protection of the uniqueness and autonomy of the individual" (ibid., p. 29). In his plea that values be reexamined, he constantly returned to this view of human nature.

In response to Tsipko's article, V. Pechenev ("Change So As to Preserve Oneself and One's Nature," *Soviet Education*, Vol. 32, No. 3, March 1990, pp. 32–36) took the view that man undergoes change because a change in a person coincides with transformation in external circumstances. Thus it seems Pechenev was not as confident as Tsipko that the peasant's creativity and autonomy would ensure the success of *perestroika*. Neither author identified the universal human values needed to forge a "harmonious combination of genuine social justice with high labor productivity and economic efficiency, thereby creating material for the realization of justice" (ibid., p. 36). Pechenev clearly believed that socialism had failed to achieve social justice and improve social and individual rights.

These articles highlighted a dilemma facing educators internationally, namely, whether the traditional virtues and values of the peasant promoted social justice and, at the same time, enabled men and women to transform a mainly agricultural society into an efficient and productive industrial society. The values embraced by capitalists may well have promoted efficient industrial production, but many observers would say that they have failed to ensure social justice.

Shadrikov, as a scholar and academician in his own right, concentrated ("Returning to the Child," *Uchitel'skaya gazeta*, No. 22, June 2, 1990, p. 8) on the development of virtues in individual children. He maintained that in emphasizing rational knowledge, Soviet educators had forgotten the child and had alienated students from both knowledge and the school. He stressed that the child should be valued in its own right. As a psychologist, Shadrikov stated that persons possess innate virtues, and it should be the task of education to realize them in behavior. The innate virtues constituted the "desire to do good, skills to do it and virtuous deeds themselves" (ibid.). If children possess these virtues, he claimed, harmony between individuals and society would be achieved.

Compared with some of the views already discussed, Shadrikov's were more child centered. He provided no vision of the kind of society for which virtuous children should be prepared. He implied, like Tsipko, that if the innate constituents of human nature were developed, society would benefit. It is doubtful that he would go as far as J. J. Rousseau in *Emile* and claim that a child's personality is harmed through contact with a vicious social environment and should therefore be isolated from it. Nevertheless, Shadrikov moved radically away from the long-held belief that a new man could and should be created for a socialist society.

Society-centered Aims

In most countries efforts are made to ensure that child-centered aims will benefit society. Political aims of education, either explicit or implicit, are found in statements by democratic governments. In the US, for example, the message is explicit. In learning how to collectively and intelligently solve everyday problems, students will subsequently be able to participate successfully in a changing democratic society. In Britain, while rarely overtly stated, it is believed that an education based on the age, aptitudes, and abilities of individual children will sustain the country's democratic institutions and way of life. Clearly, implicit in statements of these aims are the concepts of the kind of society for which children are to be educated.

Traditionally, the political aims of education were to produce competent political leaders and prepare citizens who were capable of exercising political judgement. The emergence of democracies and the development of industries resulted in the claim that education should prepare individuals for the labor market. In Western Europe, a parallel system of schools was established to train the masses from whom the carpenters, shoemakers, and skilled industrial workers would be drawn. In short, a sharp distinction was made between institutions in which future political leaders were educated and institutions in which workers were trained. The model Soviet educators inherited from Tsarist Russia was the traditional academic secondary school. The expansion of education as a human right and changes in industry-revolutionized manpower needs created problems of policy. Hence, one of the difficulties facing Soviet educators after the October 1917 Revolution was how best to secure an integrated education system and develop cultural leaders of society by means of an education geared to producing productive workers.

In America, John Dewey, recognizing that the re-creation in urban Chicago of the kind of community in which he had grown up in Vermont was impossible, proposed that primary schools should become small communities in which the vocational activities from which he had learned so much as a boy would be introduced. Dewey wished to perpetuate in large American cities the values of life in the small nineteenth-century towns of America. The notion which inspired Soviet educators was similar in that it held that a sound general education could best be acquired through polytechnical activities. For Soviet educators, such activities were not undertaken in small rural communities but in a nineteenth-century factory. One feature which distinguished Soviet educational theory from that in Western Europe and America was inspired by Marx's praise for the factory school run by Robert Owen in Scotland. Basically, in American pragmatic and Soviet polytechnical educational theory, the social aim of education was to combine academic knowledge and productive work so individuals would understand the place of industry and commerce in economic life and behave appropriately.

After years of debate, the constituents of a reconstructed and developed socialist society in the 1980s were not yet agreed upon by those advocating change. Gorbachev indicated in his Twenty-seventh Party Congress speech that changes were needed in the political system and the economy. In late 1990 there was a measure of agreement that reconstruction should create a humane, democratic, socialist society but each of the key terms was open to a range of different interpretations. It seemed unlikely that, among the societal aims of a new political system, the need to prepare young people for the workforce would be omitted. Indeed, paradoxically in view of the rhetoric, the systems of education and training in the USSR have become more differentiated rather than integrated. Unfortunately, differentiation within education traditionally has been seen as denying equality of opportunity and social justice.

Social Justice and Education

In the debates in the Soviet Union about the new society, considerable attention was paid to the question of social justice. In 1988, for example, a conservative member of the Politburo, Yegor K. Ligachev, made a speech in which he said: "The question of social justice has been raised here. It troubles me too. . . . What is the essence of socialist social justice? Some say that this principle is not observed in our society, that it is often violated" ("They're Right," *Pravda*, July 2, 1988, p. 2). The theme of social justice was taken up by several other writers. V. Kuvaldin, a well-known historian who worked in an institute of the Academy of Sciences, wrote: "As interpreted today, social justice means certain guarantees for a decent existence for all people, the opportunity for children from low-income families to try and climb the social ladder" (*Moscow News*, No. 11, Moscow, 1990, p. 7). A contributor in the *Monthly Review* stated ("Perestroika and the Future of Socialism," *Monthly Review*, Part One, March 1990, p. 1):

> True, the language of socialism prevails, usually as commitment to social justice. What this implies appears to be advocacy of special measures for the poorest and least privileged sectors of the population.

The writer went on to analyze the creation of a new class structure in a Soviet society that perpetuated antagonisms. Differences were becoming entrenched and are being "regularly reproduced by class, status and region." At the Nineteenth All-Union Conference of the CPSU, Gorbachev made reference to the low standards of housing, social and cultural conditions, and medical services in many rural areas (Nineteenth All-Union Conference of the CPSU, *Documents and Materials*, Moscow: Novosti Press Agency, 1988, p. 13) By implication social justice in the new society would equalize the provision of goods and services throughout the country.

Concepts of social justice, however, should be contrasted with another dominant value which entered Western consciousness during the French Revolution and the American War of Independence. The slogan of the French Revolutionaries was Liberty, Equality, Fraternity.

V. Stupishin claimed Americans "valued freedom of the individual over everything else." Writing in *New Times* (No. 33, 1989, pp. 15–17), he asked what kind of civic society required educating? And what interpretations of democracy were relevant for educators? His answer was:

> The time has come to revive careful attention to natural rights which, in my opinion, are the natural rights of human society, formed over the centuries of its development and based on the external moral code . . . (which means) a call for respect for parents; thou shall not kill, thou shall not steal, inform against others, lie, envy, or commit adultery . . .

He concluded that the commandments of the Old and New Testaments and equality, as the foundations on which social justice was built, were central to the rhetoric of the founders of the USSR; but he held that consideration should also be given to concepts of liberty (or freedom) in any democratic society. The historian Kuvaldin agreed (*Moscow News*, op. cit.):

> At the same time the idea of justice should effectively counterbalance freedom, to prevent freedom from deteriorating into a slightly disguised form of domination of some people over others. Only when the new system of values takes a firm hold on the people will *perestroika* become irreversible.

The balance that should be drawn in a democratic society between equality and freedom has occupied the attention of philosophers everywhere. At the same time, Old and New Testament values have been incorporated into value systems for centuries. Permanent values such as honesty, filial piety, marital faithfulness, lack of envy, and the sanctity of life have appeared in official Soviet literature for decades. Hence the main issue under *glasnost* that was debated in the USSR, as within European and North American traditions of democracy, was the role of freedom of choice in a society in which equality of opportunity in education was regarded as the sole foundation of social justice.

The values referred to above would find a place in the discourse in any humane democratic society. But what of socialism? Could the basic emphasis on liberty or freedom in Western European and North American concepts of democracy be successfully introduced into a reconstructed socialist society? By the same token could Christian values be overtly reintroduced into socialism?

The Future of Socialism

Some writers considered Soviet socialism out of touch with modern progress. Yu. Olsevich, sector head at the Academy of Sciences' Institute of Economics, in *Pravda*, October 12, 1989 (*The Current Digest of the Soviet Press*, No. 41, Vol. XLI, pp. 4–8), called for the liberation of "society from the former version of socialism." Olsevich agreed that many older Soviet ideas about socialism "have clearly come into conflict with modern scientific-technical progress," and consequently, to develop a model of socialism, a kind of bridge to the twenty-first century, is a paramount task for theory" (*CDSP*, ibid., p. 4). In an article in

Report on the USSR ("Gorbachev Aide Jettisons Communism," Vol. 2, No. 23, 1990, pp. 1–3), the views of Gorbachev's aide, George Shakhnazarov, were summarized. He opposed an official state ideology and wanted to see the social sciences taken from under the shadow of Marxism and studied as independent disciplines. Nevertheless, he sought to retain a leading place for Marx in the galaxy of socialist thinkers.

Understandably, in view of Tsipko's attitude toward peasant virtues, he went further in the rejection of Marx. As summarized in *Report on the USSR* (Vera Tolz and Elizabeth Teague, "Tsipko Urges Ridding Soviet Society of Marxist Ideology," Vol. 2, No. 23, 1990, pp. 4–5), Tsipko claimed that until it had rid itself of the domination of Marxism, the USSR would never become a healthy society. Pluralism could never take root in a country where "the monopoly on truth still belonged to Lenin, Marx and Engels." He advocated the introduction of a pluralistic Western-style democracy and a multiparty system. Even before he was dismissed as a member of the Politburo responsible for ideology, V. Medvedev, in *Soviet Weekly* (October 29, 1988, p. 5) considered that a broad network of organizations adequate to express the multitude of social interests was necessary if socialist pluralism was to be achieved and a concept of socialism for the twenty-first century was to be drafted.

G. Vodolazov reached a similar conclusion in *Oktyabr* (No. 6, June 1989), in which he wrote that it was time to stop "fooling ourselves about socialist pluralism." Moreover, he said, either there is genuine pluralism or pluralism within limits imposed by some monopolistic administrators. Socialism is best served not by predetermined correct views but by diversity and the possibility for everyone to express himself and be heard.

Gorbachev himself addressed the question of the future of socialism in an article in *Pravda* entitled *"The Socialist Idea and Revolutionary Perestroika"* (summarized in *Soviet Weekly*, December 2, 1989, p. 1) by attacking the view that the socialist idea was an artificial construction without a future and that the Marxist theory was discredited because it had created "the crisis state of our society." For Gorbachev:

> The new kind of socialism means an effective economy, the highest achievements of science, technology and culture, humanized social structures, democracy in every area of life and the conditions for each to have an active creative life.

There was no mention of the major principles enunciated by Marx about the public ownership of property and the means of production or about the unity of workers. On the contrary, general as these prescriptions of new socialism were, they were placed in the context of an international world of socialism. Gorbachev said:

> Social systems, while retraining their peculiarities, develop within a framework increasingly limited by the priority of universal human values such as peace, security, freedom and the opportunity for every people to decide its future. The world of socialism is advancing to goals common to the whole of humanity within the framework of a single civilization.

It is impossible to say if even a majority of the Soviet population agreed with the concepts of socialism represented in these quotations. What can be said, however, is that socialism needed to be redefined and that Marxism-Leninism no longer offered a completely satisfactory set of values in which to run a modern technological society efficiently. The need for alternative sets of values in the new socialism was increasingly stressed.

Many Soviet writers understood the dangers in rejecting former dogmas about, for example, ownership of property and the means of production, and replacing them with new dogmas. Academician Stanislav Shatalin was quoted by N. Andreyev in a *New Times* article as arguing, "Without dramatizing the situation, I think our aim is not simply to save socialism, communism or any other "ism." . . . It is necessary to save our people, our nation" (*New Times*, 8/90, p. 22).

The willingness of the Social Democratic Association of the Ukraine (SDAU) to join the Socialist International confirmed that some reformers were not seeking to develop a uniquely Soviet form of socialism. S. Kileyev, interviewed by A. Savysky, considered that SDAU's views were not without merit and that social democrats who rejected the violent seizure of power had achieved "good results not only in Sweden, Austria, and Denmark but in some other countries as well" ("Personal View," *News from the Ukraine*, No. 42, 1989, p. 5). The lack of consensus, however, found reflection in the large number of opposition groups. As Kileyev (ibid.) and others said, the process of eliminating the rigid ideological straitjacket from the minds of politicians and educators would take a long time. Unless based on traditional values, the establishment of a new set of societal values would take much longer.

Knowledge-centered Aims

Finally, the role of knowledge in the achievement of societal aims has been debated continuously. The ancient Greeks believed that knowledge, in contrast to opinion, could be acquired only of what, amid the ceaseless flow of experience, was permanent. Ideas, which transcended changing manifestations of them, were permanent and therefore "knowable." The position that knowledge of permanent ideas was acquired rationally or by intuition dominated the European tradition. After the seventeenth century a distinctly different theory competed for adherents when major developments in the natural sciences took place and science gained support.

Materialists believed that knowledge was acquired from impressions received through the senses by means of scientific inquiry. Galileo, Francis Bacon, Boyle, and Newton founded the modern empiricist tradition in which knowledge was acquired not simply by thinking rationally or intuitively, nor by revelation, but by observing nature. Philosophers constantly discussed the relative merits of materialism, empiricism, and induction as methods of acquiring knowledge of the real world. Rationalism and deduction were the methods of acquiring such knowledge. In Russia, N. G. Chernyshevsky (1828–1889) and N. A. Dobrolyubov (1836–1861), who received favorable mention by Marx and Engels, were regarded as materialists. The materialist tradition and the epistemology of Marx informed the writings of Lenin and subsequent Soviet writers. They were certain that by using the methods of scientific inquiry, absolute and entirely objective knowledge of the material and social worlds could be acquired. Belief in the certainty of scientific information informed Soviet education.

Lenin wrote: "You can become a Communist only when you enrich your mind with a knowledge of all the treasures created by mankind" (V. I. Lenin, "The Tasks of the Youth League," *Lenin, Marx, Engels, Marxism*, Scientific Socialism Series, Moscow: Progress, 1970, p. 116). The significance of Lenin's theory was that the scientific study of man and society would result in the formulation of objective laws. Khrushchev's challenge to the US, "We will bury you," was based upon his confidence in future societal change that would be based on the laws Marx had discovered.

Unfortunately, under *perestroika* there was no fundamental study of the epistemological foundations of Soviet education. The schools continued to inculcate scientific knowledge about the evolution of man and society from prescribed texts. The sciences received priority in terms of status and the proportion of the curriculum devoted to them. Educational reformers, however, demanded the humanitarianization of education and a shift in emphasis from science and technology to the humanities. Under the title "On the Basic Curriculum," a summary of the State Committee on Public Education's curriculum proposals appeared in *Uchitel'skaya gazeta* (December 28, 1989, pp. 1–2). The committee stressed the importance of the humanities and recommended that "more than half of teaching time should be devoted to the humanities as compared with the rigid 41 percent in the present curriculum (ibid., p. 2).

There seems to have been no major reassessment of the constituents of knowledge, its scope, and how it was acquired of the kind undertaken by the pragmatists in the US towards the end of the nineteenth century. However, Shadrikov did challenge the traditional role of science in Soviet schools (*Uchitel'skaya gazeta*, op. cit., p. 2):

> As soon as teaching the foundations of science became the main aim of the school, life disappeared from educational institutions. The maximum rationalization of knowledge has changed the child's imagination and replaced free thinking. . . . Without denying the role of science and

> concrete knowledge we must return (the child) to holistic ideas about the world, enrich the curriculum with imagination and feelings and we must not disregard explanations of phenomena which science cannot provide.

The crux of his argument was that when the acquisition of science and skills relevant to societal needs became the main aim of education, interest in personality development declined. Hence in emphasizing the importance of the humanities, the reformers seemed to reject the notion that scientific knowledge should play the primary role in understanding modern industrial society.

In this sense, the reformers returned to traditional Western European beliefs that scientific knowledge could not be humanizing. The failure of the reformers to address the problem to which Marxist polytechnical education was in theory offered as a solution implied that they had failed to tackle a problem which will arise in an even more acute fashion in the future.

CHAPTER 4

The Administration of Soviet Education

Constitutionally education did not fall within the jurisdiction of the All-Union Organs of State Power in either the 1936 or the 1977 Soviet Constitutions. In the 1936 Constitution there was no Ministry of Education named among the All-Union Ministries in Article 77. Nor was an All-Union Ministry named in Article 73 of the 1977 Constitution, although in this article the Union of Soviet Social Republics had the power to establish "the general principles for the organization and functioning of republican and local bodies of state authority and administration" (*Constitution [Fundamental Law] of the Union of Soviet Socialist Republics,* Moscow: Novosti Press Agency Publishing House, 1988, p. 2). In the 1936 Constitution each of the All-Union and Republic Ministries were listed; no mention of them was made in the 1977 Constitution. One interpretation of the above clause, however, granted to central government agencies the right to formulate, adopt, and implement policy, and this justified the centralization of power that had characterized the administration of education in the Soviet Union up to and beyond 1985.

In fact, between the adoption of these two Constitutions, many All-Union agencies were created and their powers extended. An All-Union Ministry of Higher and Specialized Education and later an All-Union Ministry of Education were established. There was also a central State Committee on Vocational Education. Many federal agencies, including Education, had taken advantage of their constitutional power to draft and approve "state plans for the economic and social development of the USSR, and endorsement of [sic] reports on their fulfillment" (ibid., p. 30).

The fact that under *perestroika* the Party was discredited and lost many of its members did not mean that the central agencies of the Party lost their power. Many features of the system remained. The hierarchical structure of the Communist Party and the influence it had on government and educational institutions made this inevitable. Its major policy-formulating body was the Central Committee. Among the committee members a number were appointed to a small executive committee named the Politburo. Each member of the Politburo was responsible for an aspect of national policy, e.g., ideology (which included education), industry, agriculture, and so on. Central Committee policies were administered by departments, several of which were responsible to a secretary. The secretaries, who formed the Secretariat, reported to an appropriate member of the Politburo. Prior to and during the early years of *perestroika* members within this structure represented, de facto, a parallel government which influenced, if it did not determine, the formulation and adoption of national policies. Party members in every institution were in a position to ensure that Party policies were not ignored.

Many foreign observers claimed that the Party actually controlled the government. The interaction between members of the parallel governments depended on the fact that leading national Party secretaries and ministers of the government were usually members of the Central Committee. In any case, all the most important executive committee documents, e.g., decrees and regulations, were issued under the authority of both the Central Committee of the CPSU and the Council of Ministers.

Within the Party, members attending Party Congresses invariably adopted unanimously proposals put forward by the general secretary of the Party. Lower Party organs and officials were expected to follow Party directives. In the absence of genuine elections, this system was not accountable to the people. To be sure, members of the Supreme and local Soviets were elected and the same was true of Party leaders at all levels. Always, however, only one person, approved by Party committees, was nominated. In neither "government" were elected or appointed officials accountable to the public through contested elections.

In saying that the deeds of the Party and government were largely responsible for the difficulties the country faced, Gorbachev apparently evoked deep and widespread but largely publicly unstated criticism. The results of an All-Union opinion poll, conducted in June 1989 by the Academy of Sciences on the attitude of people towards the CPSU (*Report on the USSR*, Vol. 1, No. 23, Oct. 27, 1990, p. 29) showed that criticism of the Party had become increasingly prevalent. One-third of the respondents doubted whether the Party could play a "vanguard role" in society.

Undoubtedly under *perestroika* the power of the Communist Party in government was gradually reduced. It was not clear, in spite of Gorbachev's expectations, how many Soviet citizens wished to see the Party reformed. While a large number of "informal" politically active groups were established, even those that had attracted the largest number of supporters were not powerful enough to offer a realistic alternative to the Party. Consequently it remained until August 1991 the most all-embracing and influential force in Soviet society.

In the field of education the situation was probably somewhat different from that in the political and economic arena. Education systems have a life of their own. Teachers may be told what they should do but are not always either willing or able to respond positively to instructions. Moreover debates about education under *perestroika* appear not to have been conducted along Party lines. Some educational reformers left the Party; others remained within its fold. A majority of those within the educational establishment who opposed change were unwilling to consider new ideals and to learn from foreign experience. Basically the conservative educators wished to run Soviet education for the most part along traditional academic lines and retain the few features of the Soviet system which were specifically related to Marxist-Leninist ideology. Even the reformist educators wished to revert to the traditional academic models of the gymnasia and lyceums.

Based on the evidence of visits by the non-Russian authors of this book to many schools in the Soviet Union between 1987 and 1992, the debate about the administration of education under *perestroika* can best be analyzed within a comparative education framework rather than one based purely on political ideology. In short, many of the problems facing educators in the former Soviet Union, including those associated with the government and management of education, were similar to those tackled in the US and Western Europe many years ago.

The Administration of Education

Both the APS and the VNIK documents placed emphasis on the need to democratize the administration of education. Democratization involved the realization in practice of some features of democratic centralism and the rejection of others. For example, under Article 3 of the 1977 Constitution, all "bodies of state authority from the lowest to the highest" were to be elected. Elections are indeed central to the democratic process, but whether all administrative bodies should be elected may be debatable. Most democrats would accept, however, as the Soviet Constitution stated, that some kind of central leadership should be combined with "local initiative and creative activity." Finally, in most democratic countries, ways have been found of ensuring that government bodies are, however imperfectly, accountable to the people through elections.

On the other hand, certain features of democratic centralism would be unacceptable to most democrats. It is rare to find in a democratic constitution that lower bodies have an obligation to "observe the decisions of higher ones," although in the US, state laws which do violence to the federal Constitution are deemed unconstitutional. Nevertheless, one of the most jealously guarded principles in a democracy is that only some responsibilities are reserved to the central government. Others lie within the province of lower bodies and the rest are the subject of negotiation between various governmental and nongovernmental agencies.

While some features of the Soviet Constitution would have been approved by democrats outside the USSR, in practice, through the agency of the Party and the way in which elections to government bodies were conducted, the acceptable aspects of the Constitution were distorted to ensure that members of the government and the bureaucracy were faithful Party nominees. The general secretary of the Party was de facto head of the government. Local initiative was in the hands of Party members who served in the local Soviets.

Throughout the world when governments state that they intend to decentralize the system of educational administration, they believe that if more and more decisions are made at the local level and in individual institutions, then education will become more democratic and more accountable to the public. In principle, this belief clearly reflects a commitment to educational processes in which teachers and those who are education's recipients (pupils and, vicariously, parents) participate in the formulation and adoption of policy.

Under *perestroika* the notion of democratization therefore included the desire to involve more teachers and the public in formulating the policies they would have to implement. In most countries, however, responsibility for the content of education and how classes are taught has been in the hands of educators with specialized skills and knowledge. Teachers, along with the clergy, medical doctors, and lawyers are members of the professions which determine for themselves who should be admitted to training, what special skills and knowledge should be acquired while in training, and what examinations should be administered before being admitted to the profession. Since teachers traditionally have been in charge of their own classrooms, in most countries teachers have had some say in determining what, when, and how subject matter should be taught. This remains so in universities throughout the world in which concepts of academic freedom and university autonomy are enshrined in universally accepted practices, which, while they may differ in detail, are intended to protect professors from interference from Church or State.

Since school teachers are committed to preserving knowledge and only marginally interested in generating new knowledge, they are inevitably conservative. As members of a profession, they are expected to possess special skills and knowledge which will enable them to perform the unique role of passing on accumulated knowledge assigned to them by members of the society in which they live and work. Once the market prevails in education, and where education is by law compulsory, democratization may require that persons outside the profession have more or a different kind of say in deciding what is taught and how it should be taught.

Critical observers of the system have, in the past, most frequently referred to the part played by Communist Party officials and members of All-Union and Union Republican governments in the formulation and adoption of policy. According to the report prepared for the UNESCO/IBE in Geneva, *Public Education in the USSR (1986–1988) and Its Development* (Moscow: 1988, p. 10), "public education in the USSR is guided by the higher bodies of state authority and administration of the USSR and its Union and Autonomous Republics as well as the local Soviets of People's Deputies and their executive committees."

Certainly in most countries, bodies with administrative responsibilities for education operate at the national, regional and local levels. The responsibilities of each of these bodies can be described and analyzed by assuming that in democratic countries each body will include a group of persons whose duty it is to protect the public interest, persons with managerial responsibilities, and technical staff who deliver the services for which the organization had been established. Usually the members representing the public are elected to these bodies. Members of the managerial group may also be elected but more frequently are appointed. Members of the staff are almost invariably appointed on the basis of their training and qualifications. Elections determine the relationships between members of the three groups within each of the organizations and relations between the three groups and groups outside the organization and also determine the extent to which the organizations are accountable to the public and therefore democratic.

Prior to the introduction of educational reform in the USSR in the late 1980s, the power of the higher bodies of state authority was unchecked, except marginally, in the implementation of policy by teachers. For example, in the sphere of education, according to the report prepared for IBE (1988), the higher bodies of state administration had the power to determine: (a) the general principles of education; (b) general principles of administration; (c) country-wide development plans; (d) types of educational establishments and other public educational institutions; (e) type and amount of material aid to persons being taught; (f) enrollment age and terms of study; (g) procedures for controlling public education; and (h) staffing, work quotas, and the salaries of personnel. These bodies had the power to approve policies relating to: (a) country-wide plans for the development of the educational and material basis of schools and other public educational establishments; (b) the statutes (rules) for educational establishments; and (c) curricula and syllabi (*Public Education in the USSR (1986–1988) and Its Development*, op. cit., p. 10).

Finally, the All-Union agencies of administration were required to perform the following tasks: establish, reorganize, and close institutions of higher education, specialized secondary and vocational education establishments, and general schools; control public education; set up an internal system of statistics and accountancy; and attend to other matters related to public education that were within the competence of the USSR under the Constitution and fundamental laws of the USSR and Union republics.

The powers of the constituent Union republics replicated those of the central government and, in addition, included the power to attend to "other matters related to public education that were outside the competence of the USSR" (*ibid.*, p. 54). The constitutional position of the higher bodies of administration in the USSR was not significantly different from that enjoyed in some democratic countries. For example, France is a democratic country in which many of the responsibilities, such as those assigned to the All-Union higher bodies of state administration in the USSR, are undertaken by central governmental agencies. In England and Wales many of these responsibilities are undertaken by the national Department of Education and Science even, since the 1988 Education Reform Act, to the extent of deciding what should be taught. On the other hand, in the US, since education is constitutionally a state responsibility, the power of the central government is limited. Gorbachev had suggested that central government organs of power should restrict themselves to the formulation of policy and that local authorities, institutions, and enterprises should be free to put policies into practice. A series of Central Committee consultations in 1987 had prepared the way for the Central Committee's Special Plenum on Education Reform in February 1988. The Plenum proposed to cut the educational bureaucracy but not reduce its power by merging the Ministry of Higher and Specialized Secondary Education, the Ministry of General Secondary Education, and the State Committee for Vocational Education into a powerful All-Union State Committee on Public Education. Although this reduced the size of the education bureaucracy, it did embrace in an advisory capacity a council made up of the heads of the republican ministries of education or committees for public education, the two first deputies, and some of the staff members. It became, in effect, the cabinet of ministers of public education. Growing demands for sovereignty by the Union republics necessitated widening the representation of the constituent entities of the USSR. Decisions by the State Committee were made on the basis of consensus or mutual agreement. Hence one of its main functions was that of coordinating educational activities of the various republics ("The Cabinet of Ministers of Education," *Izvestia*, October 25, 1990).

The proposals of VNIK were very much in line with Gorbachev's suggestion. VNIK contended that the fossilized system of educational administration was the main impediment to educational reform. The key to reconstructing education had to begin with effecting changes in the administrative system which was undemocratic, extremely centralized, and aggressively bureaucratic. The system had excluded participation of the public and ignored regional sociocultural differences and regional needs of schools.

The decentralization of decision making is by no means the only criterion by which to judge the degree to which a system of administration is democratic. Some aspects of educational policy can most appropriately be formulated and adopted in central agencies; other policy issues may well be usefully resolved in local organizations or in individual institutions. Accountability is also very important. In the case of educational policy in the USSR most aspects of it had been formulated by members of a political party who were neither elected by nor officially accountable to the public. Democracy, however, calls for government officials who will listen and respond to the views of the parents, community leaders, industrialists, and others.

VNIK proposed a radical democratization of the schools that would transfer some power from government agencies to nongovernment public bodies. It suggested that the schools should be administered jointly by government and non-government (public) councils for education. The highest level of councils should be established in regions and cities. In order to overcome any tendency towards the bureaucratization of these bodies, the council members should serve for only a limited period of time. Other school councils should be established at all levels within the administrative system, thus making way for the public self-management of educational institutions. They should include representatives of teachers, students, parents, and citizens.

The most pressing need in democratizing school administration cited by VNIK was the decentralization of decision making. The main task of the central administration should be to provide the conditions under which the required development of education could take place. Central agencies should work out the ideology and strategy associated with a continuous system of education. They should also establish an order of priorities by carrying out major social and educational experiments, developing a practice-oriented science of education, and analyzing public opinion. Central agencies should continuously disseminate information to the public about the conditions, problems, and future development of education.

Regional and local authorities should be responsible for taking into account state requirements, local socioeconomic conditions, and national peculiarities in determining the process of education and the types of schools which should be provided. The administration should organize financial and material resources, including staffing, and tackle problems in the region's schools. It should coordinate various school activities and organize the in-service training of teachers.

School staff (the collective) and councils should be responsible for ensuring that students' rights were respected and for adapting education to the psychological and physiological development of children. The pedagogical council was responsible for academic decisions such as approving of specialized in-depth profiles of subjects in the school's curriculum.

Many of VNIK's proposals were included in the draft legislation on the administration of education reported in *Uchitel'skaya gazeta* (No. 15, April 1990, p. 9). Article 8 laid down that the administration of public education would have a state-public character. Under this principle, the administration included state and public bodies, such as education and school councils, which were to operate within the constitutions of the USSR and the republics. The most significant change was the establishment of public bodies to bring decision making nearer to the public.

Article 9 laid down the state agencies of administration; the USSR State Committee for Public Education was the highest of these agencies. It was responsible for ensuring the implementation of basic curricula and syllabuses establishing policies and standards of education, and solving problems that were referred to it. The administration of education in each republic was to be undertaken in accordance with the policies of the highest administrative bodies of the republic.

The public administrative bodies were named in Article 10. They included an All-Union Council of Public Education whose members were to be elected by the USSR Congress of Education Workers. Regional, city, and district councils were to be responsible to the various soviets of people's deputies. Along with parents (or their representatives), students and education workers were to participate in the self-government of educational institutions.

General leadership within an educational institution was to be in the hands of the school council (Article 11). However, the director, principal, or headteacher was to manage the affairs of the institution. Article 12 stated that educational institutions were to be subordinated to state agencies of administration, to other state bodies, or to the public and cooperative organizations.

These articles clearly gave local public councils and councils within individual institutions an important role in running schools. In theory the draft legislation radically changed the command system of administration. The hope was that public councils would make government agencies more responsive to public demand. Without having the power to formulate or approve legislation, they were to serve as bodies to advise the government bodies that were responsible for passing laws and issuing decrees and orders.

Regulations were issued by the State Committee providing for the establishment of regional, city, and district councils of education, which were to report to their appropriate governmental soviet (*Regulations on Public Education Councils*, Moscow: State Committee, 1989). Thus, under the General Principles of the Regulations on Public Education issued by the State Committee in Moscow in 1989, the council of a region, city, or city district was to be an elected and periodically renewed state-public organ of educational administration for all the educational institutions.

The main task of the councils was to create and administer a regional system of continuous education of which the general education school was the main part. The councils were to be responsible to an appropriate region, city, or district soviet of people's deputies (ibid., p. 2) which was to provide the councils with the resources needed. A local education authority would constitute the executive branch of a council.

The specific tasks of the education councils were to identify the educational needs of the area, determine educational priorities, and prepare programs for educational development. In implementing policy, councils were permitted to organize collaborative educational research with teaching institutions, governmental bodies, enterprises, cooperatives, families, and individuals. They were to be responsible for developing a network of educational institutions to help teachers improve their methods of teaching, encourage innovations, and facilitate psychological services. To counterbalance the power of established bureaucracies and the Party, councils were expected to democratize the management of schools; defend the rights of teachers, pupils, students, and parents; control educational experiments in the schools; veto council election results if school regulations were violated; and supervise the salaries fund (ibid., p. 5). Each year councils were to submit a report of their own activities to the appropriate committee.

Members of the education council (which included students over fourteen years of age) were elected for a term of three years as representatives of the school councils, local enterprises, public and cooperative organizations, Komsomols, and trade unions. The number of members was decided by an educational conference which had the authority to elect the chairman of an education council and the head of a local school council. Although the intention in creating these councils was clearly to introduce accountability by engaging a wide range of people from the community in monitoring educational policy, only a few of them operated successfully. For the most part they did not live up to the expectations of those who designed them.

The Internal Management of Schools

Regulations dealing with the internal management of general secondary schools were issued in 1989. They defined the school collective as consisting of pupils, teachers, and other workers on the school staff. The intention of the regulations was to make each school a self-governing institution with a governing conference designated as the highest committee in the management of a school. Its members were elected by the school collective (which included students in the junior and senior grades) and representatives of the public. This conference determined the number of members to serve on the school council and supervised the election of the members and the chairman. The school principal served on the council.

Since the conference was required to meet once a year, the school council actually served as the highest organ of self-government and was expected to meet not less than four times a year. Members were not paid for their work. Decisions of the council were legally binding if at least two-thirds of the members were present. Another body, a pedagogical council, consisted of teachers who decided on matters relating to the curriculum, syllabi, textbooks, and methods of teaching.

Effectively, as in the past, the day-to-day management of a school was undertaken by the principal, who planned and organized academic affairs and was responsible for the quality and effectiveness of the work of the school. The principal was responsible for establishing conditions in which teaching and learning could take place. The principal appointed his deputies and determined their duties. He also appointed teachers, tutors, and other members of the teaching and non-teaching staff. The principal was responsible for the budget of the school. Disagreements between the school council and the administration were to be resolved by the conference or by the education council. Only a few principals immediately took advantage of the new powers conferred upon them.

In 1989 a long list of duties dealing with the management of general secondary schools, powers previously exercised by the state and municipal authorities, were delegated by the USSR Committee of Public Education to members of the school's staff and councils (ibid.). They dealt with most aspects of school life, including the election of the school council; conditions of service and promotion; opportunities of staff to innovate; general organization and rules of the school; allocation of 30 percent of the general curriculum, teaching methods, and special curricula to the needs of slow learners and gifted children; medium of instruction; examinations and promotions from one class to the next; expenditure and provision of services for payment; relationships of staff and students with outside bodies; and finally the use of bank credits and conduct of foreign trade. Unfortunately many of these proposals of the State Committee to delegate responsibility to the school's staff for managing their own academic and financial affairs were never fully realized.

School visits by the authors in 1990 and 1991 confirmed the extent to which some school principals and their staffs had accepted responsibility for making academic and management decisions. It was obvious that some Soviet teachers possessed, in spite of the events of the past seventy years, a degree of professionalism which enabled them, under conditions of greater freedom, to make administrative decisions.

The USSR State Committee for Public Education

The USSR State Committee for Public Education became effectively a Cabinet of Ministers of Public Education that recognized the need to engage republican representatives in decision making. Its main spokesman was its chairman, G. Yagodin. Clearly, its policies, while not as radical as some educators would have liked, were reformist in that they emphasized democratization, differentiation, humanization, integration, and individualization of a system of continuous education. The policies of the USSR State Committee were outlined in some detail in private meetings with Professor Vladimir Shadrikov, first deputy chairman of the State Committee. He expressed the hope that the republics would cooperate with the State Committee and reach agreement on all aspects of educational policy. The curriculum was a case in point. Having given a large measure of autonomy to the republics, the State Committee proposed to establish a curriculum structure under the control of three entities: (1) Union, (2) republic, and (3) school. It was suggested that for the first nine grades 55 percent of the curriculum should be controlled by the republics and 45 percent by the USSR State Committee. In the upper two senior grades, however, only 35 percent of the curriculum should be determined by the republic and school.

The State Committee believed that the allocation of 45 percent of the nine-year curriculum to the USSR State Committee would guarantee that appropriate international, national, and regional content would be included in a unified core curriculum. In this core, Russian would be a compulsory subject; although teaching could be conducted in forty-four languages with textbooks published in these languages. Unresolved, however, was the issue of how many and which foreign languages to offer. This in fact became a political issue.

Most republics did not require the entire curriculum to be taught in a local language. In the struggle for sovereignty, most republics realized that they would be isolated without the use of Russian as the common language. There were indeed practical reasons for its retention; Russian was usually needed for entry into any Soviet institution of higher learning. Constitutionally, of course, parents had the right to choose the language of instruction for their children. Wherever a republican language was the state language, bilingualism was encouraged.

As for the distinction between the gymnasia and lyceums, which were introduced in the late 1980s, Shadrikov pointed out that in a large country with fifteen republics both terms had been used in the past. Therefore the republics and regions could choose which term to use in the light of their traditions. The gymnasia, lycées, and lyceums were nevertheless grouped together as general education secondary schools preparing students to enter higher education. If a distinction was to be made, it was that gymnasia emphasized mathematics and modern and classical foreign languages in preparation for entrance to the university. The lyceums, on the other hand, stressed modern languages, mathematics, and the sciences in preparation for a technological institution of higher education. The State Committee declared its intention to clarify the differences between these two types of general secondary schools. Unfortunately, the issue of finance between the Center and the republics was never resolved. With growing support for a free market in the finance of education, there was no guarantee that such a market could support schools adequately. Previously the policy was clear and unambiguous: Every child was guaranteed a free basic education. It is interesting to note that to achieve this goal the percentage of the GNP spent on education in the USSR (7 percent) was similar to that spent in the US; although in terms of actual amounts, much less was spent in the USSR. At least some agreement was reached on one phase of the free market: Schools were permitted to engage in money-raising activities and projects.

Shadrikov defended the controversial 1989 Regulation 540, which allowed a student to be promoted from one class to the next with as many as three failing grades. The State Committee recognized that not more than 50 percent of students could cope with the previous curriculum and that most teachers were opposed to students repeating an entire year of study. Consequently many teachers awarded a pass mark to students who really knew very little about a subject. This led to grade inflation. The State Committee decided that until schools were reorganized and the curriculum was revised in terms of the interests and achievements of individual children, grade inflation would continue. The decision was made to permit students who had followed the required subjects but had not received pass marks in three to move on to the next higher class. The hope was that in the future, when differentiated school types and differentiated curricula were introduced, students would be able to take subjects geared to their interests and abilities. Social promotion would then cease.

Of course a commitment to different school types and differentiated curricula would lead to the abandonment of the traditional unified school for all Soviet youth. The State Committee's decision was to make paramount the wishes, interests, and abilities of the child. However, to meet the needs of all students, a research project was initiated in 1988 at the Moscow State University. It resulted in a thesaurus of school knowledge. This thesaurus provided a framework and rationale for a departure from an obligatory program for all Soviet students to an acceptance of two levels in each discipline in the curriculum. The more difficult level was geared to prepare students for higher education; the lower level led to a certificate of secondary education which would not likely qualify for advanced study. Hence pupils could study all subjects in accordance with different goals and levels of achievement.

The RSFSR Ministry of Education

Many differences existed between the Russian Ministry of Education and the USSR State Committee, although the Ministry's general position was not very different from that taken by the committee, in spite of the fact that the RSFSR (Russian Soviet Federated Socialist Republic) had declared its sovereignty in mid-1990. Within the Russian Federation some of the national republics issued declarations of sovereignty. Over the years the Russian Ministry had issued many regulations and orders for the entire Federation. Under the new policy, the Ministry granted greater freedom to the republics, provinces, and territories to determine their educational policies. This had considerable implications for language policy and for the republican and local curriculum components.

A Russian Federation Council on National Problems of Education was formed in December 1990. Membership, made up of representatives from the republics and regions, was not restricted to professional people. Three cochairmen presided over its meetings. A scientific research institute was established to deal with nationality problems of the Federation. Branch laboratories were staffed with national minorities to address problems in (1) preparing teachers for national schools, (2) publishing instructional materials and textbooks for national schools, and (3) raising the quality of the teaching personnel.

Committed to nurturing ethnic diversity, the Ministry sponsored programs to revive national cultures. In 1990 there were more than 120 ethnic groups in the Russian Federation. The smallest of these consisted of 420 inhabitants with only 20 pupils in the local school. Only 66 of the 120 ethnic groups had schools in which all subjects through the eleven grades were taught in the native language. About twenty native languages were taught only as a second language throughout the eleven years of school. Most of the rest were taught only in the first four years of schooling, and indeed some were taught only in the first grade. More than ten languages had no alphabet, but plans were underway to develop them. Russian was the only language permitted in Russian institutions of higher learning.

Because of the many different numbers and types of minority pupils, the cost of preparing textbooks was enormous. These textbooks were given free to all pupils however small the minority group. The USSR State Committee had certain reservations about the viability of introducing native language teaching and textbooks for all national minorities but the Russian Ministry of Education did not share this view.

Another important controversial policy in the Russian Federation had to do with boarding schools. For many decades boarding schools were established for children living in sparsely populated areas. In the 1980s the Russian Ministry decided that boarding schools in the Far North were harmful in that children were separated from their families and minority culture. Instead, distance learning programs through radio, TV, and peripatetic teachers could be employed to bring education to families of reindeer herdsmen and thereby protect the culture of the minority people.

A menacing question was, "How could the state protect public education under market conditions?" Under the new reform it was possible to use state funds more freely. Principals were given freedom to spend funds in ways they thought best. The local community was given the right to determine policies for its own schools and support them in various ways. Independent and religious schools could be sponsored by collectives, enterprises, parents, societies, and joint ventures. As early as 1991 evidence was mounting that differentiation might well be achieved at the expense of equality of provision.

Under *perestroika* a revival of religion had occurred. Sunday schools and some general education schools were established by religious organizations. The Russian Ministry insisted that schools should be separated from politics and religion, but religion in church-sponsored schools was permissible. Permitting religion to be introduced into state schools would be substituting the ideology of the church for that of the Party. On these grounds and given its limited resources, the state was prohibited from giving direct financial help in establishing private, independent, or religious schools.

Although there were not many policy differences between the USSR State Committee and the Russian Ministry of Education, relationships between them reflected a struggle for power. The tension lessened somewhat with the signing of an agreement between the Russian Ministry and the State Committee which stated that any function not specifically delegated to the Constitution as a federal responsibility could be undertaken by individual states. The agreement stipulated that the State Committee could set standards throughout the country as well as a basic core curriculum. It was agreed that the Russian language would be included in the All-Union component of the curriculum, and the republics and regions would require both Russian and the native language.

Agreement was also reached on the provision of the curricula for the national entities of the Federation. The Supreme

Soviet of Yakutia, for example, worked out its own curriculum. Stress was placed on the national language, culture, and history of the region. Less attention was paid to that of the Russian Federation and even less to that of the Soviet Union. National and universal human values were included.

It was agreed that the State Committee would be responsible for some special programs such as those for gifted and handicapped children. Also, the All-Union government jointly financed with the RSFSR the training personnel for the armed forces, transportation, energy, and communications. Although schools in the Russian Federation were not forbidden to have Party committees, beginning in 1991, it was recommended that there should be no Party organizations in state schools. The role of the Party youth organizations such as the Pioneers and Komsomols was restricted but not abolished. Indeed the Ministry in 1990 had no power to abolish them. Other youth organizations were permitted to operate within schools as long as their activities did not violate the RSFSR Constitution. The Ministry expressed a willingness to cooperate with all youth organizations.

The Moscow School Board

Under *perestroika* the Moscow School Board introduced many changes in the way its schools were administered and financed. The fact that it was able to introduce reforms indicated that a devolution of power had truly taken place. At a meeting with representatives of the Moscow School Board it was stated that administrative changes had brought about new relationships between the schools, the district authorities, the Moscow School Board, the Russian Ministry of Education, and the USSR State Committee for Public Education. For example, school principals had complained that with so many regulations, they had little freedom to effect change; they were forced to consult with the local district and city school boards before any innovations could be introduced, and frequently these boards were too busy to consider proposals submitted by the principals. Therefore, in principle, the Moscow School Board decided that its schools could introduce any innovations they wished, provided that they did not violate Moscow/Russian laws or the Constitution. Unfortunately, some principals introduced changes which were either in conflict with the good of the child or did not make sense under prevailing conditions. In order to protect children against foolhardy principals and teachers, the Moscow Board established an expert commission to check and evaluate innovative proposals and, if necessary, suggest alternatives. If the commission approved a new practice, it was labeled an experiment and the school, or a section of it, was designated experimental. And, if needed, additional funds were made available to support the experiment. At the beginning of 1991, about 50 percent of the Moscow schools had various experiments underway. A department in the Moscow School Board had to certify that in each school All-Union requirements were being met.

In discussions with the Moscow education authorities, principals, and teachers it was evident that the command-authority structures in at least one large city of the USSR were undergoing change. Many differences of opinion were expressed which previously would not have been revealed to foreign visitors. These differences were openly expressed and indeed vigorously debated at all levels within the system. For example, with the decentralization of All-Union services, questions were raised about the Moscow Board's responsibilities in providing for the educational services, health care, cafeteria catering, and many other of the children's welfare services.

A Moscow city-wide professional education council was established to deal with the local educational problems. The new democratic climate, requiring that the public should be involved in formulating solutions to these problems, called for the council to be made up of principals, academics, other professional people, parents, and lay citizens. In fact many well-known people served as members of the council, which met about once a month, or more often, if necessary, to discuss pressing problems and recommend courses of action. The director of the Moscow schools served as deputy director of the council.

From the start, the council raised questions relative to the degree of independence that had been granted to the Moscow

Board. It demanded that the RSFSR Ministry and the USSR State Committee grant it autonomy. Dneprov, the Russian Minister of Education, complied in November 1990 and, in good measure, appointed Mrs. L. P. Kezina, the director of Moscow schools, RSFSR Deputy Minister of Education to coordinate the Moscow School Board's administrative functions with the Ministry.

In the past the Moscow Board developed a budget for the entire city which was then distributed among its various districts and individual schools by prearranged allocations. Under the new arrangement the budget was set by the number of children in the district and a minimum per capita allotment was guaranteed. Principals were free to spend the allocation as they saw fit. For example, each school had the authority to decide where to buy its computers and enter into contracts for servicing them. Moreover, the Moscow Board set up a center to teach school administrators how to enter into and enforce contracts.

Principals were permitted to raise extra money from the sale of products made by students in school workshops and contributions from donors. Teachers could give extra lessons for a fee; there was a great demand for tutoring, especially the English language. Because of the fear that teachers and principals might pay too much attention to earning extra money, the Moscow Board set down rules to prevent abuse.

Schools were given much freedom to run their own affairs. Councils could develop their own regulations and, if they wished, elect the school principals. There was some question as to the advisability of this practice. The Moscow Board was forced to assist a number of schools in removing unsuitable principals from their posts.

In recent years teacher salaries have been much lower than those earned by many laborers. Teachers threatened strikes and some actually carried them out. Several district boards found money in their budgets to supplement the salaries paid from the USSR allocations. The district boards demanded more money from the Moscow Board in order to raise teachers' salaries. The Moscow Board transmitted the appeal to the Russian Ministry of Education and the RSFSR Soviet. Still other boards in other cities entered into joint-ventures with enterprises and institutes hoping to make a profit. Some districts with surplus apartments to house the teaching staff sold them to raise money. Still others introduced cost accounting to eliminate waste. Money was saved by dismissing school inspectors, who traditionally monitored the work of classroom teachers, and principals were given the authority to monitor the work of the teachers. Parents and teachers who believed that the quality of education in a school had declined or complained of serious problems were encouraged to complain directly to the Moscow Board and request assistance to deal with the problem.

In the late 1980s about 100,000 students each year entered Moscow's 1,300 general education schools. Of the students who completed the ninth grade, some 10 percent entered traditional trade schools which did not provide general education and were not under the control of the Moscow Board. Supposedly the interests and achievements of children determined whether they went to these schools. While the vocational schools offering high-level and specialized-skill courses were in great demand, in general, most of the trade and many of the vocational schools were held in very low esteem.

Hence the traditional administrative system of the Moscow schools was in a state of transition in January 1991. The system of control by the centralized bodies and the monitoring by inspectors and Party officials of the work done in every school and classroom had ceased. Teachers, principals, and district boards were able to challenge the orders and regulations of superior authorities. Lower bodies could decide for themselves those functions they wished to delegate to higher agencies, implying that the real power, under a process of democratization, resided in the schools under the authority of principals, teachers, and school councils.

CHAPTER 5

The Finance of Soviet Education

Once education became compulsory in Europe and the US, it could not be financed through a free-market economic system. Consumers were not free to accept or reject what the market offered. Parents were obliged to send their children to school for a specified number of years. Their ability to choose the kind of education their children should receive was strictly limited. The producers of education enjoyed a virtual monopoly. They decided what subjects and courses should be offered and consumers were compelled by law to accept them.

In ancient Greece a free market existed in education with parents paying teachers for the instruction their children received. Pupils were free to enter into or withdraw from teaching and learning relationships by mutual agreement. Only when public authorities began to establish national systems of compulsory education in the late eighteenth and nineteenth centuries was it necessary to decide how the costs of educating a small proportion of the total population should be met. In most cases it was believed, since primary schools served local communities, the members of such communities should pay for the cost of the education. On the other hand, some governments considered that the second and third levels of education also served the larger national interest and should be funded nationally. Hence compulsory education was socialized in the sense that it was not considered proper for the free market to determine the resources placed at the disposal of teachers. And the parents of those benefitting directly from education should not be the only ones to pay for it. Education should be financed through public funds raised nationally and locally.

Private Education

For centuries the place of private and fee-paying schools in systems of compulsory education has been controversial. If education is a public service, should there be a monopoly on its provision? Should parents and organizations, such as the churches, be allowed to set up and run schools to promote their own interests if they pay the costs of providing such instruction? Should they be eligible for public financial support? Not all governments agree that parents have the right to send their children to private schools. Some governments accept the principle of private schools but refuse to grant them financial support from public funds. Still others with systems of compulsory education believe private schools should receive financial support from public funds for the contribution they make to the whole enterprise of schooling. Moreover, this issue is also part of a wider debate about the relationships between church and state.

Historically, a distinction is made between the right of parents to ensure that their children receive an education of their choice and the obligation of the public authorities to support private schools. Against the view that private schools should receive public support is advanced the argument that, since education bestows benefits on its recipients, the public generally should not be expected to subsidize schools designed to promote the interests of special groups.

The status of private schools depends on the view taken by government as to the role of these institutions in promoting equality and freedom in education. Policies designed to maximize equality in education can only be pursued at the expense of liberty. Liberty, in turn, can be achieved only at the expense of equality. National ways of financing education mirror the relative importance governments place on student and parental freedom of choice in education and on the equalization of education provision. The success of financial policies has to be judged in the light of the extent to which they promote in practice one or other of these irreconcilable objectives. The Soviet system of financing education was designed to promote equality.

While recognizing that education is open to all, decision makers in the US, for example, have traditionally tried to maintain a balance by adopting policies that promote both equality and liberty. Hence while private and parochial schools are not prohibited, as in the USSR, federal, state, and local authorities consistently refuse to subsidize private education. Since the educational system in the US is not financed by the central government but by the constituent states, local school provision has been very unequal.

The proposals to individualize and democratize education in the USSR in the late 1980s called into question the previous absolute preoccupation with equality which had meant that private schools were forbidden and church schools prohibited. The power of central government over the educational system was supreme. Differentiation in terms of school type (see chapter 6) and curriculum (see chapter 8), with a few exceptions, was rejected. Financial policies were designed to promote for the most part identical education for almost all of the pupils undergoing compulsory education in spite of the enormous differences in circumstances. With the onset of *perestroika*, democratization, individualization, and differentiation proposals were advanced, and the existing financial arrangements came under criticism. Within the framework of parental choice, private schools entered the reformer's agenda. Subsidies to parents sending their children to independent and privatized state schools or even abroad were seriously considered.

The Public Finance of General and Vocational Education

The stress on equal provision made it less necessary in theory to distinguish between community and national schools in the USSR. The predominant role of the State in the financing of general education was not questioned. In contrast, in the US, federal support for schools was constrained by interpretations of the Constitution. Only during the 1950s was the interpretation of the common welfare clause in the preamble to the Constitution extended to allow federal funds to be spent on educational activities beyond those already granted to advance agriculture, industry, commerce, mathematics, science, foreign languages, and military training.

Throughout Europe the apprenticeship system has dominated the training of skilled craftsmen. In Germany it still plays a major role. In England and Wales, although training through apprenticeships is less prevalent than it was, industrialists continue to provide vocational training and to a large extent determine its character and quality; not until the Manpower Services Commission was established did a national organization, through the national government, influence vocational training programs. In Germany there have always been close relationships between governments and the chambers of commerce in the training of apprentices for a very large number of specific occupations. In 1919 the Astier laws in France obliged industries to pay a levy to support vocational training. In the US vocational education has been more fully incorporated into general education than in continental Europe.

The control of vocational training in the USSR was more in the continental European model. Responsibility was shared between the Ministries of Education, for general education content, and the State Committee for Vocational Training.

Vocational schools came under increasing criticism when, in the spirit of *perestroika*, an attempt was made to accelerate and modernize industrial production. The schools were considered to be in very poor condition and in need of modernization and more financial assistance. Detailed statistics were not made public as to the amount of financial help factories contributed to specialized vocational-technical schools, factory-based training programs, and kindergartens for the children of their workers. However, the factory-based schools reflected the low levels of technology in much of Soviet industry and the poor quality of many of its manufactured goods.

When the USSR State Committee of Public Education was established in 1988, it assumed responsibility for general and vocational education. The practice of factories and collective farms giving schools equipment, stock, workshop materials, and money for capital and recurrent maintenance costs was continued. The emphasis given to this kind of support clearly made vocational training institutions a part of a differentiated school system. However, enterprises were not obliged to give this support. Consequently, with the transition to a market system many industries and farms ended their contributions and assistance. The residual principle of funding vocational education came under criticism and demands were made for complete government funding.

The Residual Principle in Financing Education

In any country a high proportion of the costs of education goes to pay teachers. Under a compulsory system of education, the total cost is largely determined by the authorities responsible for ensuring that there are enough teachers. In the US each state, which is constitutionally responsible for education, determines the number of teachers required by establishing the period of compulsory education and awarding certificates to teachers. Local school boards determine how many teachers to employ and what they are to be paid. In England and Wales, although local authorities employ and pay teachers, the latter's salary scales are on an increasingly flexible national range. Although school governors now have much more freedom to negotiate salaries and to balance their own budgets, a major part of the national school budget is still determined by the national government.

In some countries socialized education was costing taxpayers more than defense and health care because of the post–World War II government-inspired expansionist policies that raised not only the age of compulsory attendance but also the salaries of trade union teachers. Parents and other members of the public were asking whether in education they were receiving value for the taxes they paid. Even in the USSR, because parents could not opt out of a compulsory system and they were not able to directly influence the place of education in the market, in the late 1980s some parents tried to exert political pressure on those who produced and funded education to permit tuition-charging private schools. The argument given was that parents could thereby be in a better position to influence the provision of education.

The State Committee recognized that changes in the Soviet system of financing education were needed if the reforms in education were to succeed. However, no alternative to the residual principle of educational finance was legislated, in spite of the criticism that not enough resources had been provided for education. Moreover, Soviet educators were learning that in a free market the education sector would have to compete with other interests for resources which would then have to be allocated in accordance with consumer preferences. While confidence in the educational system was declining, Russia still remained a country in which education was held in high esteem.

The USSR State Committee was forced to agree that during the transitional stage, the main source of educational finance would have to continue to be the allocations from All-Union, republican, and local taxes. But school and university councils and school principals were given permission to raise additional money, including hard currency, for their own needs.

Taxation Policies

Soviet commentators claimed that a major advantage of the Soviet budgetary system was that, in contrast to those in capitalist countries, it was unified. As in other countries Soviet budgets were prepared by estimating what would be needed and what funds should be raised through taxes to meet these costs. Since taxation policies determine how the burden will be distributed, in most democracies they are highly politicized. Under *perestroika* and *glasnost* taxation policies in the USSR became highly politicized.

On the issue of direct and indirect taxes there was previously no debate. Socialist policy favored direct taxes. When levied on individuals and enterprises on the basis of the income earned and profits, direct taxes depend on the ability to pay and cannot legally be avoided. Indirect taxes are not dependent on what individuals earn but on how much they spend. Consumers have some control over the indirect taxes they pay by limiting their spending. Socialist governments tend to favor direct taxes because they differentiate between the rich and poor in ways that indirect taxes do not. In moving to a free-market economy, the USSR authorities had to modify the taxation system. There was a shift from the unified system to practices which resembled budgetary policies in Western countries. Shadrikov agreed that national, regional, and territorial government bodies would have to participate to a greater extent in the control and finance of Soviet education.

A widely accepted democratic principle is that the people from whom money is raised should have some say as to how it is spent. Some democrats maintain that locally raised taxes increase democratic participation in government institutional activity. Before 1985 parents in the USSR had no effective say on how money should be raised and spent on education. Local authorities, through which in most countries parents could exert some influence, had no real power to raise funds or discretion in the use of resources. Soviet salary scales were nationally set by members of the state bureaucracy with little or no public discussion. Hence it was a radical departure to legislate that school councils should raise their own funds and spend them as they saw fit.

The Soviet Budgetary System

School budgeting procedures showed how, through the power of the purse, the central government agencies had been able to control the Soviet system of education. These procedures were the same throughout the whole country. They started with the annual submission from each school of a detailed estimate of its financial requirements for the coming year in accordance with the price lists, salary schedules, staffing standards, equipment, and accommodations laid down in the regulations of All-Union agencies. In a planned economy, with very low inflation, these estimates were not difficult to reach. Budget estimates from all schools in a local area were brought together to form a local budget for the education sector. The next higher level of administration constructed a budget from the estimates of the smaller administrative units. The aggregate of these budgets formed the republic's budget and they in turn formed the All-Union budget.

In years past, schools and local authorities had little discretion in drawing up estimates. Items of expenditure established by the central authorities and the hierarchical relationships between the three levels of administration ensured that the estimates prepared by schools followed a clear, centrally defined pattern. Soviet commentators claimed that, unlike those in socialist countries, most capitalist budgetary systems failed to bring together into a unified pattern national, regional, and local budgets.

There was no education tax as such. The central authorities determined the proportion of tax revenue to be allocated to republican agencies in terms of the estimates, which in turn decided the revenues to be given to local authorities. In the case of education, no matter what the source of income raised, it had to be spent according to items specified in the state budget.

Noah, a professor of comparative education at Teachers College, Columbia University, summarized the tax system in 1960 in these words: "By retaining control over budgets of inferior organs in the hands of the superior authorities, by giving local authorities virtually no initiative in taxation, and by reducing them to the status of mere recipients of tax revenue assignments determined at a higher level, the Soviet system ensures that control over the pace of development of the school system is kept firmly in the hands of top levels of government" (Harold Noah, *Financing Soviet Schools*, New York: Teachers College Press, 1966, p. 62). Under *perestroika* proposals to democratize education inevitably implied that the highly centralized financial arrangements in a unified system should be modified to increase the power of inferior agencies (including schools) to raise funds and spend them in accordance with locally determined policies.

Assigning Revenue

In the case of the Soviet Union less information is available about the precise ways in which taxes were raised than on how, by whom, and to whom funds were allocated. Noah dealt almost exclusively with how the costs of education were distributed among the Union republics, the autonomous republics, and local administrative units such as *oblasts* (districts), *gorods* (towns), *raions* (regions), and still smaller centers of population. Each of the 50,395 separate units of Soviet government had its own budget. As stated previously, as late as 1991 the state budget of the USSR was the aggregate of this enormous number of national, regional, and local budgets. Each of the many budgets specified the amount of rubles to be spent on education, culture, and scientific research.

Distinctions were made between the types of institutions financed through national and regional budgets and those financed through local budgets. In the Soviet Union, All-Union institutions like the USSR Academy of Pedagogical Sciences, other large scientific research establishments, and national broadcasting services were financed through the national budget. Kindergartens and general education schools were funded through local budgets. Technical and other specialized academic schools and institutes of higher education were financed through republic budgets.

Under democratic centralism the central authorities had the authority to ensure that the funding of schools was equalized. The sources from which local authorities received their revenue were receipts from enterprises, collective farms, and other bodies under the Council of Ministers of the Union and republics, as well as from taxes levied by the soviets on each level of government. The proportion of rubles raised from taxes in a particular area and sent to the All-Union and republic budgets varied considerably. Likewise, the variation in the proportion assigned from the state-planned budget to the different local authorities was particularly great. Noah reported, however, that "as much as two-thirds of the money spent through local authority budgets for general education is ultimately derived from the proceeds of taxation imposed at nonlocal levels" (ibid., p. 61).

Under the traditional Soviet system, local school authorities enjoyed no significant discretion in the way assigned revenues could be spent. The norms of expenditure were precisely established through general legislation which laid down the standard provision to which local authorities were expected to adhere. By retaining control over school budgets, the central authorities determined the pace and territorial distribution of development.

This centralized Soviet system of financing schools, based on incentives and the willingness of local citizens to pay nationally imposed taxes to support local services in other parts of the country, probably went part way toward achieving the goal of equality of provision. However, it reduced the ability to raise tax revenues locally for education through voluntary contributions from collective and state farms, enterprises, trade union organizations, and cooperatives to promote educational services desired by the donors.

The changes introduced in the taxation system raised two questions: how to afford a compulsory system of education, and how to promote equality of educational provision while allowing parents and local authorities to choose the kind of education they wanted. A decentralized financial system maximizes freedom of choice but almost inevitably leads to considerably greater regional and local inequality in the resources available for education.

In the US, education is a state responsibility. Financial responsibility is delegated to local authorities that raise taxes specifically to support education. Capital expenditure is usually raised by issuing bonds. Local people can protest an education tax they regard as too high; they can refuse to buy bonds or support school levies. The emphasis placed on local freedom and initiative in the US means that among states and within states, the public resources made available for education vary enormously. Freedom of choice is emphasized at the expense of equality of provision.

In England and Wales, the power of the central government to control education has been limited. Yet for many years central government funds were used to equalize provision throughout the country. In France, when it proved impossible for a nationwide network of primary schools to be financed locally, the national government agreed to subsidize local authorities.

None of the above systems is perfect, but in reforming the financing of education under *perestroika*, comparative studies offer some insights into ways of raising, allocating, and spending funds democratically. If the political will is there, features of the old system can be retained while ensuring greater local participation in decision making.

Administrative Control

Administrative methods of control were associated with methods of financing Soviet education. In some democracies, like France, many policies are formulated and adopted nationally. For example, teachers in state schools are civil servants and receive salaries according to their position on a civil-service scale. The content of education is decided centrally. Methods of teaching are monitored by national and local inspectors. In some respects the French model is similar to that of the Soviet Union. In England and Wales, on the other hand, fewer aspects of educational policy are formulated and adopted by the central government. National legislation leaves a great deal of freedom for local authorities to run things as they think fit. Only recently was a national curriculum introduced, and even then the opposition of teachers forced the government to retreat from its original position. Yet teachers are paid in accordance with national salary scales.

In the nineteenth century the federal government in the US legislated very few educational policies. The interpretation of the Constitution was translated into national policies only after the most careful scrutiny. There were constant debates about the federal government's constitutional authority to aid general education, finance religious schools, and equalize support for schools throughout the country. Curricula were not laid down by the central government. Salary scales were determined locally and differed widely from one state and local area to another. Examinations were not monitored by federal inspectors. Policies were, in short, formulated and adopted to a large extent by local boards of education and influenced by members of the teaching profession.

Hence there is no absolute relationship between the way money is raised to meet the costs of education and the power of the revenue-raising agencies to determine policy. Nevertheless, no government is prepared to abandon all control over the ways in which public money is spent. By the same token, few governments are willing to allow market forces and consumer demand to determine what money is spent on education and how it is distributed. Methods of financing Soviet schools under democratic centralism allowed patronage rather than market forces to determine the ways in which funds were allocated.

Serious thought was given in 1989–91 to the dangers of abandoning a financial system which had given Soviet teachers security, modest standards of living, and reasonable conditions of work in favor of one designed to promote democratic participation in a wide range of decision-making processes. It was easier to criticize the ways in which the system was run than the principles on which it was based.

The USSR State Committee was very conscious of the need to explore the alternative ways of financing education. This was revealed in its report to the IBE in Geneva ("Public Education in the USSR: Its Development under *Perestroika* in Soviet Society," Moscow: USSR State Committee for Public Education, 1990) in which the consequences for education of centralized financial arrangements and the residual principle were fully analyzed. The Committee reported that while expenditures on education had grown in absolute terms between 1970 and 1986, the proportion of state budget assignments had "dropped markedly from 11 percent in 1970 to 8 percent in 1986" (ibid., p. 58). Until this trend was reversed in the late 1980s, the educational system suffered from severe shortages in technical and material provision and low salaries for teaching and staff personnel.

The IBE report revealed that only 60 percent of children under seven were assured places in preschool nurseries and kindergartens. Almost 23 percent of pupils in general education schools were obliged to attend in either two- or even three-shift schools. The provision of equipment such as computers lagged behind demand. Only 11.5 percent of the schools in 1988–89 had information technology laboratories and computer equipment, in spite of the fact that a resolution had been adopted by the CPSU Central Committee to introduce a new course, "The Fundamentals of Information Science and Computer Technology," into all Soviet secondary schools. Not surprisingly the report stated that the Soviet government saw the reform of educational finance as one of its central tasks. Chances of success, however, depended as much on improvements in the economy as a whole as on the system of taxation.

Education and the Economy

In the late years of *perestroika* the stagnation of the Soviet economy was the subject of much comment. For example, in an article in *Moscow News* ("Democracy a Burden on the Poor?" No. 19, 1990, p. 7), Timur Pulatov stated that "[p]overty is gradually acquiring global dimensions in this country." Sixty-five million people, a quarter of the population, were below the poverty line; this comprised an inert force capable of slowing down or aborting any reform or revolution. In Central Asia, the poorest region, the number of people living below the poverty line had reached Third World levels. In recent years it had grown to 60 percent in Tajikistan, over 46 percent in Uzbekistan, and 40 percent in Kirghizia and Turkmenia. Seventy-eight rubles a month was considered a subsistence minimum; the average monthly income for every working citizen in these regions was between forty and sixty rubles. There was mass unemployment. Sixty percent of children in Central Asia suffered from malnutrition and diseases caused by low living standards. In contrast, an average of 3.5 percent of the populations in the Baltic republics lived below the poverty line. Pulatov concluded that "[t]he transition to a market economy was likely to throw new millions of low-income citizens into the throes of poverty."

Indeed economic equality throughout the country had not been achieved. At the Second Congress of USSR People's

Deputies in December 1989 (*Izvestia*, December 1989, CDSP, Vol. XLI, No. 52, 1989, pp. 24–25), M. M. Mirkasymov, chairman of the Uzbek Republic Council of Ministers, pointed out that while the economic situation in the country as a whole was unfavorable, in Uzbekistan it was much worse. The system of state allocations had not promoted equality. Indeed over the past 30 years, the state capital investment per capita for housing and social, cultural, and consumer services was at a rate only half the average for the country as a whole. Equalization policies had failed to provide fair starting conditions for different regions. Curiously, in view of the overall decentralizing thrust of *perestroika* reforms, Mirkasymov still urged that an All-Union program should be undertaken to equalize starting conditions with the participation of the Union republic's central economic agencies and research organizations.

Under *perestroika* proposals were made to introduce a market economy. At the same time, attempts were made to remedy some of the failures of the old system without abandoning it. For example, L. A. Voronin, first vice-chairman of the USSR Council of Ministers, was quoted in *Izvestia* as saying that in 1990 subsidies from the Union budget to the Union-republics budgets would be made in order to equalize social facilities and services within the population. These subsidies were to compensate some regions for the uneven distribution of revenue under the existing price system. Approximately eight billion rubles were to be distributed to Uzbekistan, Kazakhstan, Kirghizia, Tadzhistan, and Turkmenistan. In addition, Armenia was to receive 100 million rubles for repair work after the earthquake (*Izvestia*, December 18, 1989, pp. 8–9).

The Union authorities sought to equalize revenues regardless of the productivity levels of individual republics. The plan for 1990 was to increase Estonia's budgetary revenues by 11.6 percent and to allow Estonia to retain only 1 percent of any surplus at its disposal. The central authorities objected to the Estonian Supreme Soviet's decision to fix surcharges on alcohol, cigarettes, and beer for additional revenue. They claimed that Estonia's self-willed action had resulted in individual Estonians going to Russia to buy these items in large quantities at a very low price. Unilateral action of this kind against the decision of the USSR Supreme Soviet not to raise the price of goods on an All-Union scale created tensions which encouraged other republics besides Estonia to retaliate as well.

Clearly the power of the Supreme Soviet of the USSR to pass legislation which stipulated the amount each republic had to pay into the Union budget was a source of conflict between republics and the Center. The Estonians complained that under the old budgetary arrangements they did not benefit from the additional income derived from their more efficient organization of production. Upon declaring its sovereignty Russia decided not to pay a proportion of its tax revenue into the All-Union budget. But, in turn, the Russian Federation's central government soon had difficulty in collecting taxes from its own national republics and regions.

It was increasingly clear that the traditional budgetary methods made it impossible for the central authorities to equalize production and income throughout the country. It was clear that the central allocation of funds from a budget to which each republic contributed was resisted and resented by republics in which production was well organized and profits were high. It was also clear that some sovereign republics wished to manage their budgets independently of the All-Union budget. Inevitably the differences in economic levels between the various republics had widened during the *perestroika* reforms. Nor would political sovereignty guarantee economic prosperity as many of the republics had hoped for.

In the Soviet Union, education, health, and other cultural activities fell under the heading of social services. These services were paid out of social consumption funds and had to compete with other government agencies for revenue. A major consequence of this was that the entire school system suffered financially.

During the years of *perestroika* complaints were heard that education's share of the residual income was far too small. At the Second Congress of the USSR's People's Deputies in December 1989, Yu. A. Ryzhov, chairman of the USSR Supreme Soviet's Committee on Science, Public Education, Culture, and Upbringing, stated that "when the committee asked for additional financing (in the process of working on the 1990 budget) for teachers in particular . . . so as to give them a right to bonuses on a par with employees of other non-production branches such as public health, we were refused." He went on to say that the salaries of instructors in higher schools had not been raised for forty years, and any increase added had already been eaten up by inflation ("Ryzhov Reports," *CDSP*; Vol. XLII, No. 2, 1990, p. 10). While government allocations to the social sphere were increased by about 10.7 percent in 1990, aid to education was raised by less than 4.3 percent. Yagodin told the Supreme Soviet's Committee on Education that his ministry needed 20 percent more than the amount allocated in 1990 from government funds (Patricia Legras, "Soviet Union Gives Too Little Emphasis to Education under *Perestroika*," *The Chronicle of Higher Education*, November 1, 1989, pp. 42–43).

The Leftover Principle Questioned

The principle of leftover or residual budgeting for the social services came under intense review during the meeting of the Twenty-eighth Congress of the Communist Party in 1990 (*CDSP*, Vol. XLII, No. 27, pp. 1–13). A communiqué reported that steps had been taken to overcome the defects of the leftover principle. For example, over the past four years, thirty-four billion rubles over and above the five-year assignments had been allocated for the construction of nonproduction facilities. The annual growth rate for nonproduction investments had almost doubled from 4.7 percent under the Eleventh Five-Year Plan to 8.8 percent under the later plan. Thus, 38 percent more schools were commissioned annually than during the previous period. Overall, health facilities, clubs, and houses of culture had also experienced higher annual rates of growth. Still, Yagodin made it known that construction delays were affecting the entire Soviet educational system. As a result, the equivalent of more than eleven million dollars was unspent from funds allocated for 1986, 1987, and 1988. Obviously, appropriated money alone was not enough to make a system efficient that could not properly organize state construction projects.

Social sphere allocations were also increased to safeguard families against the effects of the changeover to a regulated market economy. *Izvestia* (*CDSP*, Vol. XLII, No. 31, p. 30) reported that the USSR Supreme Council of Ministers had adopted a resolution "On Urgent Measures for Improving the Position of Women, Safeguarding Mother and Child and Strengthening the Family," which provided that every family in which a child was born after December 1, 1990, should receive a one-time payment amounting to three times the minimum monthly wage, which was at that time 210 rubles. A monthly allowance for children between the ages of one-and-a-half and six years of age was established for families whose income was not more than twice the minimum wage.

These were some of the changes made under *perestroika* in an attempt to remedy the failures of the old financial system. They were seen as necessary to protect sections of the population from the consequences of the changeover to a market economy. However, the rate of inflation continued to erode the value of these awards before they were made. Nevertheless, as inflation grew in the USSR, the intention was to improve the social and economic security of educational personnel and students by linking their salaries and grants to the index of consumer prices (*Public Education in the USSR*, op. cit., p. 59). Boris Yeltsin, on assuming the presidency of the Russian Federation, promised teachers as much. Among the resolutions passed by some 1,600 delegates to the USSR Student Forum, reported in *Soviet Union* (No. 2, 1990, pp. 54–55), were those designed to improve the living conditions of students. Although higher education was free of tuition, the annual grants to students were inadequate. Because there was a chronic shortage of free dormitory accommodations, many students were forced to arrange off-campus rooms whose rents were not controlled.

To meet these problems, student grants were raised to equal the minimum wage. Indeed, Susannah Massey reported in *The Chronicle of Higher Education* ("Soviet Ministers Agree to Broaden Aid to Students," April 25, 1990) that in response to complaints from university students, the Supreme Council of Ministers agreed to broaden the program of grants to include students with passing grades instead of limiting them to students with better-than-average grades. The best students received more than the minimum grant. In addition, students were allowed to earn extra money in their fields of specialization while studying.

Frequent complaints were heard about the low level of teachers' salaries and the fact that they were overtaken by the wages of unskilled workers. A program was worked out (*Public Education in the USSR*, op. cit., p. 59) to ensure the salaries of school teachers would match the average wage of industrial workers.

As early as 1989 some of the newly established private institutions of higher education required foreign students to pay part of their fees in convertible currencies (*Moscow News*, No. 38, 1989, p. 7). All institutions of higher education were encouraged to enter into contracts with foreign institutions and individual entrepreneurs. Several such programs were operating at the Krupskaya Pedagogical Institute in 1990. Freedom from the former state controls encouraged such initiatives.

Likewise, schools attempted to make money through commercial activities in a variety of ways. One source of revenue listed in the temporary regulations on USSR general secondary schools published in *Narodnoe obrazovanie* (No. 7, 1989, pp. 10–110) was the leasing of school premises and equipment. Another was offering seminars and tour programs at a fee to foreign delegations of teachers. Schools were encouraged to solicit voluntary contributions from state, communal, and cooperative organizations and businesses and even to secure bank loans to meet emergency situations.

Minimum salaries were based on the qualifications of different categories of teachers and other workers. Additional payments and bonuses could be paid by schools in accordance with the individual teacher's qualifications and high achievement in fulfilling important assignments.

Many teachers earned additional income by conducting private tutoring and cram sessions in preparation for entrance exams to higher educational institutions and by providing tutorial assistance to students in demanding courses. The market determined the price students or their parents paid. Many cooperatives and individual teachers publicly advertised for students. Some claimed that a language could be mastered in groups of twelve to fifteen pupils over a period of one month.

Since schools were free to determine their own programs and make money in order to supplement the pay of staff members with special skills, Simon Soloveichik suggested in *New Times* (No. 38, 1988, p. 30) that schools should receive cash rewards for every graduate achieving high marks at college entrance examinations or performing well on the job where he secured employment.

Alternatives to public schools, with their income-raising commercial and industrial activities were the private fee-paying or joint-venture schools. They introduced the free-market element into a sphere which traditionally was financed exclusively from public consumption funds. Also, as a result, some students with low qualifications were admitted not on the basis of examination results but because of parental influence.

A not unrelated proposal was that in privatized schools, parents should be subsidized and not the schools. This principle was applied in some aspects of federal funding in the US, namely, parents and children should receive subsidies but not the organizations which own and run the nonpublic schools.

Timothy Frye found in *Report on the USSR* (Vol. 2, No. 31, August 3, 1990, pp. 16–19) that Moscow City Soviet had adopted in principle a voucher plan to improve the service of day-care centers. Under the plan, each family in the capital received an allowance per child which could be spent on cooperative or state-run day-care centers or used to cover the costs of raising the child at home.

The emergence of a private sector clearly increased the choices of parents who could afford to pay fees determined by the market. It brought Russia into line with countries like the US and Britain, where private education is regarded as socially acceptable. In the US and Britain, some private schools have a higher status than publicly maintained schools. Pupils graduating from them are at an advantage when applying for admission to the prestigious universities, whose graduates, in turn, have distinct advantage when seeking employment. On the other hand, in France state *lycées* enjoy a far higher status than the private schools. Hence the introduction of a private sector in the USSR meant that the principle of a common "unified" school embraced by the post–1917 Revolution authorities had been abandoned.

The point has been made that democratization of compulsory education seeks to give consumers and producers greater say in the formulation and adoption of policies. Under *perestroika* the financial management of schools, based on state economic planning, was changed to that of self-management and self-financing as in industrial, agricultural, and government operations. The crux of the change in economic management was, according to E. Dolot ("From the Republic and the Country: Byelorussia Prepares for Regional Management," *Soviet Union*, No. 8, 1989, p. 8), linking the national interests and advantages more closely to every region and work group. To achieve these links, republican agencies of the USSR were put in charge of the social sphere—health services, housing construction, ecological programs, education, and culture.

Nikolai Pivovarov ("More Funds to the Soviets," *Soviet Weekly*, August 12, 1989, p. 15), chairman of the parliamentary committee on local self-government, maintained that the essence of political reform was to make republic soviets masters of their own destiny. Obviously, without economic clout the soviets would have no real power. The newly sovereign state found this to be the case. But republic soviets soon found that their ability to raise revenue from taxes was limited because so many enterprises in their areas were under the jurisdiction of All-Union ministries and frequently refused to pay to the local budgets certain sums of money for the land, water, and other natural resources made available by the local authorities. Consequently, many republics demanded that these enterprises be transferred to the sovereign states.

In 1989, *Soviet Weekly* (September 2, 1989, p. 15) reported that, under a new budget policy, Kazakhstan proposed to grant to local soviets those resources which were generated directly from their local activities. In this case, all payments from enterprises situated in a particular region were to be diverted to that regional budget in order to provide the soviet with material resources on which to maintain a sound budget. Under local economic self-management, local committees were supposed to raise their own revenue and maintain a balanced budget. This was not so easily accomplished in some regions because the levels of economic development were depressed. Hence local financial management meant that the gap widened between the more prosperous regions and those in which a majority of the people lived below the poverty line.

The introduction of a free market in the USSR in the late 1980s was not an easy undertaking, especially in view of the economic crisis. Political opinion ranged from those who said the reforms were not sufficiently radical to those who claimed that the maintenance of an economic and educational system under democratic centralism would have prevented the crisis conditions.

No industrial country has permitted education to be financed entirely through the mechanism of a free market. Most are attempting to introduce a measure of local self-government. Those who oppose such reform measures fear the growth of greater inequalities between schools in affluent and those in depressed areas; between schools for the rich and those for the poor; and between schools for the gifted and those for the masses. By 1991 evidence was mounting that the local financing of schools in the USSR was in practice eroding the principle of equality on which the Soviet school system had been founded.

CHAPTER 6

Soviet School Types

In 1917 the Soviet authorities inherited a traditional system of education in which there were several types of schools. According to Nicholas Hans in *History of Russian Educational Policy, 1701–1917* (London: P. S. King & Sons, 1931), the Russian university preparatory schools were started by Peter the Great in 1701 when he founded the School of Mathematics and Navigation in Moscow. It was based on the model of the Mathematics School of Christ's Hospital in England and initiated the secular scientific, utilitarian school movement in Russia that combined common European features with the Russian traditions. The humanism in the Russian schools was broader than the classical religious humanism of many Western grammar institutions. Later, the system of popular coeducational secondary schools created by Catherine II continued the secular, scientific, utilitarian, and Russian features. However, there did exist church schools which offered courses in literacy and religion. As in the Western European tradition, the schools through which pupils moved on their path to a university also constituted a stream different from the terminal elementary schools and the technical vocational schools that trained pupils for specific jobs in industry.

Soviet policy from the start was designed to minimize differentiation by school type. A common unified school was compulsory for all Soviet youth, although a small number of children attended special schools for ballet, music, art, sports, foreign languages, armed forces, and impaired learners. Later, the Khrushchev reforms introduced other special academic terminal schools for talented children. However, the Soviet authorities rejected the Western European models which selected children between the ages of ten and twelve to enter academic schools.

Compulsory basic education for all Soviet youth took many years to achieve in the Soviet Union. Prior to 1939, seven years of schooling was the norm for the majority of children. By 1950, the period had increased to eight years. In the 1970s, Soviet education was geared to the achievement of ten years of schooling for all. Within this stage of compulsory education, minimal differentiation took place. As early as the Khrushchev years, the common curriculum, which was designed to meet the needs of pupils seeking admission to higher education, created the same kinds of problems faced by teachers in the secondary schools of the US and Western Europe. After phenomenal expansion of educational facilities in those countries in the late nineteenth century, differentiation by school type was gradually replaced after 1945 by comprehensive and neighborhood institutions to which all pupils, regardless of interests and achievement, were admitted. Since common secondary schooling lies at the heart of educational policy in most socialist countries, it was not until the onset of *perestroika* that the issue of differentiation was debated in terms both of curriculum and school types. It was recognized that the ideological commitment of Soviet educators to the common unified compulsory school had created dilemmas which could only be resolved by a return to differentiation.

The All-Union Law on Freedom of Conscience and Religious Organizations, legislated on October 1, 1990, reenforced this trend toward school type differentiation. The role of private and religious schools was furthered by a law that provided for the separation of church and state. It prohibited the state funding of church facilities or premises ("New Religious Law Comes into Effect," *Soviet Muslims Brief*, Vol. 4, November/December 1990, pp. 3–6). However, the establishment of alternative private and religious schools was encouraged by the USSR State Committee for Public Education. The Russian Orthodox in Russia and the Muslims in Central Asian republics and Tatarstan were most anxious to regain the dominant role they had enjoyed in the prerevolutionary period.

Stages of Education

Originally, the Soviet educational system consisted of kindergartens, unified general secondary education schools, special secondary education schools, specialized secondary education schools, vocational schools, and institutions of higher education that embraced universities and specialized institutes.

In the 1970s, the general unified secondary education schools were reorganized into three-year primary, five-year junior, and two-year senior stages (3 + 5 + 2). Then in 1984, an extra year was added to the primary stage by bringing the last year of the kindergarten into the primary school (4 + 5 + 2).

In large cities there were special academic schools that offered two years of concentrated study in pedagogy, medical science, mathematics-physics, biology-chemistry, humanities, or social science. These schools differed from the special schools devoted to the early study of foreign languages, music, art, theater, and ballet. By law, admission to all of the special schools was competitive and based on the discerned potential of individual applicants. Pupils in these schools had to complete the curriculum of the regular unified schools. The special foreign language schools started teaching a foreign language, most frequently English, in the first and second grades, a few in kindergarten. The reputation of these schools, particularly among professional parents, was so high that the demand for places exceeded the number available. Under these circumstances, however, the principals of the schools had some discretion in admitting pupils. The charge was made that influential families had secured places for their children, even those who were less qualified than others applying. At the same time there were special schools for the deaf, blind, physically-handicapped, brain-damaged, and tubercular children.

In practice, various school types existed to meet the needs, interests, and talents of individual children prior to *perestroika*, but in limited numbers. Beginning in 1989 the practice of differentiation and selection was gradually expanded. A major issue was the age at which differentiation by school types within the general education system should take place. Some educators supported selection and possibly allocation at the end of the fourth grade of schooling, but there was minimum support for this policy. There was much wider approval for selection at the end of the ninth grade.

Vladimir Shadrikov, the USSR deputy Minister of Education, verified in a 1990 interview with the authors that there were differences of opinion among psychologists as to the age at which differentiation by school type should commence. Should the new type of gymnasium and lyceum admit pupils after the fourth, sixth, or ninth grade? Shadrikov believed a fairly long period of common schooling was needed to enable children to reveal their interests, talents, and needs. He opposed selection at the end of the primary stage. As a psychologist, Shadrikov took the view that at some point in schooling, selection was necessary and tests should be developed to assess the development of children at various ages. These tests, he believed, were neither valid nor reliable when administered to young children. The younger the child, the less reliable were the tests.

In the mid-1980s proposals were made to the Ministry of Education to introduce differentiation by profiles in some schools after the fourth grade, and by 1989 a few of these gymnasia and lyceums offered specializations in mathematics-physics, chemistry-biology, and humanities. Also, specialized technical profiles were offered in some vocational-technical general education schools. Indeed in many schools in the last two years of schooling, special profiles were introduced alongside the regular unified school program. Still another form of differentiation in the primary school was advanced by Shadrikov. He proposed that children should be permitted to enter the first primary grade either at six or seven years of age, depending on the learning readiness of the child. Some talented pupils entering at six could complete the primary stage in three years; others would take four years. The assumption underlying this arrangement was that while there were common tasks and learnings to be mastered, children matured at different rates and ages. While the content of primary schooling was the same, the speed and tempo at which pupils passed through the various grades should be different.

Even before 1990 some Soviet psychologists, such as Ravich Shcherba and others at the Institute of Educational

Psychology of the USSR Academy of Pedagogical Sciences, conducted research based on the theory that children had innate differences. This theory had been rejected by Stalin. Research in child development in those years was based on the theory that when children engaged in activities, their abilities were formed. In the 1980s some features of Piaget's theory of child development were accepted and supplemented by the findings of Russian research psychologist Vygotsky and his students Davydov, Zankovy, and Galperin that supported the growing demand for differentiated programs at the early stage of schooling.

Soviet psychological theorists had for many years drawn a distinction between brain-damaged and normal children. Youngsters who attended kindergartens were observed by the teachers, and those children with learning disabilities, after conferences with parents, were referred to commissions made up of psychologists, doctors, and physiologists in order to determine whether these children were to continue or to be assigned to a special kindergarten. Children suffering from minor brain damage were expected to complete the course of study offered in the regular school. Although many of these children devoted more than eight years to completing the course, this physiologically based theory optimistically assumed that all children had the potential, given the appropriate pedagogical and medical help, to complete satisfactorily the compulsory course.

On December 8, 1990, the Council of Ministers approved a law providing for a special Psychological-Medical Commission to examine mentally impaired children if the district population reached more than 120,000. If there were twice this number, two commissions were to be formed. Under this program, extensive diagnostic procedures were used to determine the age at which children should enter the primary school and the number of years they should spend there. Futhermore, in the month of May, parents could bring their children at the age of six to undergo an assessment to determine whether they possessed the talents and maturity needed to enter the special schools of art, music, foreign languages, ballet, and sports. Some psychological tests as well as oral questions and drawings were used in making these assessments. Since school districts frequently did not have enough trained psychologists available, teachers and medical personnel were permitted to carry out the tests and make the assessments. However, each boarding school was required by law to have a psychologist on its staff to deal with behavioral problems.

The Second Stage

In Western Europe the selection of pupils entering the second stage of academic university-preparatory schooling traditionally took place between the ages of ten and twelve. Those who were not selected completed their education in an extended general elementary school or were transferred to a vocational school. Throughout the years of Soviet rule, differentiation into complete general secondary, specialized secondary, special secondary or vocational schools was deferred until after the completion of the eight-year school except for the above-mentioned special secondary schools. Students at an early age were admitted to the latter schools, usually located in large cities, if they demonstrated special talent in art, music, foreign language, sports, or ballet. Still other special secondary schools admitted children who were found to have severe speech, physical, or mental handicaps.

Under *perestroika* the tendency was continued for the most part to defer differentiation by school type or profile within a school until pupils entered the final years of the complete secondary school. The most common of the newly created school types were the gymnasia and the lyceums. In Western Europe if a distinction was drawn between these and the other types of schools, it was based upon the position of the classical languages—Greek and Latin—in the curriculum. Both Greek and Latin were taught in the classical gymnasia in Germany and classical lycées in France. In other academic secondary schools Latin but not Greek was taught. This distinction was not made in the USSR; the terms were used synonymously. In regions where prerevolutionary grammar schools were called gymnasia, this term is now applied in Russia. By the same token, lyceums are found in regions in which schools had been traditionally called by that name. Profiles refer to groups of subjects representing quantitatively and qualitatively, specialized academic areas that are geared to meet individual interests and abilities as determined by competitive tests or previous classroom achievement.

Institutions of Higher Education

Under communist rule higher education underwent rapid expansion. The structure of this stage of education in the USSR was similar to that in continental Western Europe. Parallel to the liberal universities, specialized institutes emerged in the nineteenth century offering post-secondary level courses. Institutes in the Soviet Union, with few exceptions, never achieved the status of the best-known universities, but they offered a wide range of highly specialized courses in engineering and allied subjects. Moreover, admission to higher education in the USSR differed from Western Europe in that candidates were required to take a competitive entrance examination conducted by the institution. The number of candidates seeking admission to prestigious state universities such as those in Moscow and Leningrad was far greater annually (more than 12:1) than the number of places available. Competition in the secondary schools to attain the highest marks was intense. These marks were taken into account along with the results of the admission examinations.

A third type of institution offering specialized secondary and higher education was the pedagogical school in which young people who intended to teach in the primary schools were trained. These institutions had their early counterparts in American and Western European normal schools. Much of their time was spent mastering the content of subjects they proposed to teach and strengthening their ideological commitment. On the next level were pedagogical institutes which trained teachers for the junior and senior stages of the general education schools. As in the US and Western Europe earlier, some of the best-known pedagogical institutes after 1990 were renamed universities, e.g., the Lenin Pedagogical Institute and the Maurice Thorez Pedagogical Institute of Foreign Languages in Moscow.

Schools of Moscow

Reforms seldom are introduced swiftly and effectively into all schools. The authors were privileged to visit many schools in Moscow in May 1990 and January 1991, to talk to principals, teachers, and staff members, and to visit classrooms. Clearly some schools differed from the stereotypical Soviet school even before *perestroika* and were continuing with their innovative programs. Others took advantage of the new freedom to introduce significant changes. Indeed the freedom to innovate was accepted by many of the local district authorities and individual principals. The following accounts give some idea of the nature and extent of the changes introduced in some of the schools in Moscow, but it is impossible to generalize about how widely such programs were being adopted throughout the city. Certainly fewer innovations were introduced by schools in Moscow Province than in the city of Moscow.

School No. 825, Principal V. Karakovsky

This school, described as a school for children of the masses, had 960 students and 42 teachers. It was typical of schools in purely residential areas of Moscow. Because most parents were employed, they saw their children off to school in the morning and greeted them upon returning from work in the evening. The prolonged-day program of this school, catering to children who did not enjoy much in the way of family life, emphasized an all-round upbringing (moral education in the broadest sense). Upbringing included teaching and learning, extracurricular activities, nonformal relationships between children and adults, everything in fact which contributed to the moral and personality development of children. Indeed the ethos of this school was designed to develop the personality of the child.

Generally, Soviet schools were integrated into the administrative command system; this was clearly reflected in the methods of teaching in most classrooms. School No. 825 abandoned the administrative-command model before the onset of *perestroika*. Previously, uniforms had to be worn and children had to learn the same material in the same way. However, the staff of this school believed early on that not all children should be taught the same things in the same ways. By individualizing the teaching process, knowledge was accommodated to the child; teaching methods were chosen that were appropriate to different stages of development. Interests were taken into account and material objects were frequently personalized. Some knowledge was gained through engaging in activities. For example, in order to understand Archimedes' principle, a play dramatized the king who demonstrated ways to ascertain whether his imperial crown of gold contained any other metals. Karakovsky maintained that pupils appreciated teaching approaches which gave them the right to choose and integrate knowledge. Students were assessed by achievement tests, but they were allowed to choose their own test items from a list of questions. Difficult questions carried 5 to 6 points for a correct answer, while very difficult questions rated 10 to 12. Each child had to decide the final mark he or she hoped to attain by choosing easy or difficult questions. To receive a final mark of 5 on a report card, 60 points had to be accumulated. For a mark of 4, 50 points were needed and for a mark of 3, 40 points had to be obtained.

This school had in the tenth and eleventh grades two profiles that concentrated on pedagogy for those students interested in teaching as a career. For these pupils stress was placed on drama studies, psychology, and teaching experience. Those students in the nonprofile classes followed the regular general education curriculum. A proposal was under consideration to convert the school into a pedagogical gymnasium in which all pupils would be required to study the principles of psychology and pedagogy, together with a broadly based human-knowledge curriculum. A cautious approach was taken to integrating subjects since such courses were being developed on the basis of scientific studies at the Academy of

Pedagogical Sciences, but the school's interdisciplinary experiments reflected a preference for integrated courses. For example, sections on music and art in history courses were no longer taught by historians but in collaboration with teachers of music and art. Chemistry, biology, and physics were taught in such a way as to develop an understanding of the world. These new approaches in the teaching in the primary school stage were based on the view that children should have an integrated view of the world. The teachers maintained that only in adult life were themes differentiated into separate subjects.

All pupils who completed the ninth grade were required to take a leaving examination to qualify for a certificate of basic education. This was needed to assist the student in deciding upon one of the many options available in the third stage of education. Karakovsky believed that academic overloading of the pupil was a result not of how much was taught, but how of the subject was taught. Overloading was, he maintained, a psychological rather than an intellectual problem. Children grew tired of receiving knowledge they could not understand. Consequently, a careful selection had to be made from the mass of traditional content in each subject so that pupils would not be overburdened with minutiae.

In 1990 the council of School No. 825 had 100 members made up of representatives of the school's administrative staff, education trade union, Communist Party, Komsomols, and Pioneers, together with heads of the primary and senior sections, teachers of various subject areas, class leaders from grades five through eleven, and parents. Because parents had to work, relatively few of them were able to attend meetings. The council was responsible for developing and adopting a school plan and serving in an advisory capacity when pressing problems were referred to it by the administration. The council had no authority to appoint teachers; a decree issued in late 1989 authorized principals to select them. Prior to this, the local school authority allocated teachers to the schools. If a teacher wished to transfer from one school to another, the principals had to agree to the transfer. If the principal did not agree to the transfer, the teacher had to spend at least two months at the school before being allowed to transfer. Moreover, it was very difficult to dismiss a teacher, partly because the education trade union had to be involved in the process and partly because it was very difficult to prove incompetence.

As late as 1990 the Party organization still existed in this school, but plans were afoot to phase it out, partly as a result of the pressure from parents. Although its Pioneer organization was in the process of being transformed, the school-sponsored scout movement was gaining in popularity.

In summary, the key to the success of this school was found in the friendly relationships between adults and children. The school embraced two principles: (1) pupils should participate in planning and carrying out the school program and (2) subject matter should be integrated in an effort to lessen the overloading of pupils.

School No. 1201, Principal M. Voitsehovskaya

When the USSR State Committee decided to renumber schools, School No. 6 became No. 1201. Students and teachers continued to call it School No. 6 because of its long history of specializing in an in-depth study of the English language and literature. Its first graders were observed very closely for the first several months in order to identify and screen out those with speech and hearing defects and minimal linguistic talent. It was a very popular educational institution with some one-third of the students coming from outside the district.

As late as January 1991 it was still a ten-year school with a three-year primary division, but plans called for it to become an eleven-year (4-5-2) school when it accepted six-year-old children. It was a relatively small school with 836 pupils. With seventy-two staff members it compared very favorably with a regular school, but twenty-two were English teachers. Some teachers of English preferred to remain with their students throughout all of the grades. In the eighth grade physics and geography were taught in English.

Although specializing in the English language, this school offered two profiles: science and humanities. Recently two others were added: economics and general education. The economics profile featured a Junior Achievement course which was imported from the US but adapted to Russian conditions. A proposal to drop some of the required subjects in the humanities and sciences from the economics profile had to be abandoned because the universities informed the principal they would not approve the change. Students in this profile are now burdened with an excessive load of subjects.

History was one subject that had undergone significant changes in the school. Formerly Soviet history was interpreted in terms of a worldwide class struggle. Now more attention was being given to personalities and cultural roots. There were, as yet, no appropriate textbooks. Teachers had to prepare their own teaching materials and lectures while pupils took notes. An Association of Young History Teachers was organized to provide discussion opportunities for teachers of the school district, and the executive committee of the local board of education encouraged teachers to attend lectures and discussions on history subject matter for teaching their courses. Many of the lectures focused on the role that socialist realism had played in Soviet education and the need for an ideological reorientation of the teachers.

All teachers in this school were permitted and encouraged to design their own courses. In the cases of history and literature, some problems arose when students applied for admission to institutions of higher learning to study these subjects. University teachers often had different ideas as to what should be taught in preparatory courses in secondary school, and students were made to feel that they were not well prepared for the entrance examinations. Since 65 percent of the pupils in this school went on to higher educational institutions, the innovative approach to curriculum content created problems for teachers, students, and parents.

In the tenth and eleventh grades, there were typing courses for girls to become secretaries, while boys were directed into computer courses. Pupils, after completing the tenth grade and not going on to higher education, entered vocational schools, the armed forces, and employment. Military training had been abolished in this school.

There was considerable opposition to the introduction of integrated courses in both the humanities and science profiles in spite of the overburdening of pupils by the previous curriculum arrangement. Science and astronomy were combined but there was no intention of extending this integration beyond the fifth grade. Since pupils and teachers wished to avoid political controversy, the study of history and social studies was not popular. Homework assignments were limited in an effort to reduce the pressures on students.

This school refused to accept Regulation 540, which permitted pupils with up to three failing marks to be promoted from one class to the next. Since this was only a recommendation, the school was permitted to define its own policy. Many examinations were administered. If a grade average was poor and the student failed an examination at the end of the academic year, another examination was given in August. In this school, a student with more than one failing mark had to repeat the entire year. One of the vice-principals monitored the examinations to ensure that high classroom standards were maintained. Any teacher who was regarded as not sufficiently rigorous in grading students received guidance in raising standards.

In a ninth-grade literature lesson students sat in rows. The teacher conducted the lesson on the basis of questions and answers. Some students stood up to answer; others remained seated. The teacher lectured for the most part but she did read with great feeling a poem by Pushkin. Only a small number of students answered questions and entered into the discussion.

A much less traditional atmosphere permeated the seventh-grade class in physics that was taught in the English language by a very articulate teacher who had been an exchange teacher in a secondary school in Princeton, Ohio.

School No. 1158, Principal G. Metlik

This school is surrounded by many research institutes. There were 1,200 students enrolled, and one-third of them studied in the second of two shifts. The principal had the support of a psychologist and three deputies who supervised the primary division, the upper divisions, and extracurricular work. All seven-year-olds due to start school in September were interviewed on April 1 to assess their emotional level, speech, and other behavioral patterns. Then they were assigned at the point of entry into streams. About sixty-three to sixty-five applicants had some difficulties in adjusting to the academic demands of the school, and later in the year some of these were placed in a special class geared to their needs. It was found that in many cases the latter students came from disadvantaged homes in which parents did not talk to their children very much and the cultural level was very low.

The principal had introduced two three-year lyceum profiles of English and mathematics, which grew out of the school's experience with in-depth classes in these subjects. A nearby higher institute joined in the planning and made some of its staff members available to develop and assist in the teaching of the in-depth profiles. Inasmuch as only two profiles had been introduced and extra money was not needed, the Moscow Board had no need to get involved in the details of this reform.

Once the three-year lyceum profiles (ninth through the eleventh grades) were announced, the school attracted applicants from all over Moscow. The one entrance examination was limited to mathematics. Since English and mathematics were stressed in the lower grades of the school, the principal had a good idea of how many pupils would qualify for its ninth-grade profiles. In addition to English, German was also offered to those students in the regular general education stream. The usual pattern of extensive examinations no longer prevailed in School No. 1158; teachers were free to choose their own methods of assessment. Every half year, however, pupils were placed in rank order and some at that point were transferred out of the lyceum profile to regular classes. The school had plans to introduce lyceum profiles at the fifth grade and to abolish the regular general education program.

At the end of the eighth grade, certificates showing the cumulative averages in class work were given to all school leavers. At the end of the tenth grade, examinations in mathematics and the Russian language were given by the school prior to graduation. It was then up to the higher education institutes to administer their own admission tests.

To earn extra income, its sports hall was rented to community groups; parents and some enterprises made voluntary contributions. The sponsoring institute was not able to contribute money but it did send some furniture, workers to maintain and repair the school building, and instructors to teach courses. In the tenth grade, for example, of the thirty-six lessons during the week, eighteen were taught by regular teachers and eighteen by lecturers from the institute. By a special agreement with the institute, all pupils graduating from the lyceum took the institute's entrance examinations in mathematics, Russian, and geography.

The school had additional links with several other nearby research institutes. Fourteen of the school's teachers received advisory assistance and ruble subsidies from the Institute of Cybernetics. A team of researchers, teachers, students from a nearby pedagogical institute, and some of the school's pupils were involved in a project with the Academy of Pedagogical Sciences's Institute of Theory and History of Education to determine the extent to which computers helped to shape the personality of children. Two groups of pupils of the same age were chosen for the research project. One group used computers in all of their subjects; the other studied without computers. Using psychological and achievement tests, the researchers assessed the relationship of computer use to motivation, values, and attitudes of children.

The school council was made up of thirty-three members, eleven parents, eleven teachers, and eleven pupils. Previously the local Communist Party had exercised considerable influence in running the school. The district Party in the past had recommended and approved all nominations of teachers eligible for awards, sanctioned the appointment of the director, and monitored the work of the teachers. Important Party views and policies were imposed on all subjects including mathematics. However, the district education authority in Moscow ruled in 1990 that the Party should no longer interfere in the operation of its district schools, and the teachers were instructed to reflect all points of view in their teaching. Indeed many of the teachers in the school had left the Party; the Pioneer and Komsomol organizations had been abolished. No longer was there a Pioneer

Palace in the district. Some of the teachers in this school joined Eureka, a club to discuss a whole range of possible societal reforms, but the school itself was never associated with the movement. Although the teachers were encouraged to use innovative teaching methods, some resisted. In February 1991 a few members of the staff were involved in a district teacher strike which resulted in a 40 percent increase in salary.

Classroom visits revealed the extent to which some teachers adapted their methods to meet the needs of individual children. In the tenth-grade lyceum mathematics lessons, for example, pupils worked in groups of four. It appeared that the teacher directed most of the difficult problems under discussion to the best students in each of the groups. Individual assessments were made once a month. In a very relaxed manner, a student read a question or topic from a card and questioned the other pupils. On the other hand, a sixth-grade biology lesson was conducted in a traditional manner. The girls were casually dressed but most of the boys wore navy blue uniforms.

School No. 1106, Principal Lidya Selezneva

This school was established in 1988. From the start it faced difficulties because the families in the district came from very different backgrounds. Although many of the parents were university lecturers, research workers, and army officers, 70 percent of the local population were construction workers. The principal commented that the children of workers were less disciplined and more inclined to criminal acts.

The principal graduated from the Lenin Pedagogical Institute as a teacher of Russian language and literature. She had twenty-two years of teaching experience before becoming a deputy principal in a Moscow district school. Upon becoming the principal in this school, she developed a relationship with the Oil and Gas Institute in which some of the parents worked. The institute sent instructors to assist in teaching eighth-grade subjects, and the school's senior students were invited to work in the institute's laboratories to apply what they were learning in their mathematics, physics, and chemistry classes. An evening school in mathematics, physics, and chemistry was established;

instructors from the institute taught the in-depth classes free of tuition.

A pedagogical profile was available for students interested in becoming school psychologists and social workers. The USSR Academy of Pedagogical Sciences and the Lenin Pedagogical University collaborated in this effort. When students graduated from this profile they were admitted to the Lenin Pedagogical University to pursue psychology or social work. Other in-depth courses were English and theater. Teachers from the Lenin Pedagogical University taught the English courses. The theatrics course was taught by staff members of the innovative Tanganka Theater in Moscow and a local music theater. The school sponsored two children's theaters; one for young children and the other for older youth. A special eighth-grade course on World Literature and Culture was introduced to further the humanization of education. The principal was in favor of introducing similar courses at an earlier age.

Through close contacts with local institutions of higher education students were able to take their entrance examinations instead of the school's final examination. All of the students who completed the eleventh grade in this school entered institutions of higher education. Most of the children were from families of the intelligentsia with a commitment to follow the academic traditions of their parents.

A special feature of this school was the qualifying examinations given to all students in the six classes of the seventh grade to determine which students would be qualified to pursue the two in-depth profiles in mathematics, physics, and chemistry. Those who did not qualify continued in the four regular general education classes.

Members of this school's staff were convinced that the real tragedy of Soviet education in past years was that all children with different life goals were taught the same courses in the same classes. They all approved of the practice of separating those who were not intellectually inclined from those who were capable of going to an institution of higher education. At the end of the ninth grade, about half the students left the school with some 50 percent going to vocational schools and somewhat fewer going to specialized secondary schools.

The Radonezh Religious Society's School

A usual feature of state School No. 1106 was the Radonezh Religious Society's private religious school that was housed on one of the unused floors. The Radonezh Religious Society's seven-year Russian Orthodox parochial school enrolled 175 students; parents paid fees directly to the Society, not the school. A priest taught courses on religious art and the Bible and conducted a religious service each school day. The principal of School No. 1106 was reprimanded for renting floor space and allowing a religious service in a state school. Yagodin, the chairman of the State Committee, demanded that the principal be fired.

A commission from the Moscow School Board investigated the so-called violation of separation of church and state. The Moscow regional education committee under its director, Mrs. L. I. Kezina, supported the principal in her right to rent to the Radonezh Society the unused floor of the state school in that this parochial school was organized not by the church but by a public religious organization. The principal, who was herself not a religious person, was committed to innovations in education and saw this as the beginning of a movement to establish parochial schools in the USSR. In fact, the Radonezh Society had raised enough money to design and construct its own school building. The principal of School No. 1106 confided that she had no desire to be a director of a parochial school, although she would consider an offer to become a principal of a private secular school. She considered religion to be a matter between the individual and God, without the intervention of a priest.

The fifth-grade history class in the Orthodox school had 30 pupils, all wore the traditional school uniform. Religious music was introduced in history lessons and the study of ancient Slavic culture was included in the course on the Culture and History of the World. Icons and portraits of sainits were displayed in the classrooms and hallways. Each school day was started with a religious service, sprinkling of holy water, and singing of hymns. All of the basic general education subjects were taught as well as physical education. A foreign language, the fundamentals of religious education, sacred music, and religious art were introduced in the second grade. Russian philology and classical Greek language and culture were taught from the fifth through the seventh grades. Latin, rhetoric, and Old Church Slavonic language were assigned to the eighth grade.

The teaching of general education subjects was financed from the state budget, but all other subjects not in the state curriculum were supported by fees paid to the Society by the parents. Six members of the Society made up the Board of Trustees. For the 175 school places there were over 1,000 applicants. Children of Society members and those from religious homes were accepted first, but the majority of pupils did not have religious parents. The following year the Radonezh Society's new Russian Orthodox Gymnasium opened with all courses firmly rooted in religion and the traditional classics. The school issued its own graduation certificate but students had to take state examinations to qualify for a state certificate.

School No. 109, Principal Evgeni Yambourg

This school, sponsored by the Institute of Theory and History of Education of the USSR Academy of Pedagogical Sciences, served a community on the outskirts of metropolitan Moscow. Its building, compared with older school construction in Moscow, was modern, open, and airy. As one of the Academy's experimental schools, it was in the vanguard of reform. The principal and staff were receptive to new ideas and innovations. They fully understood the erosion that had taken place in the physical, social, moral, and psychological life of children in the USSR. For a number of years the school had a close relationship with a medical clinic because of the large number of pupils suffering from illnesses. The lack of spiritual roots left many children without a moral purpose.

Yambourg and his staff believed that under these circumstances physicians, educators, and psychologists should cooperate closely to help those children whose condition was marginally pathological. Unfortunately, Yambourg said there were not enough pediatricians and psychologists to look after the needs of children. In this school diagnostic testing was undertaken in the kindergarten for all four-year-olds in the district. When the pupils came to the school at the age of six physiotherapy was available for them all. For those who were physically and mentally normal, there were daily physical-education activities. Having rejected the old-fashioned Prussian gymnastics, the children were taught to breathe properly according to thirty-two systems of breathing and Yoga practices in relaxation.

The school was organized on the principle of integrated stages of education from the kindergarten through the primary grades, lyceum, and university. The kindergarten and primary grades combined the focus on the child, dance, folklore, the Bible, national culture, and different kinds of psycho-motor skills. In terms of tactile development, the methods of Montessori were used in the kindergarten. Starting in the primary grades, an intensive method was used in the teaching of foreign languages. Large blocks of instruction were repeated several times. Role playing was an important way of introducing pupils to Russian tales; acting out plays was part of this method of teaching. A broader view was taken of the time limits imposed on learning and on fixed and narrow standards used to measure achievement. To reduce the constraints placed on learning, Yambourg experimented with (1) improving the teaching methods, (2) integrating the content of education, and (3) utilizing all the new technology. In seeking answers to problems associated with teaching writing skills, the teachers turned to international educators who had researched this area.

Montessori's method was adapted to facilitate tactile learning. In fact, much of what Montessori wrote was available in the USSR as early as 1920, but few had read her books. Vygotsky had two reservations about the use of Montessori's methods. First, he questioned the feasibility of teaching children to write at the age of four. Second, he did not accept the view that at this age the tactile perception and memory of children were very strong. In Vygotsky's time children in the USSR entered school at the age of eight, so his views were probably well grounded. Nevertheless, Montessori was right in thinking that children could be introduced to writing at the age of four. Some fifteen teachers in this school worked along Montessori's lines. One of them had published books on the Montessori teaching method which were widely read by Soviet teachers.

Although the objectives of secondary education in School No. 109 were directed to individual development through a program of elective subjects, a basic common core curriculum was mandated for all students. Each adolescent designed his own individual study program upon entering the junior stage with the help of teachers and psychologists, and upon entering the lyceum he chose one of the profiles.

In School No. 109 there were three profiles: (1) medicine, (2) science and mathematics, and (3) humanities. Each of these profiles was sponsored by institutions of higher education, namely, the Institute of Medicine, the Institute of Radio-Electronics, and the Institute of Historical Archives. Instructors from these institutions gave lectures in senior classes. Within the profiles were subdivisions which enabled small groups to study nontraditional subject matter with the help of an instructor from one of the institutes. All of the profiles contained a basic core of humanities, the Great Books, and the Bible. The humanities profile required the study of Latin and Greek; the medical profile offered Latin but not Greek. The science profile had no classical languages.

In addition to the lyceum profiles, the school had the regular general education classes found in all state schools. Because the level of work and expectations in the latter classes were lower than those in the lyceum, every effort was made to overcome attitudes of snobbishness that might be displayed by the more able students. This was a concern of those responsible for moral education. Common activities were organized to draw together pupils of all levels of ability. The five theater groups involved all of the students of the school.

Another question was raised relating to differentiation by school type. What should be the catchment area from which pupils could be admitted to this school? Pupils coming to the kindergarten of this school and subsequently to the primary and first level of the secondary grades were drawn from the immediate neighborhood. Pupils from all over Moscow applied to enter the lyceum classes which started at the tenth grade. All applicants were interviewed each spring and selection followed.

However, all pupils who studied in the junior division of this school but were not capable of entering one of the lyceum profiles could continue in the regular general education stream.

School No. 299, Principal Eleanor Baral

The principal taught to a group of senior pupils in her office a class dealing with aspects of life in Poland and the concentration camps during the Second World War. Some of the pupils had participated in exchange programs with Poland. The lively interaction suggested that this would have been regarded throughout the world as successful teaching and learning in any school.

After dismissing the class, the principal and two members of the staff gave their personal views of the impact that *perestroika* had on their school. Both the content and methods of teaching had undergone change. In the social studies classes, for example, discussions involved active participation of students, and many questions were raised. Teachers sought to understand what pupils already knew about current issues and problems, and they tried to penetrate students' thoughts through the medium of theater performances that the class members had attended. The students produced different plays with the object of portraying human problems. These plays included themes about the Stalin years and involved military people, poets, scientists, and Party people. One of the difficulties in working with teenagers on these themes, according to the students, was that some of their parents and teachers had suffered persecution during this period and preferred not to recall those days in classroom situations.

One of the goals of the school was not only to revive the lost spiritual traditions but also to develop more humane and moral personalities. The principal commented that this was a very difficult goal to achieve since it involved releasing inner feelings and beliefs of pupils. Children were encouraged to discuss political issues, not in black-and-white terms but in asserting what was good and what was bad in general terms and exploring in depth all facets of issues. The teachers hoped that through this approach students would realize that there were no

"Good Czars" who could be trusted to bring into being a better era.

Attitudes of students towards the church and theology were undergoing great change. Since the 1930s, the teachers of Russian history only referred to churches as examples of great architecture. Now pupils needed to learn about Christianity and other religions. In School No. 299 a priest had given two lectures which aroused wide interest among students and teachers in the subject of religion. A course was given on the Bible in which problems of morality were discussed. One day each month pupils in grades eight to eleven were free of lessons to visit museums and other cities.

In spite of these innovations, however, it was difficult to overcome the authoritarianism and command system which had existed for so many years. Not all of the sixty-three teachers in the school were open to the changes brought by *perestroika*. The principal encouraged the teachers to reject authoritarianism and to develop a new style of teaching so children would be free, happy, relaxed, and joyful.

Children were regularly tested psychologically. The teachers were free to organize their own curricula and individualize instruction by introducing their own teaching materials in all subjects.

Differentiation and individualization were also achieved by varying the number of lessons per week in accordance with the interests and abilities of individual children. For example, in 1989 each of the four groups in the ninth grade had three introductory lessons in history during which an attempt was made to discover which students had a deep interest in the subject. On the basis of this assessment, those most interested in history took more lessons in the subject and four lessons in mathematics instead of six after the first year. Some pupils elected in the tenth grade to take more courses in the humanities; others opted for more mathematics; while others preferred to follow a balanced course in the humanities and mathematics.

The teacher of an optional tenth grade course in literature, which included the study of the Bible, reported that 90 percent of the pupils in her course came from one of the groups that had opted for in-depth study of history. The principal emphasized that pupils and teachers worked closely together in making the choice between the humanities and mathematics-physics. Selection was based not only on the interest shown by pupils in the subject, but also on their abilities, which were determined by tests. Some students exhibited interest but did not have the necessary ability to pursue the specializations of their choice.

In the teaching of the Bible, teachers were cautioned not to stray from the officially sanctioned syllabus. Pupils did not have to agree with the teacher's interpretation but were encouraged to interact and to examine various opinions through frank and open discussions. The aim was to develop the moral qualities of individual pupils through the study of world religions, literature, and culture. Highlighted were the general moral values and ethical points of view portrayed in novels and cultural artifacts. The moral values of Christ and the Sermon on the Mount served as the criteria to evaluate the moral principles which were expressed in Russian and Soviet literature. The rationale was that in order to understand Russian history, a knowledge of Christianity was needed. The principal explained that current Russian literature could be understood only if prerevolutionary writers were studied, and these, in turn, could not be understood without knowledge of the principles enshrined in the Bible. A course on world literature was introduced in which the relationship between church and state and Christian values was examined. Teaching these new spiritual values proved difficult because many of the former Soviet institutions were still in the hands of conservatives who were tied to the old era and values.

Other Moscow Schools

An inspector of the Moscow City Committee on Public Education, N. Vagamova, described the creation of seven alternative schools in Moscow *(Uchitel'skaya gazeta,* No. 2, January 12, 1991, p. 3). Three experimental preschools were dedicated to the all-round development of pupils in a noninstitutional environment. In another instance, a Slavic gymnasium sought to revive Slavic culture. In the "School of Cooperation" the main form of learning in grades one through ten was through laboratory activities. Children conducted investigations and acquired their own knowledge independently. Parents took part in the laboratory work. Each day there were special-interest activities. In this school children could specialize in English, French, German, or Swedish as their foreign language or follow a history profile. Inspector Vagamova reported that a new chemistry lyceum selected its students at the end of the eighth grade from the entire city of Moscow. Preference was given to the winners of chemistry olympiads and outstanding members of chemistry clubs. Quite unique was the "IBC" school, which was sponsored by the Society of Women for Social Development. "IBC" stood for "Intellect, Beauty, and Conscience." It had several other sponsors including the A. Solzhenitsyn fund, the Isadora Duncan Fund, and the Bank Association "Menatep." The principal of "IBC" school, Ul Zavalsky, believed that the most important goal of education was to develop the individual abilities of children. In seeking to achieve this end, the school was later converted to a lyceum for gifted children.

Throughout 1987–1991 the Soviet media reported on many other newly established and innovative schools. The "MTL" Technical Lyceum in the Kirov district of Moscow was founded by Sergei Pomerantsev, a graduate of Moscow Institute of Railway Engineers (MIRE). He chose to become a teacher of mathematics and drawing at Moscow school No. 259. There he encouraged students to take courses that prepared them for MIRE entrance examinations. In 1987 N. S. Konarov, USSR Minister of Railways, and L. I. Kezina, the innovative director of the Moscow City Board of Education, invited Pomerantsev to create a new four-year Moscow Technical Lyceum-Institute (MTL) complex in cooperation with MIRE and the Moscow Cast Alloy Plant. MTL entered into a contract for their students to use MIRE laboratories and its computer center, attend lectures by its professors, exercise at the MIRE's Sport Palace, and take tests twice a year that combined school examinations with entrance examinations to the institute. In the summer of 1988, the first pupils from Moscow and nearby towns took competitive entrance examinations to enter the eighth grade of the MTL, which was modelled after the Tsarskoye Selo (Pushkin) lyceum.

Prior to deciding between the in-depth special subjects of information and computer technology, physics, and mathematics, all eighth-grade pupils, upon entering the MTL, were enrolled in an orientation course to determine their interests and abilities. Teachers were contracted to design their own courses and were paid in accordance with their success in recruiting students. The daily schedule of classes started in the morning and continued into the evening. The regular state-mandated subjects were required of all students together with a special-interest cycle of optional subjects leading to a lyceum diploma. Two foreign languages, dancing, and swimming were obligatory. Girls enrolled in aerobics; boys took track and field, gymnastics, boxing, and fencing. Later, grades five, six, and seven were added to the MTL; students were selected by competitive examinations at the end of the fourth grade. An annual olympiad sponsored by MTL was designed to test the students' achievements in physics, mathematics, literature, a foreign language, history, and sports.

At the start of the school year of 1991 there were some 6,600 Russian schools (or 10 percent) offering in-depth courses, double the 1990 figure. The number of gymnasia, lyceums, and colleges had trebled to over 500, most of them in large cities. The common features of these newly created schools were:

1. Financial and intellectual sponsorship by higher education institutions
2. In-depth optional profiles in addition to the regular state-mandated subjects
3. Creative, dynamic, and scholarly teachers with freedom to innovate
4. Freedom from bureaucratic constraints
5. Flexible, creative, and scholarly directors.

Rural Schools

The gymnasia and lyceums described above certainly were not typical of the 130,000 schools in the former Soviet Union in the 1990s. Some 70,000 of these were rural. According to staff members of *Narodnoe obrazovanie*, a public education journal (interview, January 14, 1991), the rural schools were less well financed than city schools. The financial problems, depressed living conditions, and a lack of incentives explained why teachers were reluctant to take positions in rural areas. But with the food shortages in 1990–91, there were reports of a growing number of teachers requesting posts in rural schools.

Of the 70,000 rural schools, many had only four and others eight grades. Among the former were many one-room schools. An order of the Russian Ministry of Education in 1990 required that all schools had to maintain separate classes even if there were only a few children in any age range. However, in the transition, one teacher was permitted to teach two grades. It was hoped that an improvement in the quality of rural education would forestall the movement of peasants and their children to towns and cities and even encourage some families to return and take up private farming. During the 1960s, many villages were consolidated and small schools were closed. But many villages in isolated regions continued to exist. Boarding schools were established but they were not well received by the students and their parents. Hence many one-room schools continued to operate. Young children were expected to walk no more than two kilometers to the nearest school, or, for older children, three kilometers. In practice, students frequently walked up to five kilometers because there was no bus transportation due to the poor condition of the roads in the autumn, winter, and spring months of the year. Moreover, to encourage peasants with children to continue their residence in villages, all rural secondary school graduates were granted the right to apply for admission to higher education institutions and certain concessions were extended to ensure their admission.

The residual principle on which school financing was based placed rural schools at a great disadvantage. Under this system cities had far more money for education than villages. Republics with more affluent collective farms than Russia, such as the Ukraine, the Baltics, and Byelorussia, had better rural schools. To attract them to rural schools in Russia, teachers were offered higher salaries, reduced teaching loads, free flats with electricity, and vouchers for scarce goods. Collective farms promised to supply teachers with food.

Rural school teachers in 1990 were trained in either specialized secondary schools for teachers or pedagogical institutes. Some pedagogical institutes in cities maintained links with rural schools by sending out lecturers to meet with teachers and students, assist them with their problems, and encourage students to take up teaching as a career. As a result of these added incentives, more male teachers were induced to take teaching positions in rural schools.

Not only were city schools better financed than rural schools, they also had more equipment. For this reason, throughout 1990 Russia placed great emphasis on improving rural schools. Because many of them, unlike city schools, did not have the complete eleven grades of a secondary school, many of the new policies designed to foster differentiation did not apply.

What is clear is that in 1991 the dogmatic acceptance of the ten- or eleven-year common unified school, a central feature of Communist Party policy since 1917, no longer commanded universal acceptance in the USSR. It was too early in 1991 to predict with confidence that a new structure of common schooling would emerge and be accepted throughout the country. It was clear, however, that the principles of differentiation and humanization, at least as slogans, were accepted. It was also clear that the principle of democratization found expression in the freedom granted to local authorities and school councils to run some schools in accordance with the demands of parents and representatives of the local community. No doubt, however, most principals and teachers retained a controlling voice in formulating and implementing policies for their own schools.

Two features of differentiation were evident. The first, which appeared to be widely accepted, was the differentiated curricula, particularly in the final classes of the complete secondary schools and in the gymnasium and lyceum profiles. The second, differentiation by school type, was less wholeheartedly agreed upon since it necessitated selection of bright students at the point of entry, and rejection, at some point in their school careers, of students who were not deemed capable of following a curriculum leading to an institution of higher education.

Selection by school type after the fourth (or even the third) grade constituted a return to the traditional Western European model of selective schools for potential university entrants. The postponement of selection to the end of the eighth grade permitted a degree of reconciliation with the previous Soviet common school ideal. A major unresolved question continued to be whether or not the final stages of the complete secondary school should be selective. Attempts under the Khrushchev reforms to introduce work-related training into general secondary schools failed. Subsequent attempts to require all adolescents to complete ten or eleven years of schooling in a unified school without differentiated methods and curricula gave rise to now-acknowledged difficulties. Similar difficulties and problems were experienced in most Western European countries where, under pressure from the universities, governments were reluctant to undertake radical reform of traditional selective systems of schooling.

Acceptance of the theory of innate differences was the turning point in the USSR in determining structural changes in the school system and the role of vocational schools within it. The freedom granted to school councils and principals to make their schools more selective and more manageable encouraged them to introduce innovations and reforms.

Undoubtedly the emergence of selective lyceums, gymnasia, and private and religious schools was the most profound of the many changes introduced under *perestroika*. Some indication of the future for these schools was revealed by the USSR State Committee for Public Education's draft regulations on the lyceum and gymnasium, issued in 1990 in Moscow, encouraging the establishment of these institutions. Specifically this required the identification and development of individual talents and abilities, formation of a scientific outlook, inculcation of humanistic values, and cultivation of creative thinking together with knowledge about society, man, and his world. The lyceum and gymnasium applied the principles of self-government and democracy while taking into account unique regional and local conditions. They could be established in cities, districts, and regions and in cooperation with cultural centers and institutions of higher education.

The emergence of private and religious schools was certainly another of the profound changes introduced under *perestroika*. The religious school established in School No. 1106 set a precedent and a model that was later followed by other religious societies and churches that wished to cultivate a religious ethos in a school and to teach those subjects that would reflect certain sectarian religious beliefs.

CHAPTER 7

The Politics of the Soviet Curriculum

There were two main aspects to the curriculum debates with the onset of *perestroika* in the Soviet Union (see p. 27). The nationalities issue was closely linked with problems of decentralization, the position to be given to the native languages, and the emphasis to be placed on local geography and history in the curriculum.

Constitutionally, republics were granted many rights to govern themselves. Article 76 of the 1977 Constitution provided that, apart from those responsibilities conferred in the Constitution of the USSR, each republic had the right to "exercise independent authority on its own territory." However, the twelve sections of Article 73 of the Constitution directly conferred considerable powers on the central government. The right to retain and exercise these All-Union powers was used by opponents of democratization under *perestroika* to resist the republics' demands for decentralization.

The central issue for Gorbachev was how to realize Lenin's principle of self-determination without reducing it to secession from the Union. It was, for Gorbachev, a complicated multi-faceted process of affirming national dignity, developing language and culture, consolidating political independence, and advancing economic and social progress. The powers of the central government agencies had to be limited in order to enable regions to control all aspects of their own existence except those which they voluntarily delegated to the Union.

The rights of the central government of the USSR included its power to establish general principles for the organization and functioning of republican and local administrative bodies, to pursue uniform social and economic policies, and give them direction, and to determine the budget, taxes, prices, and wage policies throughout the Union. In practice, these rights legitimatized the centralization of power.

Constitutionally power resided in All-Union, Union-republic, and autonomous region and area entities. In the 1977 Constitution, no distinction was made between the All-Union and Union-republic ministries as was the case in the 1936 Constitution, which provided for a number of All-Union ministries. Each ministry was entrusted, according to Article 75, with the direction of the "branch of state administration delegated to it throughout the territory of the USSR either directly or through bodies appointed by it."

Between the passage of the 1936 Constitution and the adoption of the 1977 Constitution more power was granted to the All-Union agencies in the field of education, including the curriculum. An All-Union Ministry of Education was established. The Russian Academy of Pedagogical Sciences was transformed into an All-Union Academy. In effect, power to determine the curriculum of the general education schools throughout the whole Union had been taken over by the All-Union Ministry, and the authority of the academicians of the Academy of Pedagogical Sciences to advise on the curriculum content, especially in mathematics and the sciences, had been greatly extended.

A Federal State

When the Soviet Union became a federal state, Lenin wisely chose a form of federalism or "internationalism " that included unfailing regard for ethnic interests, respect for the identity of every ethnic group, recognition of all peoples as equal, and an irreconcilable attitude to any forms of national oppression. The Treaty of 1922, in which the formation of the USSR was concluded, and the first Constitution, adopted in 1924, were landmarks in the establishment of a nation-state based on Lenin's principles. Lenin stressed the need to create a federation of republics in which the rights of particular national groups would be safeguarded. In multicultural states all citizens do not speak the same language, do not hold the same religious beliefs, and do not come from the same racial or ethnic background; yet they live in politically defined territories, under national laws, and under conditions which require them to cooperate with one another economically. The USSR was such a multicultural nation.

The freedom of Union republics to secede from the Soviet Union was seen as a way of ensuring that the rights of particular groups would be respected. In the USSR Constitutions drawn up under both Stalin and Brezhnev, this right was granted to the republics. Article 17 of the 1936 Constitution stated that "the right freely to secede from the USSR is reserved to every Union republic." Moreover, Article 72 of the 1977 Constitution stated that "each Union Republic shall retain the right freely to secede from the USSR."

Prior to *glasnost* no overt claims to secede were ever publicly revealed. Covert dissent, when detected, was ruthlessly suppressed. For this reason the revival of aggressive nationalism under Gorbachev's *glasnost* was perhaps not anticipated by him when he referred to the rights of nationalities in his address to the Twenty-seventh Party Congress. He blamed Stalin and his henchmen for transforming a federal state into a unitary state extending over 100 ethnic groups. Diverse interests—including educational—of these groups were inhibited by a system of political and administrative controls which emasculated the substance of the Federation and held back the progress of an entire society. *Glasnost* prompted calls for self-determination and placed the Union of Social Soviet Republics in jeopardy, when after 1985, informal groups emerged demanding political, economic, and cultural independence.

Supreme Soviets in the Baltic republics were at the forefront of self-determination movements. These republics had been part of Tsarist Russia but were not republics of the original Soviet Union. This was a Union of many cultural and linguistic traditions, nationalities, and religions. Although the Baltic republics of Estonia, Latvia, and Lithuania were incorporated into this Union in 1940, the legality of this incorporation was never accepted by the Baltic republics. *Perestroika* and *glasnost* enabled the presidium of the Estonian Academy of Sciences to form a committee in July of 1989 to review the events of 1940. One month later the Estonian Communist Party daily, *Rahva Haal,* published the reasons why two of the commission's members concluded that Estonia had not joined the Soviet Union voluntarily (*Rahva Haal*, August 11, 1989, p. 33).

Understandably, since 1987 the concept of republican sovereignty was openly discussed in Lithuania, Estonia, and Latvia. On November 16, 1988, the Estonian SSR Supreme Soviet declared the republic's sovereignty. This meant that the highest authority in the land was transferred to the republic's executive, legislative, and judicial bodies. Six months later, in May 1989, Lithuania declared its sovereignty by stating that only laws adopted or approved by the Supreme Soviet of the Lithuanian SSR were valid in the territory of Lithuania. Although the issue had been discussed for nearly three years in Latvia, its Supreme Soviet finally declared its sovereignty on July 28, 1989.

The constitutions of the three republics were amended to mandate that all relations with the USSR would come under the authority of the highest bodies of their respective nations. However, as late as 1991, the sovereignty of the Baltic republics was not recognized by the Soviet Union government. Hence there was considerable unrest in January 1991, with intimidation of the population by Soviet troops. The governments in these three republics refused to participate in the national referendum held in April 1991 on whether the Soviet Union should remain one nation and they were among the first six of the republics to declare their independence.

The Baltic republics, to be sure, were not alone in seeking a measure of independence from the USSR. In the Ukraine, the "Popular Movement of Ukraine for *Perestroika*" (RUKH) had been active in the campaign to gain sovereignty for the republic. In 1989 it held a conference at which Roman Solchanyk ("Constituent Conference of Kiev Popular Front," *Report on the USSR*, Vol. 1, No. 32, August 11, 1989, pp. 23–25) reported that there could be no talk of two state languages, namely, Ukrainian and Russian. He said that the state had to not only guarantee the Ukrainian language "the right to priority functioning in all spheres of production and spiritual and administrative life," but also had to ensure the practical implementation of it. This task was not a simple one. For example, in the Odessa region the linguistic diversity was extreme. Ukrainians, Bulgarians, Gagauzes, Moldavians, Russians, Byelorussians, and many other nationalities were living there ("No Peace in Bessarabia," *News from the Ukraine*, No. 32, August 1990, pp. 1–4).

Along with representatives of other progressive political movements, RUKH organized a campaign in February 1990 to demand that the republic's government should seek genuine political and economic sovereignty for the Ukraine. The *Report on the USSR* (Vol. 2, No. 30, July 27, 1990, pp. 17–19) announced the "Declaration of the State Sovereignty of the Ukraine" had been issued on July 16. In addition to guaranteeing "the supremacy of the Constitution and Laws of the republic on its territory," sovereignty gave the Ukraine sole dominion over its resources and security forces. With its sovereignty assured, the Ukraine voted to remain within the Soviet Union.

Another example of a political self-determination movement was the Byelorussian Popular Front whose electoral platform was described by W. Stankevich in *Report on the USSR* (Vol. 2, No. 2, January 12, 1990, pp. 20–22). It called for economic and cultural pluralism, the elimination of the Party's *nomenklatura* system, and the revival of Byelorussia's cultural heritage. The compulsory teaching and use of the Byelorussian language was to be enforced. It rejected the view that there was a need for Russian as a language of interethnic communication and supported the principle of "national cultural autonomy for all nationalities residing in Byelorussia, regardless of their number and their length of residence. Moreover, it called for legal guarantees for national schools, press, cultural centers and organizations" (op. cit., p. 22).

Bess Brown, in "New Political Parties in Kazakhstan" (*Report on the USSR*, Vol. 2, No. 35, August 31, 1990, p. 10), reported on the emergence of political parties in Kazakhstan demanding republican sovereignty. The draft law in Kazakhstan required officials and those dealing with the public to know both Russian and Kazakh. The draft was modified by stipulating that public officials would be required to communicate in either language by 1995, and by 2000 they would have to speak both Russian and Kazakh. Later the deadlines were removed. Since large areas of the republic were predominantly inhabited by Russian-speaking people, there were almost no facilities nor incentives for them to learn the Kazakh language.

Among the republics that had by 1991 adopted declarations of sovereignty could be counted the Supreme Soviets of Russia, Ukraine, Lithuania, Byelorussia, Georgia, and Armenia. Geoffrey Hoskins in the *New Times* stated: "The most urgent problem is the national one. I believe it is essential to convene a conference of Union republics in order to renegotiate the Treaty of 1922 which originally set up the Soviet Union." There was, however, a possibility of further disintegration even if a new treaty was concluded. Marina Shakina felt ("Will the Phoenix Rise from the Ashes?" *New Times*, No. 26, June 30, 1990, pp. 25–26) that even if a new federal treaty was agreed upon, the constituent sovereign republics might break up along ethnic lines.

USSR Law on Languages

Throughout history language has been the foundation of nationalism. Hence the curriculum issues concerning what should be the medium of instruction and the other languages which should be taught were highly politicized ones. The political status of the native language was thoroughly debated in the republics and the USSR. Some republics gave the native language the status of a "state" language. In some cases Russian was accepted, as suggested by Gorbachev, as the medium of interethnic communication.

Some uniformity, at least in terms of legislation, was reached when in May 1990 a USSR Law on Languages was passed ("USSR Law on Languages," *CDSP*, Vol. XLII, No. 22, 1990, p. 15). The preamble stated that the Soviet state would protect the right of citizens to use their languages in various spheres of public life and preserve, revive, and develop them. The law also laid down the general principles of language policy in the USSR but did not regulate the use of language in interpersonal and nonofficial relations. Within the administrative structure in which distinctions were made between the powers of the federal government and the Union and autonomous republics, language policy was delegated to the republics. The federal government was given the power to establish general principles for the use of languages and development of language policy based on the need for a Union-wide medium of communication. Beyond this it was for regional authorities to decide "on the development and use of languages on their territory, taking into consideration the interests of the peoples residing there." The educational implications were spelled out. Regional agencies were required to develop appropriate languages by setting up programs of instruction, by training teachers, and by publishing dictionaries, reference books, textbooks, and literature on teaching methods. While these activities were to be financed from regional funds, programs for numerically small groups of people would be able to draw on central funds.

Articles 6 and 7 of the law were of great significance for education. Article 6 guaranteed citizens the right to choose the language of instruction. It stated that preschools and primary and secondary general education institutions should present the content of the curriculum in various languages. Although parents had the right to choose an appropriate school for their children, in practice, the Russian language continued to dominate school instruction, in part due to parental preference.

Article 7 went further in asserting the right of the republics to create conditions which would allow citizens to study their own language and the languages of other peoples in the USSR. However the Russian language was to be studied in order to meet the needs of communication among the nationalities within the Union. The nature and extent of the teaching of the native language and culture were to be determined by the regional authorities in terms of the needs of people living in the region. Although the freedom of choice of languages was somewhat circumscribed, particularly since the mass media and armed forces had to operate in the Russian language, there were local language newspapers, magazines, radio, and TV programs in all national republics.

The educational implications of this law were tremendous given the fact that each of the many nationalities based their claim for self-determination and independence to some extent on the right of parents to educate their children solely in their native language or mother tongue. In regions in which several indigenous languages were spoken, the law required that instruction in the native language be provided only upon the request of the parents. In sparsely populated areas, the provision of schools, or special language courses within schools, for relatively small numbers of pupils placed heavy demands on such resources as trained teachers, suitable textbooks, dictionaries, and other materials. In heavily populated areas containing groups speaking many different languages the recognition of this right depended on whether members of each language group lived in sufficiently close proximity to allow for the establishment of specific language schools or the provision of classes in which specific languages were used. Hence the practical implementation of the law depended, in part, on regional conditions.

The Law on Languages represented a political solution to a political problem. In theory, it may well have put an end to previous school language policies which were openly criticized under *perestroika*. In practice, the demands placed on the independent systems of education were enormous. Successful implementation would depend not only on the determination of parents to have their children educated in a native language but also on the distribution and number of people speaking the same native language and the availability of teaching resources such as trained teachers and textbooks.

The Language Problem

In most world empires parents have been faced with a language dilemma. Should they, for nationalistic and cultural reasons, expect their children to be educated in an indigenous native language? Or should parents accept that in the interests of educational and occupational choice and mobility, their children should be taught in a language with a wider currency than the native language, namely, an imperial language? Faced with this dilemma, many parents in former British colonial countries chose if possible to send their children to schools in which the medium of instruction was English. The same may be said of parents in the French Empire.

In nineteenth-century America, in the absence of legislation, English became the medium of instruction and intergroup communication for people from many linguistic groups who came from the old nations of Europe. A new nation was created out of people from many different nationalities. Parents were persuaded that in order to become Americans their children had to learn English.

The strength of feeling against the Russification of language instruction in the USSR and the complexity of the language situation guaranteed that the adoption of a "melting pot" solution would generate resistance. Russification was seen as a major threat to the maintenance of national identities. However, since the 1930s Russian as the medium of instruction was promoted at the expense of native languages in many of the republics. During the 1950s and 1960s parental pressure also influenced language provision. Parents preferred their children to learn the dominant state language rather than their native language ("Problems of the National Schools in the USSR," *VNIK "Skhola,"* Moscow: 1989, pp. 26–27). Because many non-Russian-speaking parents preferred to have their children taught in Russian and because Russian speakers were widely dispersed throughout the Soviet Union and frequently occupied the most important managerial and professional positions, in many republics instruction in many schools was conducted in the Russian language. Hence major non-Russian and minority languages suffered. Population movements added to the complexity of the demographic situation. The net effect of out-migration of Slavs from the southern republics was that they had become relatively less Slavic, while the movement of people from the three Slavic republics into the Baltic states placed the indigenous people at some disadvantage. The net migration into the Russian republic was far greater, though not percentage-wise, than any other movement.

Over the years population movements helped to Russify schools throughout the country. Some sixty million people lived outside their national republics. In Latvia, immigrant groups—

mainly Slavs—accounted for one half the population. Four in ten persons in Estonia and two in ten persons in Lithuania were immigrants. Not only did very few of the Slavic settlers in Turkmenistan know the Turkmen language, many Turkmen sent their children to Russian-language schools. Instruction in many institutions of higher learning and the upper secondary schools was entirely in Russian. In the capital city of Ashkhabad, 40 percent of the pupils did not study their native language. The quality of instruction in Turkmen deteriorated, and since knowledge of Russian among the Turkmen was poor, many members of the group did not have a sound knowledge of any language. Since a similar situation existed in Uzbek SSR, demands were made to restrict Russian in-migration to this Asian republic ("Uzbeks Demand Halt to Russian In-migration," James Critchlow, *Report on the USSR*, Vol. 2, No. 9, 1990, p. 15). For many years Russians and other Europeans occupied the senior positions in the republic, but the Russians never troubled to learn the Uzbek language. Between 1979 and 1989 more than half a million people left the republic, and some 20,000 moved in each year to take sought-after jobs for which local people were not qualified. Understandably, anti-Russian feeling found expression in resolutions calling for limits to be placed on hiring workers from other regions.

Immigrants aside, by no means were all of the republics inhabited by indigenous people speaking the same "republic" language. The Russian Federation was a case in point. In spite of the Russification of schools, instruction in the Federation was conducted in twenty-one languages, and forty-three native languages in all were taught. The movement of people from various parts of the country to the big cities like Moscow further complicated the situation. In September 1989 ("Moscow Schools Widen the Language Option," *Soviet Weekly*, September 9, 1989, p. 6), it was reported that ten Soviet languages were being studied in a total of forty courses in Moscow schools at the start of the new year. Under *perestroika* Ukrainian, Byelorussian, Tatar, and Yiddish were among the free extracurricular courses open to children of any nationality. Nevertheless, in 1989 the situation of the ethnic languages in the RSFSR was described (*VNIK "Shkola,"* pp. 26–27) as serious, thanks to the process of Russification which had been going on for many years. The process had seriously affected ethnic schools in various autonomous republics and regions. In many cases of consolidation the schools were completely Russified. In other cases all teaching in the native tongue stopped in the fourth grade. In yet other autonomous republics the Russian language was introduced in the first grade in some schools. Under these circumstances the teaching and use of Russian was strengthened while the native language was relegated to the position of an ordinary school subject. These developments were particularly obvious in cities and industrial towns where all-Russian schools predominated.

Frequently in these schools the native language was not included in the curriculum even as a school subject. For many nationalities these developments heralded the end of their ethnic schools. Thus as reported in *VNIK "Skhola,"* six nationalities had schools in which the native language was used only in the first two grades. Eight nationalities retained native language instruction at the primary stage, while in the second stage of schooling instruction was conducted completely in Russian. Ten nationalities had completely Russified schools from the first grade.

During the 1950s and 1960s some fifteen nationalities in the RSFSR lost their ethnic schools, while in the 1970s at least five nationalities suffered the same fate. These changes took place in accordance with the population's wishes, but at the same time it must be recalled that several of these groups were persecuted and deprived of their homeland under Stalin. It is possible that free choice and persecution combined to destroy ethnic schooling not only in many parts of the Russian Federation but in other republics as well (Martha B. Olcott, "Language Training and Nationality Relations," *Soviet Education,* Vol. 31, No. 10, October 1989).

In the Russian Federation not everybody was pleased that Russian was the medium of instruction. As reported in *Uchitel'skaya gazeta* (No. 33, August 18, 1990, p. 7) in the article "Our Schools Have Been Declared Russian," the author, who was raised, lived, and worked in Chuvashia (one of the autonomous republics), complained that all the schooling in her village was carried out in Russian. Many pupils communicated at home and in extracurricular activities in their native language (Chuvashian). In regular classes, however, only Russian textbooks were used, and in contrast to previous practice, when essay examination questions touched on topics relevant to nationality, all questions were those used in the Russian schools. The writer asked: "Why should I assess the progress of Chuvashian children according to criteria applied to Russian children?"

The plight of many ethnic groups was similar to that of the reindeer herders. In an article entitled "Russian Without an Accent" (*The Literary Gazette International*, Vol. 1, Issue 5, April 1990), Valeri Sharov, having heard of the utterly hopeless position of the languages of the ethnic minorities in the Soviet Far North, went to a newly opened school where the children of Chukcha and Evenk reindeer hunters could attend school and stay with their parents for most of the year. Over the years in areas like these, the percentage of people speaking the native languages had steadily diminished. For example, in the 1950s the percentage of Chukchas speaking their native language was 94.3 percent, in the 1970s it had dropped to 82.6 percent, and at the beginning of the 1980s, to 78.3 percent. The languages of the Evenks, the Nenetzs, and the Udeges were in danger of disappearing unless schools of the type visited by Sharov were opened. Russian had become the language of the younger generation. In 1990, A. L. Vugaevoee stated (*Narodnoe obrazovanie*, No. 5, 1990, p. 23) that "[o]ur society is so guilty as far as small minorities of this country are concerned, that verbal repentance does not satisfy anybody." Some peoples had not yet acquired a written language, and the authorities did nothing to help, while others had lost their written language.

The languages of still other groups within the Soviet Union were also the subject of considerable controversy. The reindeer herders who lived in the north of the country were frequently nomadic and subsisted by hunting. They had no written language and for many years Soviet policy was to create written languages for native peoples and to educate them in their own language. This remained the policy of the RSFSR in the 1980s, and while some groups still did not possess a written language of their own, attempts were made to educate all pupils in their own tongue.

In the Caucasus, in the Kabardin-Balkar Autonomous SSR, the Kabardin language was relegated, according to B. Bakuyev ("Native Tongue," *Moscow News*, No. 9, 1990, p. 6), "to the kitchen sink." As elsewhere, Russian was used for meetings, conferences, and business correspondence. To know Russian was to be an internationalist; to speak Kabardin was to be a nationalist. Nonindigenous persons were appointed to important positions in the Party and government. This confirmed the view of parents that their children would only succeed as speakers of Russian. None of the nurseries and schools in the capital city taught the native language, but the Institute for Advanced Teacher Education now offers classes in Russian and Karbardin.

The Tadzhik republic offered another example of a native language which had lost its status. Even among the intelligentsia there were a good many who were unable to read or write Tadzhik. During debates on the Law of Languages, therefore, great importance was attached to the role of Russian as the language of communication among nationalities of the USSR and in the schools of the Tadzhik republic. In spite of the fact that the law provided for the study of old Tadzhik texts in Arabic, they were not available. Some of the issues were debated with such passion that police squads had to control those in attendance (A. Karpov, "Law on Language Ratified," *Izvestia*, July 23, 1989, p. 1, *CDSP*, Vol. XLI, No. 29, 1989, pp. 31–32).

In the face of this failure to make it possible for minority groups to learn in their native language, how was it possible to regenerate the languages of the small minorities? Policy needed to be directed to the revival of local cultures and languages. Although the language issue was more and more politicized, small minority peoples did not, in general, present a serious threat to the central authorities since the advantages of learning Russian were so obvious.

Protests in the Baltic republics, Byelorussia, and the Ukraine against the Russification of schools were a different matter. These republics supported claims for self-determination. The situation in the Baltic republics was fairly clear. In Riga, the capital of Latvia, for example, where many Russian-speaking workers from other parts of the USSR lived, there were two systems of education, one for Latvian-speaking children and the other for Russian-speaking children. The same was true in the other Baltic republics which had large Russian-speaking populations. In the big cities, the Russian-speaking schools were attended by Russians; the Latvian, Estonian, and Lithuanian schools, only by native speakers. Leonid Mlechin, in an article "The Russians in the Baltic Republics" (*New Times*, No. 24, 1990, pp. 31–34), wrote that this educational division had created a "friend or foe" identification system. Mixed schools with instruction in different languages had not solved the problem, and the government had washed its hands of the whole business. Thus, in the Russian schools a curriculum compiled in the RSFSR was followed, facilitating admission to higher institutions in Russian cities. Local languages were not studied since it was much more expedient to study Russian. According to Mlechin, the passions of Lithuanians, Latvians, and Estonians had been roused. They claimed that 300,000 hostile strangers were living among them. Nationalists claimed that the Russians were responsible for destroying their culture.

The pressure to defend native languages against the inroads made by Russian must be seen against a long period of decline in the teaching of the native languages. In Byelorussia in 1989, for example, the state of the native language was described as disastrous (*National Language Relationships in the USSR: State and Prospects,* Moscow: Novostí Press Agency 1989, pp. 105–107). The decline of the Byelorussian language was reported in *Soviet Weekly* (March 29, 1990, p. 12), where it was claimed that "[t]oday one can only hear Byelorussian spoken at the Union of Writers, the Academy of Sciences, several libraries, universities, and some of the drama theaters." Until recently the capital city of Minsk, a "capital of a sovereign republic with a population of 1.5 million, did not have a single Byelorussian-speaking school, nor did any other city or town in Byelorussia (population 10 million)." The native language was taught to only 20 percent of school students.

The secretary of the Minsk City Party Committee of Byelorussia, Pyotr Kravchenko, gave the reasons for this decline in an interview for *News from the Ukraine* (No. 12, 1990, p. 9), in which he claimed that the Stalin purges in Byelorussia in the 1930s "destroyed the flower of the republic's intelligentsia." Subsequently, Byelorussian schools were scrapped in some towns, so that during the Brezhnev years the native language had fallen into disuse in state and public life. According to Jan Zaprudnik ("Byelorussian Reawakening," in *Problems of Communism,* July–August 1980, pp. 36–52), during the Second World War the Party in Moscow launched a campaign to thoroughly Russify Byelorussia by depriving the inhabitants of their language and traditions. Z. Paznyak, a historian and archaeologist, supported his indictment of the process by pointing out that by the mid-1970s, in Byelorussia's ninety-five cities and in almost all of the republic's towns, in not a single school or kindergarten was Byelorussian the language of instruction. Reaction to this situation predated *glasnost.*

In 1981 an informal patriotic movement was started by students from the state university, the Institute of Theater and Arts, and some other professions and schools. On October 19, 1988, the Byelorussian Popular Front for Restructuring (Renewal) was founded. In December 1986, twenty-eight eminent Byelorussian scholars aired their grievances in a petition, one section of which dealt with the closure of Byelorussian schools. As a result of this kind of pressure, in 1989–90 Russian-language primary schools once again were beginning to teach Byelorussian in the second instead of in the third grade. The authorities also announced plans to increase the publishing of books in the Byelorussian language.

A similar situation had arisen in the Ukraine, except that, as in the Russian republic, many languages were spoken. The use of the Ukrainian language in schools had been substantially reduced. In 1989, only 46 percent of students studied it as their first language. In many regions, due to the movement of population, members of other language groups feared they might be swamped by the immigration of Russians. An example of the Russification was reported by Natalya Kraminova in *Moscow News* ("A Ukrainian Exile Returns," No. 43, 1989, p. 16). She recalled that when Shevchenko returned after his arrest in 1980 for anti-Soviet propaganda, he realized that at the university everything, even agricultural courses for the people who were supposed to work in villages, was taught in Russian. He noticed that the Ukrainians were ashamed of their language, speaking it only at home. Suspicion, indeed, fell on anyone who was brave enough to speak the Ukrainian language in official contacts. This led to the proposal of a draft law of the "State Ukrainian Language" (S. Tsikora, "Facts and Commentary: Month for Reflection," *Izvestia*, September 6, 1989, p. 1). It stipulated that the Ukrainian language was to be given state-language status but all citizens were to be given the right to freely use any other of the languages that were spoken in the republic. Russian had always been the language of interethnic communication between the peoples of the USSR.

This draft law recognized that the republic was multinational and every child should have the right to be educated in the language of one's nationality. However, Article 24 made the study of Ukrainian and Russian mandatory in all general education schools regardless of the language of instruction used. Moreover, all individuals applying to enter specialized secondary schools and higher education institutions had to take entrance examinations in Ukrainian. The extra burden on non-Ukrainian-speaking students was evident. The draft law promoted heated debate over the position of Russian as the interethnic language of communication (*News from the Ukraine*, Vol. 40, 1989, p. 1).

Tribal loyalties exerted a strong influence on the inhabitants of Turkmenistan and were reenforced by the persistence of dialects (Annette Bohr, "Turkmenistan under *Perestroika*: An Overview," *Report on the USSR*, Vol. 2, No. 12, March 23, 1990, pp. 20–30). The status of the Turkmen language was of paramount importance for the Turkmen and had "strained relations between the republic's indigenous and nonindigenous inhabitants" (ibid.). Turkmen officials were reluctant to support legislation that would grant state status to the language of the majority for fear of creating backlash from the sizeable nonindigenous populations of whom the Russians formed the largest group, 9.5 percent. Slavic settlers supplied the Turkmenistan economy with much needed skills. This was also true in many of the other republics, and few of these immigrants wanted to learn the native languages.

Reaction to the Language Problem

Politically the nationalities problem was clear. Gorbachev, recognizing that the language problem had become "very acute," proposed that the indigenous peoples of all the republics should have the right to establish their mother tongue as the state language. At the same time he recognized the need for a means of interethnic communication and insisted that Russian was the appropriate common language across the USSR. In an aside he pointed to the use in Switzerland of three languages and in Finland, with a small percentage of Swedish-speaking people in the population, of Swedish as a second language. He failed to make clear that the far greater complexity of language and population patterns in the Soviet Union made it unlikely that such solutions would succeed.

Glasnost allowed data to be collected that revealed the complexity of the national language problem. Survey respondents were more ready than previously to identify their true origins and voice complaints. This new openness helped to clarify the complaints of the supporters of ethnic schools, particularly in the urban areas that for a variety of reasons had become Russified.

Russophobia reemerged on a broader scale in the RSFSR. According to A. Sinyavsky, on January 9, 1990, speaking at the Kennan Institute for Advanced Russian Studies, the recent national-religious renaissance in Russia very possibly could lead to fascism and had already taken on an increasingly anti-Semitic tone. Not surprisingly, in view of Russian history and the dominance of Russians, a powerful militant Russian nationalism emerged. Deep feelings were aroused. Knowledge of demographic trends contributed a renewed consciousness of native Russians. Differential birthrates complicated an already complex situation. In 1989 a census on the size of the some 100 nationalities and ethnic groups in the Soviet Union revealed that the Muslim share of the population had risen by 19.2 percent. In 1979 this group made up 16.5 percent of the population. Between 1979 and 1989, some 49.4 percent of the total population increase was accounted for by Muslim births. The increase in the Uzbeks was 34 percent; between 1979 and 1989 the Tajiks increased by

45.5 percent, and the Kazakhs and the Azerbaijanis each increased by 24 percent ("Ethnic Muslims Account for Half of Soviet Population Increases," *Report on the USSR*, Vol. 2, No. 3, January 19, 1990, pp. 15–18). Overall the Russian share of the total population dropped from 52.4 percent in 1979 to 50.8 percent in 1989. Many demographers predicted that the Russians in the years ahead would become a minority of the population (Ann Sheehy, "Russian Share of Soviet Population Down to 50.8 Percent," *Report on the USSR*, Vol. 1, No. 42, pp 1–5).

Associated with the rise in the Muslim population was their demand to use its own Arabic script. Many Muslims wished to restore the alphabet they used before Cyrillic was forcibly imposed on them. The Central Asian republics were upset with the legacy of anti-Arabic propaganda about their "illiteracy" ("Erika Dailey's Update on Alphabet Legislation," *Report on the USSR,* Vol. 1, No. 32, 1990, pp. 29–31). Publications regularly appeared partially or entirely in the Arabic alphabet in Tajikistan, and a new book for children had been printed entirely in Arabic. Article 124 of the Uzbek draft law making Uzbek the state language guaranteed assistance to those wishing to learn the Arabic alphabet. There were demands that the study of Arabic should be mandatory in the advanced history courses and that ideally it should be integrated into the standard common secondary school curriculum.

Regional History and Literature

Under *perestroika* the intention was to democratize the system of education by reducing the power of the central authorities. Draft legislation delegated to the republics and individual schools the power to formulate, adopt, and implement curriculum policies. However, the control and content of the curriculum were aspects of the wider problems identified by Gorbachev in his report on the Communist Party's nationalities policies at the plenary meeting of the Central Committee in Moscow on September 19, 1989. The preservation of native languages was fundamentally important if people were to retain their identity, but politicians also called for changes in the curriculum, namely, the inclusion of subjects relevant to national pride. Prior to *perestroika* there was little room in the Soviet curriculum for such subjects. Soviet educational theory mandated the entire socioeconomic and historical experience of mankind, suitably interpreted, should be passed on from one generation to the next through an encyclopaedic curriculum.

In practice, Soviet ideology determined selection of all curriculum content. In the humanities each item of knowledge had to be interpreted from the standpoint of Marxism-Leninism. Even in the natural sciences political commitment from time to time influenced the presentation of scientific material. Under these circumstances the histories and literatures of non-Russians received far less attention in Soviet schools than was thought proper by critics of the curriculum that had been laid down by the central authorities under the eagle eye of Communist Party officials. The trend under *perestroika* was to include more local history and regional literature in the curriculum. The inclusion of such material depended on who determined the curriculum. The draft curriculum prepared by the USSR State Committee for Public Education in the late 1980s in principle allowed republics, regions, and individual schools to select from history and literature the material they thought relevant to their own schools. The draft plan was published in *Uchitel'skaya gazeta* (December 28, 1989, p. 2). The State Committee encouraged republics to establish a core component of their own choosing. Naturally some republics wanted this component to constitute a greater part of the curriculum. This also raised the question of what the content and extent of the All-Union component should be through which the legitimate needs of the USSR would be met. This component, suggested by the State Committee, had to be decided in consultation with, and agreed upon by, ministries of education in the republics. Once agreed upon, the state component was to be the main curriculum in that it would be common throughout the country. Although the list of specific subjects was not rigidly laid down, subject areas were identified. The subject content could be decided upon in each of the republics, regions, and schools. The State Committee prepared and presented syllabi for use as examples in the light of which republics, regions, and schools could then develop their own.

The State Committee promised to decentralize curriculum control even further in the long run so that the components could be determined exclusively by individual schools for their own purposes. Schools then would have the maximum freedom to adopt a curriculum relevant to the conditions within the regions and immediate environments of the schools.

The USSR State Committee's proposals and its draft curriculum legitimized calls for greater freedom of choice and went a long way to democratize what was once solely the concern of the central agencies. Greater freedom to determine the content of education opened the door for some schools to place greater emphasis on subjects associated with the promotion of cultural identity. School No. 97 in Kiev, for example ("In-Depth Courses: Experimenting with New Ideas," *News from the Ukraine*, No. 37, 1988, p. 1), introduced at the beginning of the 1988–89 academic year an in-depth course on Ukrainian literature. It was, incidentally, one of many other in-depth courses introduced in fifty-six Kiev schools. The four-year course on Ukrainian literature started in the seventh grade. The three lessons per week over this period compared with the two for the ordinary courses and included weekly discussion seminars when the class was divided into two sections. In 1987, Kiev School No. 127 introduced ethnic studies into the curriculum. In speaking to educators from all parts of the Ukraine, the principal of School No. 127 stated (Alexandr Stetsenko, "Ethnic Studies: A Step to a National School," *News from the Ukraine*, No. 20, 1990, p. 9): "We sought to involve in the ethnic studies program all the teachers of our school, irrespective of their subjects. The program embraced both lessons and extracurricular measures."

CHAPTER 8

Soviet Curriculum—Pedagogical Issues

The pedagogical problems associated with curriculum reform in the Soviet Union stemmed in part from the determination with which the Soviet authorities had pursued practices based on Marxism-Leninism ideology. Only under *perestroika* were politicians and educators prepared to consider theories that in Western countries had legitimized responses to the problems created after World War II by the explosions of knowledge, population, aspirations, and expectations.

Faced with these explosions, educators had four major curriculum theories from which to choose in order to justify what was taught in schools. The first, essentialism, had its origins in the theories of knowledge of Plato and Aristotle. In the Middle Ages these views found expression in the Seven Liberal Arts curriculum. The quadrivium consisted of arithmetic, geometry, astronomy, and music and the trivium embraced grammar, rhetoric, and logic. Later, the essentialist curriculum theory asserted that a sound general education could best be provided by a careful selection of "essential" subjects which could be identified by their inner logic and coherence. For example, a specialized English curriculum in the final grades of the secondary school contained no more than three related subjects. However, the explosion of scientific knowledge made it much more difficult to determine what the few essential subjects should be.

The second theory, encyclopaedism, did not require a selection of subjects. It had its origins in the work of Comenius. His scheme of universal learning was based on the observation of nature and the study of its laws. Encyclopaedic curriculum theory found expression in the content of education proposed for

French schools by the Napoleonic authorities. The influence of French education throughout continental Europe in the nineteenth century spread to Russia and a broad spectrum of subjects was introduced into Russian schools. Selection was avoided in the upper grades by providing for specialized clusters of subjects catering to the interests and abilities of students.

The third theory, polytechnical education, was proposed by Soviet educators as a modification of the encyclopaedic curriculum theory. It had its origins in the favorable remarks by Marx about Robert Owen's labor school in Lanarkshire, Scotland, where he combined theoretical knowledge with work experience. Soviet curriculum theory maintained that in the productive life of a socialist society the social implications and practical applications of theoretical knowledge should be made known through a polytechnical curriculum. In the Soviet Union there were continuing debates about how to achieve this ideal in practice. The 1958 Khrushchev reform attempted to introduce polytechnical education throughout the Soviet school system, but for a number of reasons the reform was never successfully carried out.

A fourth theory, pragmatism, was developed at the end of the nineteenth century by a group of American philosophers who set out to establish a new rationale for life in a rapidly industrializing society. One of these pragmatists, John Dewey, formulated a pragmatic curriculum theory based on the assertion that the curriculum should enable young people to solve social problems collectively and intelligently. Compared with the other theories, pragmatism offered a process- rather than a subject-centered curriculum theory.

The Soviet Encyclopaedic Curriculum

Soviet educators inherited an encyclopaedic curriculum from the Tsarist regime. In most Western European countries the subjects for a very small minority of pupils preparing for university entrance included Greek, Latin, mathematics, a modern foreign language, the mother tongue, physics, chemistry, biology, history, geography, and in the original French proposals, design and mechanical arts. In Tsarist schools less emphasis was placed on the classical languages than in Western schools, but in principle and in practice the content of education was European.

Lenin approved an encyclopaedic curriculum and an ideology which stressed equality above all else. This meant that a broadly based encyclopaedic curriculum, intended originally for the minority of pupils preparing for university entrance, was required for all students except for those suffering severe brain damage. This curriculum for all created a series of difficult problems under *perestroika* to which Soviet educators turned their attention less dogmatically than they had in the past.

Although in theory each republic in the USSR could modify syllabi to meet the needs of its own region, in practice a large number of subjects was centrally prescribed. At least twenty-four subjects had to be studied at some time during the course of a pupil's schooling. This encyclopaedic curriculum had to be followed by all pupils regardless of their abilities, interests, and achievements.

Another feature of the Soviet educational system was the heavy pressure under which pupils worked. Not only were the subjects prescribed, but also the time spent on them each week, throughout the year, and during the whole period of schooling. Syllabi determined the content of textbooks, which, in turn, determined examinations and assessments. Teaching was textbook- and examination-centered. Teachers had to use approved textbooks and assign a great deal of homework. After the primary grades, homework covered up to six subjects every night, and the following day the students' work was assessed by the teacher. Also, during classroom sessions students were asked questions and marks were assigned to the pupils in their class record books. A mark of 5 represented an excellent answer; 4, good; 3, satisfactory; 2, bad or unsatisfactory; and 1, very bad. The mark of 1 was rarely used; the majority of the students receive a grade of 3. Homework and class lessons concentrated on memorization of textbook assignments. A positive feature of this system was that pupils, by receiving marks in their record books, had constant feedback about their level of knowledge, which also enabled the parents to follow the child's progress in each subject.

Examinations were scheduled four times during the school year. Once or twice a month written tests were conducted, and at the end of each term written and oral tests were administered. All the marks a pupil received were averaged to arrive at term and final marks. Comprehensive examinations were conducted at the end of the ninth and eleventh grades in those schools which had incorporated the kindergarten into the system. All schools were allowed to organize examinations at the end of other years as well. The general practice was for pupils who received an unsatisfactory mark at the end of a school year and did not pass tests before the beginning of the next autumn term, to repeat the year. In 1989 the USSR State Committee issued Regulation 540, which recommended that pupils with three unsatisfactory marks be promoted from one class to the next. This would enable these pupils to graduate with a leaving certificate even though they received unsatisfactory marks. The object of this regulation was to reduce the practice of grade inflation. Later it was cancelled by the Russian Ministry of Education because of teacher resistance.

Prior to graduation, some of the examinations were written and some were oral. Questions were prepared by the republics' ministries of education; special commissions of teachers from each school conducted the exams and assessed the pupils' answers. There was much subjectivity in assessment procedures. Up to 1989, all pupils leaving school had to take examinations in all eight academic subjects. Oral examinations were conducted by offering candidates a choice of tickets, *bilety,* on each of which two or three questions were written. Few candidates studying for an oral examination dared to study only part of the extensive syllabus under this system. Conscientious pupils attempted to cover as thoroughly as possible the entire syllabus for each subject.

The encyclopaedic curriculum and the pressure of continuous assessment were highly criticized by the progressive teacher movement in the late 1980s. A well-known scholar and innovative teacher, Sh. Amonashvili, refused to give marks to pupils in the primary grades. Another reformer, V. Firsov, remarked that the system of assessment was oriented towards the "maximum level of acquisition of the curriculum by the pupil" (*The Planning of Obligatory Results in Teaching Mathematics*, Moscow: APS, 1989, p. 3).

In the 1980s, when all pupils were enrolled in upper secondary schools, such assessment caused frustration among pupils who could not get good marks. Consequently many of them lost interest in learning. Firsov maintained that the "orientation of the learning process towards the maximum level of achievement is amoral towards a lot of pupils" (ibid.). On September 22, 1989, the Russian republic's Ministry of Education sent a letter to schools No. 357/8, ordering them to organize two obligatory examinations (in Russian and mathematics) and one or two optional examinations after the ninth year. After the eleventh year there were obligatory examinations in literature, algebra, history, and social studies plus two optional examinations chosen from literature, geometry, physics, biology, astronomy, chemistry, and a modern language (*Information Booklet of the RSFSR Ministry of Public Education*, Moscow, December 1989, p. 35–36).

Only in 1977 was it admitted that different pupils needed a somewhat different curriculum diet. Electives were allowed in grades seven and eight, and after the reform of 1984 in grades nine and ten, to enable some students to raise the level of their knowledge in such basic subjects as mathematics and the Russian language and for other high achievers to learn additional information, preparing them to take university entrance examinations in subjects of their choice. The experiment received little attention. However, it did show that Soviet educators recognized even before *perestroika* that some differentiation in terms of curriculum provision was necessary if the varying needs of pupils were to be met in unified schools. Moreover, many educators and parents thought that the curriculum was grossly overloaded for the majority of pupils. They pointed to the overloading, malnutrition, and pollution as contributing to the deterioration of the health of children. According to the *Uchitel'skaya gazeta* (December 23, 1989, No. 51, p. 1) "only 20 percent to 25 percent of children were absolutely healthy." Since Yagodin made a connection between this phenomenon and the organization of the education process, his State Committee developed a national program, "Health Through Education," for the schools. It encouraged better nutrition, reduced curricular pressures, and outlined daily physical activities.

Other education critics levied attacks on the overloaded curriculum of the schools. Professor Kumarin in 1991 compared the subject load of children at school with that of cosmonauts in space. He claimed that what was going on in schools was a crime. The school, he maintained, "not only emptied us of talents, cultivated mediocrity, and promoted antisocial behavior, but burnt the health of people" (*Uchitel'skaya gazeta*, No. 5, January 30, 1991, p. 7). The data received from the first Deputy Minister of Health Care in the USSR indicated that almost 100 percent of school leavers suffered from some form of disease. The following statistics worried Kumarin even more: from sixty to eighty thousand school children from seven to seventeen years of age committed suicide annually. The main reason was the discontent of teachers, peer jokes, and authoritarian parental control (ibid.). The pressure on school pupils was further increased by the content of each subject, methods of teaching, and examination and assessment procedures.

The Polytechnical Curriculum

The unique contribution to curriculum theory of Soviet educators was their research in ways of relating the content of education to the productive life of a socialist society. Debates were endless. One group, even in the 1920s, considered that "polytechnical" implied an increased number and variety of vocational courses. Another group, under the leadership of Krupskaya, considered productive labor to be the source of a sound general education. While her analysis made it difficult for practicing teachers to translate theory ideas into action, her concept of polytechnical education could be gleaned from the following passage in her book, *On Education* (Moscow: Foreign Languages Publishing House, 1957, p. 15).

> The school will stimulate pupils' interest in production and desire to raise production to the highest possible level. On the other hand, the factory training school will acquaint the pupil with labor organization in factories and plants and, for that matter, everywhere else. It will teach pupils to create the necessary fundamentals of labor protection and industrial safety at any enterprise, particularly in a textile mill. Lastly, the factory training school will teach the history of the labor and trade-union movement at home and abroad, and acquaint the pupils with the struggle waged by workers, particularly textile workers, the world over. All that will give the pupil not a narrow profession that may prove unnecessary on the morrow but a broad polytechnical education and working habits with which he will come to the factory not as an inexperienced worker but a skillful worker who requires only a short-term specialization course.

Marx was more explicit about the general nature of polytechnical education. He wrote in *Capital* (Vol. 1, Moscow: Progress Publishers, 1958): "From the factory system budded . . . the germ of education of the future. An education that will, in the case of every child over a given age, combine productive labor with instruction and gymnastics, not only as one of the methods of adding to their efficiency of production but as the only method of producing fully developed human beings" (pp. 453–54).

It was not clear from Krupskaya's quotation whether polytechnical education was designed to train skilled workers or was a form of prevocational general education. The quotation from Marx made it clear that it was intended to produce "fully developed human beings." Most educators, including Soviet reformers, would accept this general education aim. However, the Khrushchev reforms, which centered on relating education to productive work, failed to polytechnicize the Soviet curriculum.

APS and VNIK Concepts of General Education

Both the Temporary Scientific Research Group (VNIK) and the USSR Academy of Pedagogical Sciences (APS) concepts of general education dealt with curriculum reform. The tone of the VNIK statement was more directly critical of the existing state of affairs than that of the APS. VNIK assumed radical reform was necessary; APS, that a new curriculum could be built on the existing one. VNIK's major criticism was that the curriculum was aimed at the acquisition of knowledge and not at the development of personality. In the introduction to the APS document a general comment likewise was made about the failure of the system to pay attention to the personalities of pupils. VNIK went further by complaining that educators were not interested in passing on the experience gained through various forms of classroom activity.

Curriculum improvement in the past consisted of adding more and more information geared to the requirements of higher education to syllabi. Such an emphasis, VNIK maintained, did not make a syllabus more "scientific." Furthermore simply adding material had led to a loss of coherence and the collection of badly organized information. VNIK concluded that these defects had left students and teachers bewildered and had resulted in less interest in schooling and a less thorough preparation.

The proposals of VNIK's were indeed very radical. In principle and in some practical respects, they resembled those of the American advocates of a pragmatic curriculum insofar as they suggested an activity- or an experience-centered approach. The intention of this approach was to develop cognitive abilities and creativity so that children would learn how to acquire knowledge. If this interpretation of the views briefly expressed in the VNIK document is correct, it implied a rejection of the encyclopaedic curriculum in favor of an activity-centered one. The supporters of VNIK did not, however, propose to abandon entirely the well-established encyclopaedic curriculum. Unfortunately they merely referred to the possibility of another alternative curriculum theory. This brief mention of an alternative curriculum theory suggested that the VNIK curriculum would be process rather than knowledge centered. It claimed, however, to be one in which the two basic activity components, society-oriented and creative activities, could be successfully integrated.

For VNIK the criteria on which curriculum data were to be selected were concerns of man, society, nature, and "noosphere" (the outer surroundings of the Earth). "Concerns of man" indicated the life activities which contributed to the education of personality. Under the criterion of "society," important values were elaborated about motherland, mankind, socialism, internationalism, democracy, *glasnost*, the legal basis of the state, family life, and citizenship. In the relationships between man and "nature," individuals were made aware of themselves as part of nature and given an ecological outlook so that future generations might accept responsibility for their interpretation of nature. "Noosphere" included the development of moral responsibility for using the products of scientific-technological innovations and the acquisition of the methods needed to control the activities associated with cultural transformation. In all of these suggestions were found the bases of a curriculum that was radically different from the knowledge- and subject-centered curriculum which for so long had typified education in the Soviet schools.

Some basic principles were implied in VNIK's approach to the establishment of a democratic curriculum. The first principle was that the curriculum must be child-centered and contribute to personality development. Next, the basic components of individual growth and development and the qualitative change that was possible in human potential had to be identified. Also, it was important to know what connected one individual with other individuals and with previous generations of mankind. Finally, a system of ideas and values was needed to effect mutual understanding between peoples and a mutually beneficial life. These were considered to be determinants of a general education that would guarantee the realistic achievement of new educational goals.

For VNIK the "humanization" and "humanitarianization" of the curriculum were closely linked. Usually the latter term was taken to mean that the time devoted to the humanities should be increased. However, it also involved developing man's relationship with nature by directing the attention of the school curriculum to the culture, history, and spiritual values of the world. VNIK pleaded for the humanities to be restored to their rightful position by freeing them from the cognitive realm and by revealing their spiritual character and humane essence. The curriculum's whole content needed to be restructured to provide for the development of written and oral forms of communication, a humane attitude towards nature, and an understanding of different peoples and periods of history.

The goal of the "humanization" and the "humanitarianization" of the curriculum, therefore, was the reduction of technocratic attitudes and alienation. The whole process of education was to be humanized by taking into account the personal qualities of individual students and teachers. The individualization of the curriculum called for syllabi to be established for different levels that took into account the different experiences, achievements, interests, and aspirations of students. VNIK recommended that aesthetic education assume an important role in the humanization of education, and physical education be given a more prominent place than it had previously held.

These proposals meant that the group of reformers associated with VNIK hoped to abandon a subject-centered curriculum based on the accumulation of the knowledge of mankind in favor of one that was relevant to the child's personality, moral, and aesthetic development. VNIK's proposals can be compared with pragmatic curriculum theory insofar as they implied that subject-centered aims were to be abandoned in favor of child-centered aims. Though not spelled out in detail, VNIK's proposals justified the abolition of traditional subjects and their replacement with problems or activities through which knowledge would be selected from the established university subjects. The radical nature of VNIK's curriculum proposals should not disguise the fact that they lacked specific and detailed advice on the establishment of an activity-centered curriculum.

The Academy's proposals were much less radical but, consequently, were more realistic than VNIK's. They identified the main principles of curriculum reform by making explicit the concerns expressed by educators all over the world. For example, balance within the curriculum was widely debated. The first principle of the APS document stated the need for balance among the social sciences, the natural sciences and mathematics, the language arts, the fine arts, and labor so as to reflect a wide variety of human activities and a system of human relationships. The second principle was that subjects should be integrated in order to eliminate overloading. The third principle suggested that all subject matter must be derived from scientific ideas, concepts, theories, and principles.

The APS advocated a curriculum that would promote the creative abilities and emotional-value attitudes of students and also their scientific, dialectical-materialistic thinking. It advanced the polytechnical concept to foster links between curriculum content and life, between social and industrial practice, and between socially useful productive work and the interests and aspirations of individual students. A fundamental Marxist principle was upheld, namely, that due regard should be taken of the general laws of the country's development. Finally, it recommended that curricula and syllabi take into consideration regional and local peculiarities and the differences in intellectual and emotional makeup of students.

Especially, the Academy document stated that the humanization of the curriculum was very important because such reform was designed to inculcate moral knowledge about man and society and to make the curriculum personally relevant. The APS asserted that public opinion appeared to favor increasing the time devoted to the humanities. The document then went on to identify the position and importance of various subjects. Physical education promoted health. The arts, although poorly taught, could have a powerful influence on the development of personality. It concluded that the role of science and mathematics was bound to increase in a period dominated by the applications of science and technology.

New fields of knowledge were regarded as important. Information science, computers, biotechnology, and scientific knowledge about space and the oceans needed to be included in science and mathematics syllabuses. The APS opposed any decrease in the amount of science in the curriculum, and science was not to be seen in opposition to the humanities. A synthesis between the sciences and the humanities should be sought. Other considerations suggested that new fields of knowledge should be included in the new curriculum, such as the already mentioned information sciences. The relationship between man, nature, and science demanded that the student should develop an ecological awareness and an ability to think about protecting the environment.

A most significant proposal advanced by the APS was that the curriculum should consist of two parts. The first part, the "core," should be common throughout the whole country without regard to specific regional and local conditions. This core should be determined by the requirements for a general education laid down by the state. The second part should take into consideration the individual abilities of children and the unique features of various regions and nationalities.

On the crucial issue of content the VNIK and Academy statements were very different. VNIK's document did not specifically reject encyclopaedism, nor did it spell out in detail the activities around which a new curriculum could be built. It did imply that a knowledge-dominated, subject-centered curriculum was no longer viable. On the other hand, the APS's proposals identified issues on which international comparative information was readily available. The recommendations made by the Academy could be translated into practice more readily by practicing teachers than those contained in the VNIK document because the APS was still committed to a subject-centered curriculum. The Academy document included curriculum aims which were similar to those expressed in the VNIK document, but, in contrast to the latter, the Academy document included specific references to some fundamental Marxist principles, including a polytechnical curriculum.

A radical modification in curriculum theory demanded fundamental rethinking of the kind that few Soviet teachers were prepared to undertake. The innovative teachers in the USSR, whose work was widely reported and around whom like-minded teachers collected, undoubtedly provided models that could be followed. They had an impact; but in 1991 the authors met only a few teachers in Moscow who claimed that the influence of Eureka and the "innovators" remained strong among the teachers who were taking advantage of the new freedoms under *perestroika*. The early success of the movement depended on the desire of teachers to copy what they had seen in experimental classes and schools and on their ability to translate into effective practice the accounts they had read about the new methods of teaching. Nor did the adoption by central authorities of a new, or revised, curriculum based on radically different theories and aims ensure that teachers were able or willing to incorporate the new material into their teaching or to present it in a way which would guarantee that new aims would be achieved.

Meanwhile both VNIK and the Academy's Institute for the Content and Methods of Education prepared new syllabi for subjects, some of which were still in dispute. Undoubtedly the draft curriculum prepared by the USSR State Committee and published in *Uchitel'skaya gazeta* reflected many of the views expressed in the Academy's concept of education.

On one issue many curriculum critics were agreed. A high proportion of pupils had no interest in learning. In his article "What Education Do We Have?" (*Uchitel'skaya gazeta*, December 23, 1989, p. 4), Yagodin claimed that sociological surveys showed that only 9 percent of senior school children studied with interest. Only 30 percent wanted to become real professionals, and 20 percent thought it was not necessary to study much of anything to acquire a job or profession (indeed 15 percent thought they were wasting time at school). It was not surprising therefore that the survey showed that 18 percent of pupils did not study at all in school, 63 percent studied from time to time, and only 19 percent were disciplined and committed students.

The critics agreed that effectively the aim of education was knowledge centered. V. Firsov, for example, claimed that "[t]oday's school is concerned most of all with passing on knowledge while the real level of its acquisition is of no less significance . . ." ("Unified and Various," *Sovetskaya pedagogika*, No. 2, 1989, p. 56). He was confident that for the best pupils the quality of general secondary education was adequate. However, he stated, "not many of the rest had mastered the required material satisfactorily" (ibid). He then drew attention to one of the most fundamental difficulties facing curriculum developers, namely, how to differentiate between an adequate lowest level of content and achievement and the level fixed for advanced education. He agreed that obligatory state requirements should determine the lowest level of education (ibid., p. 57). Yet in another article he maintained that this lowest level was not clearly defined. "Traditional assessment," he wrote, "is oriented to the excellent 5 level." The high expectations associated with a mark of 5 accounted for the decline in interest at school for those pupils who could not meet the requirements of such a mark (ibid., p. 13). Firsov proposed, therefore, two basic curriculum levels, a minimum obligatory level and a maximum level (V. V. Firsov, *Materials for the Concept of the General Secondary School Curriculum*, Moscow: Basic Education, 1990). The basic level would determine the lower level of the two in a worthwhile general education. Establishing this minimum level made it possible to limit the study of disliked and difficult subjects and thus reduced the load on pupils (ibid., p. 23). Only by freeing pupils from an excessive curriculum load would it be possible to arouse their interests and inclinations, create a positive motivation to learn, and contribute to their development. These two curriculum levels would enable pupils to satisfy state requirements while at the same time it would give them the right to study subjects in greater depth. The level of advanced training, for those capable of achieving it, would be determined by the depth of mastery over content and not by the addition of new topics.

Already in January 1991 two levels of physics and mathematics had been developed for general education schools. The USSR State Committee asked the APS to apply this principle to all subjects for the 1992 school year. According to Firsov, the cultural orientation of the basic curriculum required the inclusion of the main areas of culture in accordance with the child's age. Thus the basic minimum curriculum should be flexible and include the three main components of the surrounding world, namely, nature, society, and the spiritual and physical well-being of man. By reducing the total obligatory thirty periods a week it was possible to lessen the six-day week by one day; and also more time was made available for the individualization of the curriculum and activities ("The Basic Curriculum," *Uchitel'skaya gazeta*, December 28, 1990, p. 2).

There seemed to be agreement that the content of education could not successfully be improved simply by the addition of new material to traditional subjects or by the establishment of new school subjects. Curricula had to be differentiated to meet the needs of individual children. The less able had to be allowed to follow an easier course. On the other hand the differentiation of the curriculum was designed to allow pupils freedom to choose either optional courses or a special field of study in line with their interests and achievements. In general terms the creation of a core curriculum for all and the establishment of options met these requirements. Curriculum development took into consideration both the interests and the abilities of individual children.

There was no intention, however, of introducing specialization. By allowing differentiation by means of profiles and optional courses and also providing pupils with a broadly based education, future mathematicians would study the humanities. But the depth and character of various subjects would be different. Hence mathematics and physics for future engineers would be different from the mathematics and physics for future students of the humanities.

The USSR State Committee's Draft Curriculum

The first draft of the basic curriculum was developed by the USSR State Committee and was released on December 27, 1989. It included All-Union, republic, and local school components. In the All-Union core, subjects were prescribed and the number of periods per week laid down. The number of periods per week allocated each year to the republic and local school components and to the "facultative," or additional, lessons was mandated, but the subjects to be taught were not specified.

Of the twenty-two lessons per week in the first grade of the primary division in the 1989–1990 school year curriculum, four lessons were devoted to the All-Union component and eighteen to the republic component; of the twenty-four in the second grade, six were All-Union and eighteen republic; of the twenty-five in the third grade, eight were All-Union and seventeen republic; and of the twenty-six in the fourth grade, eight were All-Union and eighteen republic. As to the junior school division, of the thirty-two lessons in the fifth grade, ten were All-Union and twenty-two republic; of the thirty-two in the sixth grade, fourteen were All-Union and eighteen republic; of the thirty-three in the seventh grade, seventeen were All-Union and sixteen republic; of the thirty-four in the eighth grade, nineteen were All-Union and fifteen republic; and of the thirty-five in the ninth grade, twenty-two were All-Union and thirteen republic. As to the senior school division, of the thirty-seven lessons in the tenth grade, twenty-one were All-Union and sixteen republic; and of the thirty-eight in the eleventh grade, nineteen were All-Union and nineteen republic ("National Base Curriculum for Secondary Schools," *USSR Committee for Public Education*, Moscow, December 27, 1989, Appendix).

Throughout the entire eleven years of schooling, between four and nineteen lessons per week, depending upon the grade level, were reserved for lessons in the five general education subject areas laid down in the basic All-Union component, whereas between sixteen and twenty lessons per week, depending upon the grade level, were allocated to general courses in the republic component. This reflected the worldwide consensus that a sound general education should include subject materials from the language arts, the natural sciences, and the social sciences. Two additional group and optional lessons for each of the grades were stipulated in the republic component as well as four lessons in specialist courses in the tenth and eleventh grades.

The 1989–1990 national base curriculum for all general secondary schools, serving as a norm for the whole of the USSR, was designed to serve as an experimental first step in the transition away from the old mandatory undifferentiated All-Union curriculum to a differentiated All-Union, republic, and individual school one. The All-Union defined component set forth a uniform level of educational development for all Soviet youth to ensure a general education foundation for future professional training, life, and work. Also it aimed to provide continuity in the transition from basic schooling to higher levels in the system of uninterrupted education. Moreover, the study of the Russian language was required for all Soviet youth since it was the means of international communication between the people of the various national republics of the USSR.

The republic-defined component formed the core around which the curriculum of the republic schools revolved. The core took into account regional and local conditions and traditions, pupil and parent wishes, and creative initiatives of teachers. It was the exclusive responsibility of the Union republics to define the specific content of such courses. Therefore, the national and republic core components served as guides to achieving the level of general education required by law.

In most countries the mother tongue is given pride of place in the curriculum as the medium of instruction and the main source of the literature to be studied. The Russian language was spoken by the great majority of people in the Soviet Union but the demands for independence made the inclusion of the Russian language in a compulsory core curriculum controversial. As stated in a previous chapter, proposals that Russian should be the language of interethnic communication met resistance. One response was to suggest that Russian be made the official language. The inclusion of a core subject called the "Literature of the Peoples of the USSR," rather than "Russian Literature," in the tenth and eleventh grades avoided the impression that the Soviet Empire was to be replaced by a Russian Empire. In the absence of consensus regarding a Soviet-wide medium of instruction, Russian in the state component was seen as an attempt to establish Russian as an official language rather than as a culturally and politically unifying language.

The other subject areas in the state component were less controversial; although the content of social studies was debatable. Since the All-Union component had to be negotiated with the republics, the syllabi in social studies were not laid down by the All-Union State Committee but negotiated in ways that made it possible for there to be regional differences. The freedom granted to republics and schools to determine a considerable proportion of a school's curriculum also made it possible for schools to respond democratically to the interests of pupils and parents.

Schools were encouraged to respond to the proposals made by the All- Union State Committee in its 1989 document "On Enlarging the Rights of Secondary School Collectives, Providing Real Legislative, Organizational and Financial Independence of Educational Institutions." It recommended that in the senior high school one third of the curriculum could be determined by the school collective. In Order No. 565 (July 7, 1989), the collective was authorized to develop and use in the educational process individual curricula and syllabi for slow learners and advanced students. The school collective could determine the language or languages of instruction and the vocational training profile for students (Order No. 667, August 15, 1989). The same order authorized the collective to establish the length of the working week and lessons. Another order (Order No. 567, July 17, 1989) permitted local examinations and promotion procedures to be introduced at the second and third stages of schooling.

Optional subjects increased the number of subjects to be studied and allowed for differentiation in the last years of basic schooling and in the tenth and eleventh grades in order to develop the permanent interests, independence, and creative activity of children. All of this was necessary if children were to make conscious choices in terms of educational profiles in the final classes and their future careers. The list of options and their syllabi were developed by the education authorities in the republics.

Profile education, on the other hand, was based on a somewhat different concept. It was intended to allow talented pupils to specialize in subject areas of their choice. Students were expected to specialize in those areas in which they had developed a permanent interest and shown some ability. The USSR State Committee recommended that profiles be introduced in the tenth grade, which would enable students to study in depth those areas in which they were preparing to take entrance examinations for specific departments or faculties in a university or other institution of higher education.

Finally, perhaps the most important feature of the school-based curriculum component was the recommendation that additional corrective lessons be used at the discretion of a school to meet the needs of those who required remedial help. The school council was responsible for this component and a psychologist could be employed for remedial classes. In principle, additional lessons took into account the needs of all children, whether normal or not, from the first years of their schooling. This profound change in psychological theory legitimized proposals to differentiate curricula.

The humanitarianism of the curriculum was reflected in the recommendation that the proportion of school time spent on the humanities should be increased in spite of the APS recommendation that the time devoted to science must not be reduced. It was suggested in the *Uchitel'skaya gazeta* article on December 28, 1989, that more than half the curriculum time should be spent on the humanities instead of the existing rigid 41 percent. This increased time would allow twice as much time to be devoted to aesthetic education. Likewise, the possibility of integrating traditional subjects was seen as a possible way of humanizing the curriculum.

A major criticism voiced by the teacher innovators was that the system of assessment and examinations put too much pressure on the students. If the wider aims of the reformers were to be achieved, changes in syllabi were necessary. The APS's concept of education called for the integration of subjects in order to provide a holistic picture of the world. The opponents of integrated science in the Soviet Union, as in other countries, claimed such courses did not adequately prepare pupils to study physics, chemistry, astronomy, or biology in an institution of higher learning. The relative merits of single-subject science syllabi and general or integrated science syllabi were fiercely debated. Nevertheless, integrated science syllabi were prepared by the APS's Institute for Content and Methods of Education for courses in the first six grades and others in various subject areas were in preparation (*Biologia v shkole,* No. 5, 1988, pp. 20–57). The authors of the integrated science syllabi agreed that the traditional Soviet curriculum did not include a huge amount of scientific knowledge found in the separate sciences. It was evident, they claimed, that such a differentiated study of nature in traditional subjects does not provide children with a holistic idea about nature and man's place and role in it. Nor does it provide an understanding of the global ecological problems. Indeed it "hinders the development of the practical skills children will need in life" (ibid., p. 20).

A fifth-grade integrated science syllabus was produced by the Academy's Institute of Content and Methods of Education. Designed as it was to provide a holistic global notion of nature and man, the course for the first four grades, "The World Surrounding Us," was intended to form a pupil's first notions about nature and society and moral attitudes towards the environment. The following topics were studied: traffic rules, health and hygiene, nature around us, motherland, water, mountains, rocks, air, plants, animals in outdoor life, man and the surrounding world, and the Earth. Clearly the intention was to break with the tradition in which scientific knowledge was emphasized without regard for its relevance to the pupils' lives.

Three integrated science courses were devised for the fifth through the seventh grades and offered as electives. The first course was based on the interconnection between geographical, physical, chemical, and biological phenomena and processes. The main theme for the fifth grade dealt with the relationships between various aspects of the earth. Man's relationship with nature was the focus of the sixth grade course. The seventh year brought together the relationships between man and the physical, chemical, and biological phenomena.

Topics studied in the fifth grade included the various spheres, e.g., the atmosphere and the biosphere of the Earth. Substances and forces in nature, such as energy and living organisms, constituted the topics in the sixth grade course. Clearly the organization of scientific knowledge in accordance with its logical and historical development was abandoned in favor of topics in which man was studied in his natural environment.

The second of the three courses was based on social ecology. Topics included the Earth as a planet, objects and substances, living organisms, spheres of the Earth, the biosphere, man on the Earth, and field practice. The third course was based on the integrity of nature and its systematic organization. An historical approach was used in this course with a special topic entitled "Reflections on the Notions about Nature and Man in the Arts of Different Epochs." All of these syllabi were tried out in experimental schools in different cities and towns throughout the USSR.

The acceptance of integrated science courses by the school authorities was very slow. In 1990–91, for example, they were used only in some schools in Moscow and a few other cities and towns. At first they were established only for the primary school and the first three grades of the secondary schools. In 1991 it was not yet clear how physics, chemistry, biology, and astronomy would be studied in the final two grades in which differentiated profiles had been introduced. This was especially the case in humanities profiles, since the existing course included highly theoretical material which was too difficult for many pupils. The principle previously mentioned had been applied. There were two syllabi: a minimum and a maximum (or advanced) one. It was considered, however, that even the minimum syllabi would not allow enough time for a sufficiently profound study of the humanities in the appropriate profiles.

On the humanities side, a syllabus, "Man and Society," developed by R. A. Artsishevsky of the Lutsk Pedagogical Institute and N. N. Kovalenko of the Ukraine Ministry of Education ("Man and Society," *Prepodavanie istori v shkole*, No. 5, 1990) was a response to the need to improve education by humanizing and integrating the curriculum. The subject matter dealt with man in harmony with nature, his social environment, and his interaction with other people. The aim of the syllabus was to help school children realize themselves on the basis of a dialectical-materialistic outlook, taking into account the development of world civilization.

The syllabus concluded with a series of courses: "The World of Man" and "Science." These consisted of four parts over a period of four years starting with "The World and Man" in the eighth grade, "Man Among People" in the ninth, "Personality and Society" in the tenth, and "Man in the Modern World: Soviet Society in the Process of Restructuring" in the eleventh (ibid., p. 135).

The methods to be used in teaching these courses reflected changes in attitudes towards learning. An emphasis was placed on understanding rather than on memorizing. Information children received from the media and their daily experiences were treated in the courses. Dialogue, discussion, and independent work were the main methods of instruction.

Four lessons were devoted to "The World and Man in Historical Perspective," eight to a "Contemporary Picture of the World," seven to "Man as the Product of His Interaction with Nature and Society," and seven to "Life of Man." "Activity as the Way of Existence and Self-Realization" was given seventeen lessons and additional lessons were devoted to the "Spiritual World of Man."

The whole course represented an attempt to break away from the traditional way in which school knowledge was organized in historical sequence. Themes in which man had a central place were used to integrate knowledge drawn from history, sociology, and political sciences. In each of the four parts, sixty-eight lessons constituted the course. These courses presumably formed part of the state component of the general school curriculum. Social studies was allocated four grades per week in each of the last four classes of the eleventh-year school so that the course "Man and Society" could occupy a proportion of the time laid down for social studies.

In another article, "On the Polytechnical Approach to Social Studies" (*Teaching History in School*, No. 3, 1989, p. 8), A. B. Reznick claimed that social studies had always had a potentially polytechnical component, if not explicitly, at least under the influence of particular teachers. Its interdisciplinary character facilitated polytechnicalism, and since social studies had a large philosophical element, the laws of dialectical materialism were connected with productive life and therefore given a polytechnical character. Questions such as the role of labor in the development of man and the unity and diversity of natural and social laws were dealt with in courses of social studies. These courses provided an opportunity to integrate the humanities and the natural sciences rather than, as previously, polarize them.

These syllabi, prepared under the auspices of the Academy of Pedagogical Sciences, indicated that a lead was being taken by the state authorities to integrate and humanize the curriculum. Nevertheless, it was difficult to assess the extent to which these innovations had succeeded. N. Il'yna, writing under the title

"Fruits of the Enlightenment" or the "Power of Darkness" (*Ogonyok*, No. 22, 1990), claimed that after five years of *perestroika*, in spite of the changes needed in approaches to humanities, little had been done to improve textbooks. The textbooks on literature for senior pupils contained the same old phrases on social realism and the positive influence it had on the Soviet writers who glorified the struggle for communism and the achievements of the USSR. The best writers like I. Babel, M. Tsvetayeva, and many others were not mentioned. Il'yna claimed that the authors of Soviet textbooks "develop in children a deep hatred of literature. . . . They speak about the humanism of collectivization and our highly developed industry and achievements that brought us nearer to a bright future" (ibid., p. 8). Il'yna implied that this group of textbook authors was out of touch with the real world.

She made a very valid point. Teachers depended upon prescribed textbooks which closely followed the syllabi. The freedom of teachers and pupils to think for themselves was strictly limited. This is much less the case today. Examinations called for the students to reproduce information set forth in the textbooks. If the aims of educational reform were to be achieved, the monopoly exercised over the production of textbooks and examination answers had to be broken.

In theory constraints were being removed in 1991–92. Authors were invited to submit textbooks for consideration. Alternative textbooks in each subject were in the process of being published, and teachers were able to choose the ones they wished to use. Pressure was being exerted to allow pupils more freedom in answering examination questions with ideas that might not agree with those set forth in traditional subject matter. The USSR State Committee adopted the slogan: "What is not forbidden is allowed." Unless teachers abandon their traditional reliance on textbooks and unless there are radically different textbooks, the humanization of education by reducing the obligatory learning load and developing the abilities of individual pupils will continue to be thwarted.

Finally, the traditional Soviet curriculum was informed by a single ideology. The deliberate attempt to ensure that all subject matter was interpreted from a particular ideological position was one way of creating a "New Soviet Man." Courses such as "The History of the Communist Party," "Dialectical Materialism," and so on were used to inculcate a knowledge and acceptance of the Marxism-Leninism used by leading members of the Communist Party to legitimize the regime. The desire to reform education by making a range of textbooks available and changing the character of highly ideological subjects represented a significant movement away from the belief that education should introduce the younger generation to a totalitarian set of beliefs. Religious values were among those proscribed by the Soviet authorities in spite of the fact that Article 121 of the 1936 Constitution justified the separation of church from state "in order to ensure to citizens freedom of conscience." Soviet authorities had consistently drawn a distinction between the freedom granted to individuals to worship as they thought fit and the political power of an organized church. In practice, opportunities to worship were limited, and nonregistered churches were forbidden to operate. Under *perestroika* overt opposition to religion existed. Indeed churches attracted a great many worshipers. Outward manifestations of the revival of Christian, Muslim, and Buddhist beliefs evidenced the failure, over a period of seventy years, to eliminate traditional religions.

Inevitably some teachers wished to introduce some aspects of religious teaching into the school curriculum. The history of the church in Tsarist Russia made it possible to introduce religious values through school subjects, particularly through the humanities. Whereas in the past the Christian churches in Russia could only be studied as historical examples in such courses as architecture, teachers started to interpret history and literature from a religious perspective. The question of formal lessons in religion in the school curriculum was linked with debates about the establishment of religious schools. The example, described in chapter 6, of a school opened in Moscow by a religious society anticipated that future state schools wishing to teach about religion and Christian values would not be prevented from doing so and that church authorities would be allowed to set up schools.

The Importance of Curriculum Change

Curriculum change was vital if the aims of educational *perestroika* were to be achieved. If education was to be humanized, more freedom would have to be given to teachers to interpret the humanities from a variety of perspectives. The relevance of scientific subjects, not only to productive life but also to the cultural activities of individuals, had to be made explicit in revised science courses. Choices within the curriculum were made available to meet the individual interests and talents of pupils. The humanitarianization of the curriculum demanded that in order to develop the personality of pupils, more time would have to be devoted to aesthetics, humanities, and integration of subject matter to provide a holistic picture of man in relation to nature and society.

Although the teacher-innovators received a great deal of publicity in the early days of *perestroika,* there were many other educators who contributed to the cause of educational reform. Its future success, however, will depend on the number of teachers who are willing and able to introduce relevant curricula, teach imaginatively, and assess pupils in ways which do not stifle initiative and inhibit learning. A framework for reform has been created. Unfortunately only a small proportion of teachers are prepared to teach in a new way. The majority of them still teach as they were taught in the colleges and universities.

CHAPTER 9

Soviet Teacher Education

The structure of teacher training in the Soviet Union resembles that of systems in many continental Western European countries. Historically a university degree in Europe was a license to teach. The academic secondary schools and the universities were part of a closed system for an academic elite. Pupils from secondary schools entered a university, where they acquired knowledge of a subject or subjects from leading scholars in the field. The possession of this knowledge qualified them to teach in secondary schools and, indeed, in a university.

Some elements of this closed system remain in some European countries; for example, in Paris the leading French *lycées* are clustered round the Sorbonne. Part of this tradition lingered on in the USSR where some university professors included in their lectures advice on how to teach at the university level the subject in which they were experts.

During the nineteenth century, systems of elementary schools were set up in which reading, writing, and arithmetic were taught to pupils, the vast majority of whom had no hope or intention of entering a university. For this growing number of pupils, teachers were trained not in universities but in "normal schools," where recruits from elementary schools completed an academic secondary school education, took some courses in methods of teaching, and undertook periods of supervised teaching practice. The feature common to both systems of training was that all teachers were expected to complete an academic secondary school course of studies. The normal schools offered academic courses at a level no higher than those in secondary schools. After completing a normal school course of study, successful students returned to teach in elementary schools. Transfers between these preparatory systems were minimal.

As educational systems evolved, links were established between the two systems. These links were first established in the US and England and Wales. By the early twentieth century, in institutions in which elementary school teachers were trained, students had, for the most part, completed an academic secondary school course. Before entry it was assumed that they possessed enough general knowledge to teach young children, and, therefore, teacher training institutions in these countries concentrated on methods of teaching and the study of education. For example, in the United States, elementary school teachers were recruited from senior high schools and trained in normal schools. Senior high school teachers continued to be trained in colleges and universities. In European systems, differentiation was lessened when it became possible for pupils between the ages of ten and twelve, depending on the country, to transfer from elementary to academic secondary schools on the basis of the results of entrance examinations. The proportion of such transfers varied but was rarely more than 25 percent of the age group.

In Britain, by 1945 all future teachers were recruited from academic secondary schools. This fact influenced the character of British teacher education in ways that made it similar to that in the US. In America, after 1910 normal schools recruited senior high school graduates. Then, in the 1920s, many of these schools were transformed into teachers' colleges and finally into liberal arts colleges and universities.

After 1945 the establishment of comprehensive secondary schools in many industrially developed countries was accompanied by the demand for more and better-educated teachers. This process stimulated professional aspirations. The trend today is for the teaching profession to become an all-graduate one, with teaching thus regaining in mass systems of education the status enjoyed historically by teachers who graduated from universities. For example, in the United States virtually all teachers are trained in universities, although prospective primary school teachers usually follow different courses from those seeking to teach in senior high schools. In

England and Wales all future teachers will soon possess higher education degrees. There are differences, however, between the way future secondary school teachers are trained in well-established universities and the way primary school teachers are trained in institutions which were formerly colleges of education.

Prior to *perestroika* the system of teacher training in the USSR was basically similar to that of Western Europe, in spite of the fact that the unified secondary school had been founded immediately after the October Revolution. In order to introduce compulsory elementary education, many new teachers had to be trained in specialized secondary pedagogical schools which offered a three-year course. These institutions, although much smaller in number, continue to operate in Russia.

The system of teacher training did undergo some changes. Teachers for the primary stage (the first four grades) of schooling continued to be trained in specialized secondary schools for teachers, where they completed a secondary school course and were shown how to teach. Teachers destined for the secondary schools were trained either in five-year pedagogical institutes, which were equivalent to university-level institutions, or in pedagogical or pedagogical psychology departments in universities, as a service to those university students who were majoring in history and philology and intended to teach in secondary schools. Not more than 10 percent of teachers were prepared at the universities.

The expansion and extension of the common unified school in the USSR made the problems associated with the development of teacher education more pressing. Nevertheless, even before *perestroika* some of the issues debated in Western countries had emerged in the USSR. In the Khrushchev era, the desire of all teachers to be members of an all-graduate profession found expression in policies requiring all teachers to complete a course of study in an institution of higher education. This implied that the specialized secondary schools for teachers would be phased out. Unfortunately, this was never achieved. However, departments were established in pedagogical institutes in which kindergarten and primary school teachers were trained. As the difficulties of teaching all of the pupils of

Russia proliferated, the need became more and more pressing to find a new balance between subject matter and pedagogical studies. Some critics of overloading in the middle and upper secondary schools claimed, for example, that the cause lay not in the amount of knowledge that pupils were expected to acquire but in the methods used to teach it. Hence, there was a need in the USSR, as elsewhere, to adapt methods of teaching to take into account mixed-ability classes. In Western Europe and the US, the autonomy and freedom enjoyed by university academics raised questions about the desirability of allowing persons subject to minimal public control to exert a major influence over the training of personnel for a major public service such as education. Under *perestroika* in the Soviet Union, the principle of granting freedom to individual educational institutions to run their own affairs raised questions of control of the kind debated in the US and Western European countries.

The reform of teacher education and training was based on the assumptions that training should increasingly be provided in institutions of higher education and that administrators and faculty members in each educational institution should be free to formulate, adopt, and implement teacher education policies without interference from government authorities, in spite of the debated questions of control.

Teacher Education Issues

A great many issues were the focus of protracted discussions in Soviet teacher education in the 1980s. The first issue had to do with selecting candidates with potential talent for the teaching profession. A rather high percentage of new graduates refused to accept teaching assignments. Many of the students who were well prepared in their major disciplines were not able to hold the interest of the students nor communicate with their parents. Second, there was the question of finding a balance between the time devoted to the study of general education subjects, pedagogical studies, and other professional experiences needed for teaching in a compulsory education system. Third, how to prepare a new type of master teacher to cope with a rapidly changing world, one who would be innovative, open to new ideas, and searching for more efficient and effective teaching styles? Fourth, there was the complaint that students were forced to attend an excessive number of lectures a week and master a great deal of information unrelated to the task of teaching. In their place, subjects such as sociology, anthropology, physiology, and educational psychology were needed that would develop a sensitivity to the needs of children and an understanding of the stages of child development. Finally, there was the issue of the ideological orientation that permeated all of the courses in the curriculum. In practice a great proportion of time in teacher preparation was spent on pedagogical orientation, namely, teaching such basic primary-level subjects as language and literature, social sciences, mathematics, arts, music, dancing, and physical education. But the instruction in these subjects was also combined with how, ideologically, to teach the subject matter.

Primary school teachers have played a crucial role in imparting to young and impressionable children values and beliefs considered vital to the continued well-being of society. It was hardly surprising, therefore, that in the Soviet secondary schools for prospective primary school teachers, great attention was paid to the development of a communist or Marxist-Leninist outlook. In the secondary pedagogical school's social studies program much content was devoted to the history of the Communist Party, the foundations of scientific atheism, and Marxist-Leninist philosophy.

In an article by V. Gurevich, chairman of the Association of Instructors of Higher Education, the charge was made that such concepts as "ideological-political education," "atheistic education," and the "moral code of the builders of communism" had distorted the teacher education program. According to Gurevich, the system needed to deideologize and depoliticize the theory and practice of education by excluding outside influences, thus leaving it free to develop in accordance with its own inner logic.

The notion that there was a special Soviet theory of education was rejected by Gurevich, who argued that there was no New Zealand chemistry or English geometry. He objected to the fact that foreign educational theories were rejected in Soviet textbooks simply because they were "alien." One of the fundamental drawbacks of Soviet teacher education was the ideological straitjacket that stifled the educationists who determined the foundations of educational theory and practice. It was important, Gurevich concluded, that the search for new concrete models for teacher education should be conducted in the spirit of humanism.

In the book *Teacher Training in the Process of Perestroika*, E. P. Belozertsev, a professor in a pedagogical institute who worked with the State Committee on Education, identified quantitative rather than qualitative methods and a lack of integration as the major defects in teacher education. This concept was pursued in the research project directed by V. Slastenin of the Lenin Pedagogical University and sponsored in the late 1980s by the USSR State Committee on Public Education. Slastenin developed a concept of higher teacher education based on the system, activity, and individual-creative approaches. The system approach sought the unified development of all the components of a student's personality. The activity approach stressed learning by doing as a means of developing the pedagogical skills for teaching. And the individual-creative approach was geared to the development of creative personalities in future teachers. The activity approach was very important since the personality of a teacher could only be enriched through the development of various skills and the inculcation of certain forms of knowledge. Professional development, contended Slastenin, should be based on educational activities.

These principles of teacher education were designed to overcome severe drawbacks in the Soviet system. The teacher training curricula had greatly expanded through the introduction of more and more obligatory subjects. Moreover, in order to cope with additional subject matter, the time allocated to the study of each subject had had to be increased, even though the students were overloaded.

A second weakness in the Soviet system was the fact that professional educational courses had not been adequately related to everyday life and the activities students were likely to undertake in their future careers. Students, consequently, failed to acquire a systematic vision of their future work or an integrated concept of what was involved in educational activities. Moreover, according to V. F. Morgun in "The Experience of Restructuring the Psychological Training of Teachers" in *Voprosy psychologii* (No. 2, 1988, p. 84), the requirement to master professional experience in pedagogical institutes did not go beyond the ability to reproduce prescriptions. For this reason, the majority of young teachers, drilled as they were, did not use the experience they had gained in the pedagogical institute, but simply repeated what their own school teacher used to do. One reason for this was that educational studies and psychology were taught separately and were too abstract (ibid., p. 36). There were no interdisciplinary links. Furthermore, there was no balance between the various learning activities, namely, between lectures, seminars, practical work, and teaching practice.

Specialized Secondary Schools for Teachers

Apart from the demand that the ideological component of teacher education programs should be eliminated, the concerns expressed by Belozertsev were voiced in somewhat different ways by many critics of teacher education. No doubt many teacher educators agreed with the principles enunciated by Belozertsev. At the same time not all those concerned with teacher education in the USSR believed that all future teachers should be trained in an institution of higher education, or that no teachers should commence on a teacher training program before completing an upper secondary school course.

At the time of the author's visit to Pedagogical School No. 2 in Moscow, senior staff members were justifiably proud of their traditions. They were convinced that students who entered the traditional pedagogical school after the ninth grade and followed the four-year course were more committed and flexible than those recruited after the eleventh grade. All too often the latter had failed to gain admission to an institute of higher education or university, and teacher education was a second choice.

Only about one-fifth of the new students at Pedagogical School No. 2 had graduated from the eleventh grade. Members of the staff did not agree with the new proposal, in line with international trends, that only graduates who had completed the eleventh grade should be admitted. Consequently they encouraged secondary schools to offer an in-depth pedagogical profile that would admit students who had completed a secondary school profile and showed a commitment to pursuing a teaching career.

Members of the staff reported that most school principals believed that primary grade teachers graduating from pedagogical specialized schools were better prepared for their work than those graduating from a pedagogical institute. Only since the 1970s were a few primary school teachers prepared in special departments in pedagogical institutes. Some principals claimed that graduates of pedagogical schools had more practical experience than graduates of pedagogical institutes, where theory courses dominated the curriculum. Students who entered the pedagogical school upon completing the ninth grade were younger and more willing to engage in activities with children. Nevertheless, most of the staff members, in keeping with the times, reluctantly agreed that the school should become a college. In the same way, some pedagogical institutes like the Maurice Thorez Pedagogical Institute for Foreign Languages and the Lenin Pedagogical Institute and many others had become universities. These changes reflected international trends to raise the status of teacher training to a professional level.

The popularity of Pedagogical School No. 2 was evidenced by the competition to gain admission to it. More candidates applied than could be admitted. Many of the mothers and even grandmothers of present-day students attended the school and many former students were principals of schools. Some famous orchestra conductors and a well-known poet were former students. The traditions of the college were reenforced on the last Saturday in January, when former students returned for a reunion with the graduating seniors. Close contacts with state schools were maintained by lecturers visiting the classrooms and even attending parent organization meetings. In view of the reputation of the pedagogical school, it is not surprising that there were between four and five applicants for every primary school place and two applicants for every preschool spot. The entrance examination to the preschool course required examinations in Russian and mathematics.

Applicants were interviewed and had to be recommended by the pedagogical councils of their schools. As in past years the majority of those admitted were girls. In 1989, three boys had entered the preschool course upon completing the ninth grade, and in the primary school program there were six boys who had completed the ninth grade and three from the eleventh grade. The career of teaching in lower school had little appeal to the male sex.

Of the 120 teachers on the staff, 40 had been trained in secondary pedagogical schools and many at School No. 2 itself. Usually such teachers had ten years or more of experience before they could be admitted to a pedagogical institute to pursue a higher education diploma. Moreover, every five years, staff members had to take a refresher course. The Moscow Institute for In-Service Training offered specialized and advanced study in each school subject. Furthermore, the whole country was divided into zones with one pedagogical school in each zone chosen to provide in-service training for teachers. Departments in the Lenin Pedagogical University also provided pedagogical courses for primary school teachers.

The course for students entering the pedagogical school from the ninth grade was different from that taken by students who had completed their secondary education. In accordance with the traditional European model, students following a four-year course at the pedagogical school completed their general education in the first two years. There was some theoretical professional training combined with practical work for one day a week over the first three years. The third and fourth years of the course were devoted to professional studies with a four-week period of teaching practice in the final year of the course. During the summer prior to their last year students spent one and a half months working in a Pioneer camp. For those students who had completed their secondary schooling, the emphasis in their two-year course was on professional studies.

The following schedule lists the subjects organized as cycles, together with the semesters offered, and the prescribed hours per week. The students were recruited for this course after the ninth grade of an incomplete secondary general education school.

The Curriculum of a Specialized Secondary Pedagogical School, May 1989

Major Field: Teaching in the Primary Grades of a General Secondary Education School

Sociopolitical Cycle

History (194 total hours)

First year	- 6 semesters, 4 hours per week

Foundations of Marxism-Leninism (198 total hours)

Second year	- 2 semesters, 2 hours per week
Third year	- 2 semesters, 2 hours per week
Fourth year	- 2 semesters, 2 hours per week

Russian Language and Literature (190 total hours)

First year	- 3 semesters, 2 hours per week
Second year	- 3 semesters, 2 hours per week

Language-Literature of the Republic (191 total hours)

First year	- 2 semesters, 3 hours per week
Second year	- 3 semesters, 2 hours per week

World Art Culture (94 total hours)

Fourth year	- 3 semesters, 3 hours per week

Special Education Cycle

Soviet Law (66 total hours)

Fourth year	- 2 semesters, 3 hours per week

Mathematics (195 total hours)

First year	- 5 semesters, 5 hours per week

Physics-Astronomy (98 total hours)

First year	- 2 semesters, 3 hours per week

Chemistry-Biology (156 total hours)

First year	- 4 semesters, 4 hours per week

Information Technology (78 total hours)

First year	- 2 semesters, 2 hours per week

Foreign Language (78 total hours)
- First year - 2 semesters, 2 hours per week

Education Studies (174 theory hours and 44 practice hours)
- Second year - 1 semester, 2 hours per week
- Third year - 2 semesters, 2 hours per week
- Fourth year - 2 semesters, 2 hours per week

Psychology (91 theory hours and 21 practice hours)
- Second year - 2 semesters, 2 hours per week
- Third year - 2 semesters, 2 hours per week

Anatomy-Physiology (62 theory hours and 16 practice hours)
- First year - 2 semesters, 2 hours per week

Safety Education (56 total hours)
- Fourth year - 2 semesters, 2 hours per week

Teaching Skills (20 practice hours)
- Fourth year - 2 hours per week

Russian Language (259 total hours)
- First year - 1 semester, 1 hour per week
- Second year - 3 semesters, 3 hours per week
- Third year - 2 semesters, 1 hour per week
- Fourth year - 2 semesters, 2 hours per week

Native Language (235 total hours)
- First year - 1 semester, 1 hour per week
- Second year - 2 semesters, 2 hours per week
- Third year - 3 semesters, 2 hours per week
- Fourth year - 2 semesters, 2 hours per week

Methods Cycle

Spelling (19 total hours)
- Second year - 1 hour per week

Children's Lit. (157 theory hours and 43 practice hours)
- Third year - 2 semesters, 2 hours per week
- Fourth year - 4 semesters, 6 hours per week

Elementary Math (226 theory hours and 28 practice hours)
- Second year - 4 semesters, 3 hours per week
- Third year - 2 semesters, 2 hours per week
- Fourth year - 2 semesters, 2 hours per week

Science (28 theory hours and 114 practice hours)
- Second year - 2 semesters, 2 hours per week
- Third year - 2 semesters, 2 hours per week

Arts (142 total hours)	
Second year	- 1 semester, 2 hours per week
Third year	- 3 semesters, 2 hours per week
Physical Education (24 theory hours and 25 practice hours)	
Third year	- 1 semester, 2 hours per week
Crafts (133 theory hours and 28 practice hours)	
Second year	- 1 semester, 11 hour per week
Third year	- 2 semesters, 2 hours per week
Fourth year	- 2 semesters, 2 hours per week
Technical Aids (38 total hours)	
Third year	- 2 hours per week
Teaching Practice Cycle (367 total hours)	
Second year	- 2 semesters, 2 hours per week
Third year	- 6 semesters, 6 hours per week
Fourth year	- 6 semesters
Qualifications Cycle	
Military Training (76 total hours)	
Second year	- 1 semester, 1 hour per week
Third year	- 1 semester, 1 hour per week
Physical Education Cycle (552 total hours)	
First year	- 4 semesters, 4 hours per week
Second year	- 4 semesters, 4 hours per week
Third year	- 4 semesters, 4 hours per week
Fourth year	- 4 semesters, 4 hours per week
Consultation	(200 total hours)

Optional

1. Russian Language and Literature	6. Scientific Atheism
2. Ethics and Aesthetics	7. Ethnic Culture
3. Scientific-Technical Creativity	8. Photography
4. Conferences with Parents	9. Foreign Languages
5. Russian Literature	10. Other options possible

State Examination
1. Educational Studies & Methods of Teaching
2. Marxism-Leninism
3. Russian (or Native) Language and Methods of Teaching

Emphasis was placed on the general education component in the first and second years. Thereafter primary school subjects and methods of teaching them received greater attention. Indeed, apart from Marxism-Leninism, Soviet Law, and World Art Culture there were no general subjects in the fourth year. Overall, nearly three-fifths of the four-year course was devoted to subject matter and how to teach it, together with teaching practice. Professional studies including psychology occupied relatively little time, but courses in pedagogy were offered in each of the four years.

Because students were recruited from the ninth grade, rather than as in the past from the eighth grade, the content of the four-year course had been reduced. Students could complete their secondary school education in one rather than in two years, and the amount of physics and chemistry they had to learn had been reduced. More emphasis than in the past was placed on educational subjects. After completing the course in a pedagogical school, students could go to a university or a pedagogical institute. With this background they could complete a university or pedagogical institute course in three years instead of the usual five.

A special feature of the course was that all students had to play a musical instrument. In fact a third of the students in Pedagogical School No. 2 were preparing to teach music. Music was taught through the seventh grade in the state schools. Of the twenty-three groups in the preschool department of this pedagogical school, two were preparing students to teach English. There were thirty students in each group. Indeed many schools were searching for teachers prepared to teach English. The number of night students was 300; there were 1,000 students in the day departments. Some overlap existed between the courses for preschool and primary school teachers because students had to know about children at each stage of their development. Consequently students studied child-developmental psychology, which stressed play as a way of learning. *Vospitanie,* the development of well-rounded personalities, called for identifying student interests and providing a wide range of activities including art and music. Teachers of this pedagogical school favored changes in the way school children were assessed. Some primary schools were no longer giving marks, and the pedagogical school staff encouraged this trend. They believed that the work of children should not be characterized simply as "good" or "excellent." Instead, more positive ways of appraising improvement should be devised. Stars were used to show progress in each subject. Since many schools now had psychologists on the staff to deal with problem students and provide a variety of psychological services, teachers were taught how to use psychological tests.

Although pedagogical schools prepared students for teaching in traditional schools, some attention was given to transformations taking place in the schools. Students learned how to teach integrated courses and incorporate music, art, and crafts into the history course. These new approaches to pedagogy were facilitated by a decree issued in 1988–89 from the State Committee that made it possible for 15 percent of the teacher education curriculum to be designed by pedagogical school instructors. Teachers had only to submit their curriculum proposals to the head of the department for comment and approval.

Pedagogical School No. 2 had not accepted many of the new reforms in teacher education, but it had incorporated the curriculum suggested by the USSR State Committee. In the past this school was given the option of following the RSFSR curriculum or the All-Union one. Two major curriculum changes provided for more attention to be given to pedagogical and psychological studies and to the study of brief digests of the subject content of the complete secondary school. Students were especially relieved to have a lighter class load than previously.

As late as January 1991 many of the staff continued to support the existence and activities of the Communist Party organization in the school even though the Minister of Education of the Russian Federation had banned communist organizations in educational institutions. The USSR State Committee chairman,

Yagodin, on the other hand, considered these matters to be for each individual institution to decide. In spite of the apparently conservative attitudes, however, members of the staff accepted in principle many of the suggested reforms in teacher education. As in other countries, they favored upgrading the status of professional education.

Pedagogical Institutes

In fact, many of the pedagogical institutes of the Soviet Union were experimenting with and introducing new professional content in their curricula in the early 1980s. In an effort to recruit professionally talented students, practically all pedagogical institutes had organized evening "Schools for Future Teachers," providing secondary school graduates with an interest in teaching a one-year course in pedagogy together with contact experiences with children in school, at home, and in extracurricular activities. Some of the secondary schools had in-depth courses combining general and pedagogical education. Students who completed these classes or participated in "Schools for Future Teachers" were granted certain privileges in being admitted to pedagogical institutes. Workshops replaced some of the classroom hours in providing students with opportunities to develop skills in communication, solving problems that teachers face in the classrooms, and holding student attention.

During the 1980s, and especially after 1985, many proposals were made to reform the existing system of teacher education. One of them was developed by a working group of professors from the leading pedagogical institutes. Their proposal was discussed at the All-Union Congress of Education Workers in December 1988. Great stress was given to having students actively participate in research projects while still enrolled at the institutes. Most pedagogical institutes sponsored "Student Scientific Societies," which provided students with opportunities to select problems and topics for independent study and to submit their findings at year-end student conferences.

A major debate in the pedagogical institutes turned on the proper balance between subject matter and methodology. The university tradition was one of teachers mastering the subject that was to be taught. This emphasis conformed with knowledge-centered objectives. The trend in pedagogical institutes, according to Professor Vassily Zhuravlev, the Chair of Pedagogics at the Krupskaya Pedagogical Institute, had been to lessen the attention paid to methodology over the years. There was, as in many countries, an ongoing debate between the subject specialists and educationists about what the balance in the curriculum should be. The subject specialists welcomed new theories and principles in their own disciplines but resisted the introduction of new teaching strategies. This resistance was attributed to traditional and deeply held internalized beliefs that were not easily changed.

The debate was not restricted to "teachers of teachers." Student choice had been introduced into the curriculum. For example, students interested in educational subjects could choose them or, if they were interested in mathematics, they could choose in-depth study in that subject. Such choices were available within a curriculum that included mandatory subjects, of which the theory of education was one, and options, of which comparative education was one.

Traditionally, teacher training institutes had to follow a curriculum ordered by the state. Under *perestroika*, the teaching staff was given greater freedom to design part of the curriculum. For example, a new curriculum was introduced in the Krupskaya Pedagogical Institute at the beginning of the 1990 academic year. There were already in 1991 plans to revise it to meet new demands and use new approaches. A measure of autonomy had already been granted and more was requested. Although the institute was no longer under its direction, the USSR State Committee still tried to exert some control, in spite of the fact that the RSFSR Ministry of Education had jurisdiction. Nevertheless, 50 percent of the curriculum still was laid down in 1991 by the State Committee, 30 percent by the ministry of education of the republic, and 20 percent by the institute. Members of the institute's staff wanted to alter the balance in favor of complete institute control.

Under the new regime, professors of the institute had more freedom. Research topics, previously prescribed, could be identified by the head of the department rather than, as before, being centrally determined. Knowledge of foreign education was accessible through the study of more objective materials on comparative education and education history. It was doubtful whether foreign theories directly influenced courses in Soviet teacher training programs, but knowledge of them was made available and frequent references were made to them in a range of different courses. Professor Zhuravlev identified a number of ongoing debates about the academic work of the institute. For example, a new generation of more informative and up-to-date textbooks was needed to replace those which had been in use for some years. Such textbooks, he maintained, would be more condensed and include more pedagogically relevant information. Bloom's taxonomy of objectives and its elaboration by Oxford University had a following. Two models of the professional teacher were debated. One model assumed that institutes would graduate teachers who followed the traditional professional education courses. The other model assumed that teachers would acquire actual teaching experience throughout the entire three-year course. This debate reflected those in some Western countries where the relative merits of training that was closely connected with working schools were compared with theoretical courses based in universities or institutions of higher learning.

It had not been decided how to combine a unified standard model of teacher training with one that prepared instructors for teaching the individual profiles in gymnasia and lyceums. It was clear, however, that the authorities were more tolerant of student views and major criticisms of the courses. In a world of changing values, what should be changed and what should remain unchanged? This was an issues under continuing debate. Some educationists maintained that there were eternal values to be transmitted in teacher education. For example, they said, the teacher should have some medical knowledge in order to protect the physical well-being of pupils.

As educational reforms were introduced, the Krupskaya Institute found that it needed a functioning data base. A number of studies were conducted. One study turned on the common behavioral mistakes, made by teachers that influenced the academic performance of high school pupils. School administrators and teachers collected and statistically analyzed these mistakes, which were then used to assess teacher performance. It was found that the most frequent and serious mistakes were the least easy to eliminate. The research revealed that the most frequently recorded mistakes related to the tactless remarks made by teachers concerning confidential knowledge about pupils and, from the pupils' viewpoint, the inadequate marking of schoolwork. Many of the mistakes could be eliminated if educational practices were brought more closely into line with educational research.

Another study sought data on what institute students thought about their own lives and their school. Fifty-one indicators were used to analyze the life and activities of pupils. In accumulating the data, researchers were looking for the answers to two questions. First, was the teachers' experience valuable? Second, did innovative teaching practices improve the quality of specialist training? If the outcome of an innovation increased the professional quality of teachers, then *perestroika* made sense. If the quality was not raised, then *perestroika* made no sense. A medical analogy was given. If a medical prescription was followed by side effects and the condition was not cured, the remedy was no good.

Some mistakes had been made in formulating policies designed to democratize the Krupskaya Institute. For example, the decision to involve students on the academic council was, in theory, in line with democratization. However, the experience of students was not up to the level of the technical questions that were raised and on which they were asked for an opinion. For example, they had been given opportunities to evaluate professors. It was far from certain that the criteria on which they made their assessments were valid. On the other hand the election, rather than the appointment, of the rector seemed to have had no adverse side effects.

The position of the Party had been radically reduced at the institute. In the past it had had great authority, and the Party secretary was the Pro-Rector. He could summon any member of staff to his office to give an accounting of any action a teacher had taken. Local Party officials also interfered with the work of the institute. Under *perestroika*, however, the rector had the authority to summon the Party secretary to his office and request an explanation of his actions. It was acknowledged that there were many good Party people on the staff of the institute as late as 1991. The rector invited them to express their ideas and make suggestions.

The institute was opened in the early 1930s with ten faculties and fifty chairs. Students were drawn from the city and province of Moscow. Postgraduates were prepared in thirty specialties. In-service programs were offered in thirty special areas. It sponsored an advanced program that brought together specialists in physical education and information technology. Besides having an outstanding geology department with a mineral museum and the first ecological department in USSR higher education, the administration claimed that its Russian Language and Literature department, which awarded a doctoral degree, was equal to that at Moscow State University and the Pushkin Institute in Leningrad.

The Center for Russian Culture in that department was largely for foreign students who wanted to study the Russian language and culture. The staff represented a vast range of languages which enabled its members to work with foreign students from a great many countries. The students paid their tuition in foreign currency. Beginning students paid US $500 per month and lived in student hostels. Students taking special courses had better accommodations and special tutorial facilities that cost US $700 per month. Additional income was received from the sale of language cassettes and arts and crafts made by the students. These commercial activities illustrated how the students implemented the USSR State Committee's recommendation that educational institutions raise money in the commercial market.

The internal administration of the Krupskaya Institute was an example of the greater autonomy enjoyed by institutions of higher education. It elected its own rector, a practice followed for many years at the State University in Leningrad, and the rector had freedom to initiate new courses. In 1990, for example, a new faculty of arts and folk arts was established. Students made and sold arts and crafts which taught them artistic skills and business practices. Departments employed visiting professors for a one-year term and renewed their contracts. The rector had the authority to grant increases in lecturers' salaries. Special courses were organized for staff members of enterprises and co-ops if they could pass the entrance examinations. In order to dismiss a professor, a special review board had to prove incompetency and agreement had to be secured from the trade union. The dismissed staff member could appeal to the courts. The institute's scientific council had to approve all reappointments. Open competitions for renewal of contracts were held every five years, which was a means of getting rid of incompetent and unsatisfactory staff members.

The institute had its own scientific council. The rector nominated 50 percent of its members. At least 25 percent of this council had to be teachers and 25 percent, students. No lay members served on this council. On the general council which governed the institute, 10 percent of the members were non-professional workers; 30 percent, students and postgraduates; and 60 percent, members of the academic staff. The institute's Communist Party organization no longer had any internal influence. The Komsomol limited its activity to the summer work program.

Comparing the status of the Krupskaya Pedagogical Institute with comparable institutions of higher education proved difficult for the authors during their visit. Moscow State University was autonomous; the Krupskaya Institute was still under the Russian Ministry of Education. The latter did not enjoy the same privileges and status as the Lenin Pedagogical University, which had the added advantage of conducting research activities. On the other hand, the Krupskaya Institute was deeply involved in the lyceum movement and sponsored an experimental lyceum. It proposed to raise the lyceums to the level of colleges affiliated with institutes. The best students would be admitted to a college upon completion of the basic ninth grade course, and the best students upon completing the college course would automatically enter the institute. The four-year college course would lead to a bachelor's degree, whereas the institute would award a master's degree after three years of study. The institute submitted this proposal to the RSFSR Minister of Education in 1991.

The Lenin Pedagogical University

Professor V. Slastenin, dean of the Faculty of Education and Psychology at the Lenin State Pedagogical University, described the diversity that was cultivated in this teacher education institution. Students in the first two years of the five-year course had to follow a fixed timetable but in the last three years of the course they were free to make choices in accordance with their interests and achievements. This radical change was designed to individualize instruction and gear it to the development of the personalities of students. In the past, the primary concern was to ensure that teachers had sufficient professional knowledge. Too little attention was given to the development of personal qualities. In the last three years students could choose three out of twelve options. Professors had to compete for students. If only one or two students chose a course it still had to be taught but it was a signal to the professor that an effort should be made to attract more students. In the Lenin Pedagogical University, 40 percent of the time was devoted to options, whereas in pedagogical institutes the proportion was no more than 20 percent.

The trend in 1990 was to grant pedagogical institutes more freedom to devise programs to meet the individual needs of students. The debate dealt with the proportion of course time that was to be fixed by the USSR State Committee and by the republic's ministry of education. In 1991 the USSR State Committee, as previously stated, determined the allocated percentages. Attempts were made to reduce the All-Union component to 30 percent and to increase the republican component to 70 percent, which would permit each institution more freedom to design its own courses. For example, in Kiev 40 percent of the curriculum was determined by institute lecturers. However, Slastenin confessed that there were dangers in delegating this authority to small provincial institutes which lacked the professional staff to design courses. This explained the reluctance of the USSR State Committee to decentralize curriculum control. On the other hand, the Lenin Pedagogical University was given the freedom to develop a curriculum that would meet international standards in teacher training institutions.

Although under the Khrushchev regime it was announced that specialized secondary schools for teachers were to be phased out, they have continued to exist. As previously stated, in accordance with international trends, all teachers were expected to have a higher education. For this reason further education of secondary pedagogical school teachers was one of the functions of the Lenin Pedagogical University, as well as the training of lecturers for pedagogical institutes, personnel for psychological services, boarding school educators, and social workers. Indeed the Lenin Pedagogical University even trained graduates from secondary schools to teach in preschool classes and the primary grades of the eleven-year schools. The integration into higher education institutions of courses for both primary and secondary stage teachers had been going on since the time of Khrushchev. Under *perestroika* it received a new impulse.

Important changes were made in the Lenin Pedagogical University's curriculum. A new block of subjects called "World Culture" was introduced. It included the history of ethical doctrines, economics, philosophy, world art, religion, and the culture of the area in which the institution was situated. Practical training was improved. Courses on the philosophy of teaching were designed, not to deal with the special methods of teaching a particular subject, but to encourage students to be more independent and creative in developing their own methods of teaching. The integration of traditional subjects and pedagogical courses was encouraged. A new course brought the preschool, primary, and adolescent stages in child development into a system of continuous education. The aim was to build bridges between psychologists and the teachers who lacked sufficiently sound knowledge of psychology to diagnose problems in student behavior. The crux of these reform proposals was that it was up to each institution to choose the courses it wished to design and introduce into its teacher education program.

The success of school reform depended very much on the extent to which teacher education changes kept pace with, or indeed were in advance of, reforms in the schools. Some leaders in the field were rather pessimistic. They believed that the self-interest of many people working within the system would inhibit reform. In spite of this, changes had been successfully introduced. For example, greater freedom of choice was permitted both for the students and for staff members. The work of well-known foreign philosophers, psychologists, and educators was widely available, as well as the monumental contributions of early and current Russian pedagogical academicians. Frequent references were made to this information in a range of new courses. The major debate about the proper balance between subject matter and educational studies still had not been resolved, nor had it been in many other countries. Certainly the emphasis on personality development rather than knowledge acquisition suggested that the professional educational component in courses of teacher education would have to increase somewhat, but perhaps not to the extent of dominating courses as was the case in some primary teacher training courses in other nations of the world.

CHAPTER 10

The Demise of Soviet Totalitarian Education

The role of Yeltsin in confronting the hard-line conspirators in the failed coup of August 1991 was extremely significant for the future of the USSR and Russia. According to one commentator (Kornid Lybarsky, "Gorbachev," *New Times*, No. 52, December 31, 1991, pp. 6–8), "We took the real freedom in August outside the Russian parliament building. We have nobody to thank for this freedom—not Gorbachev, and not even Yeltsin, who owes us as much as we owe him. This was the main significance of the August revolution."

As news of the attempted coup spread in the early morning of August 19 among a crowd of some 10,000 people that formed spontaneously outside the Russian parliament building, President Yeltsin gained the support of "the young faces of soldiers moved to Moscow by the conspirators under the pretext of an emergency situation" (Alexander Tomasz Massey, *The Chronicle of Higher Education*, September 4, 1991, p. 54). There was plenty of evidence to support the view that for some time the outcome was in doubt. Simon Soloveichik, for example, was one of the leaders of the grass-roots reform movement in education. He later commented that, as he walked to the Russian Ministry of Education on the morning of August 21 to help draw up an appeal to school teachers, which was to be produced on an underground press set up by Minister of Education Dneprov, nobody knew how long the dictatorship would exist—a day, a month, or even ten years (Simon Soloveichik, "A Land That Triumphed over Socialism," *New Times*, No. 35, September 1991, pp. 6–9). Later it was revealed, from a study conducted by a department in the RSFSR president's office, that more than 70 percent of the RSFSR's *oblasts* (provinces), *krais* (districts), autonomous republics, autonomous *oblasts,* and autonomous *okrugs* (regions) had failed to support Yeltsin during the coup and had either sided with the conspirators or adopted a wait-and-see position. Only the local authorities in Moscow, Leningrad, and three *oblasts* gave active support to Yeltsin.

The choice was stark. On the morning of August 19 people had an opportunity to choose between two powers: the old legitimate USSR communist power or the emerging legitimate RSFSR democratic power. In other terms, the choice was between the legitimate power of the general secretary of the Communist Party or the legitimate power of the president of Russia. Gorbachev interpreted the coup as an action against the president of the USSR and his family. Those who opposed the coup saw it differently. For them it was, indeed, a choice between the old guard and the pro-democracy reformers.

Gorbachev's Downfall

Personalities were involved. The rivalry between Gorbachev and Yeltsin was public knowledge. While in power, Gorbachev had treated Yeltsin with a certain amount of contempt. Yeltsin became a real challenge to Gorbachev's authority. On July 20, *Radio Rossii* announced that Yeltsin had issued a decree dismantling Communist Party cells in factories, schools, government offices, and other workplaces throughout the vast Federal Republic of Russia. The decree stated that the creation of any political organs or the activity of existing political organizations in state agencies and enterprises in the RSFSR would not be permitted (Decree No. 14, "On Terminating the Activity of the Organizational Structures of Political Parties and Mass Public Movements in State Agencies, Institutions, and Organizations of the RSFSR, July 20, 1991," *Sovetskaya Rossia,* July 23, 1991).

In disowning the Communist Party so comprehensively, Yeltsin established his own power base in the RSFSR and disavowed Gorbachev's authority. Leaders of the RSFSR Communist Party were slow in obeying the order, claiming that they could not remove the Party's cells immediately (*Tass*, August 13 and 15, 1991). Gorbachev, in turn, announced that he would take every measure necessary to reverse Yeltsin's edict against the Party and would, if necessary, issue a presidential decree annulling Yeltsin's decision ("Gorbachev Vows to Fight Yeltsin Decree," *Record Courier*, July 26, 1991, p. 19). On July 24 Yeltsin specifically justified his decree on the grounds that it would put an end to the attempts of Party officials to stonewall further reform. Later, on August 2, Yeltsin's press secretary, P. Voshchanov, told *Radio Rossii* that no specific time had been established for the demolition of the Party, but it was expected that the process would be essentially completed by the end of 1991.

Gorbachev consistently and persistently tried to reform Soviet society within the framework of socialism, and indeed, until the failed coup, some progress had been made in the leadership of a reformed Communist Party. This view was shared by some members of the Party but denied by the leading figures in the pro-democracy movement. However *Pravda* reported that the prolonged debate over the enactment of the draft Union Treaty had brought about a polarization of public opinion into supporters and opponents of the socialist choice and the Communist Party ("A. N. Ilyin's View," *Pravda*, December 12, 1991). At a plenary session of the Central Committee on December 10, 1990, Gorbachev had defended the draft Union Treaty as a way of guaranteeing the development of republics as sovereign states and the Communist Party as the only political force on an All-Union scale (Gorbachev, "For the Renewal of Our Union State," *Pravda*, December 11, 1990). Yeltsin, on the other hand, had committed himself neither to the Communist Party nor to the maintenance of the Soviet Union in its existing form.

For Gorbachev the failed coup was presumably the last straw in a struggle in which he had become increasingly isolated from the pro-democracy movement and the people, especially early in 1991 when he made known his support of the conservative Party *nomenklatura*. Later, in order to salvage his political base, Gorbachev resigned as general secretary of the Party and called on the Central Committee to dissolve itself

(*Tass*, August 24, 1991). Then, on August 23 Yeltsin issued a decree, "On Suspending the Activity of the RSFSR Communist Party," and, on August 25, another decree, "On the Property of the CPSU and the Russian Communist Party," nationalized property that was either owned by the CPSU or was managed by it.

The suspension of the CPSU and the freezing of its assets were ratified by the USSR Supreme Soviet, but a proposal to ban the Party altogether was rejected ("Has the Communist Party Been Legally Suspended?" *Report on the USSR*, vol. 3, No. 40, October 4, 1991). In a *Pravda* article, A. Petrushov and others argued that the suspension ran counter to the USSR Constitution and the Constitution of the Union Republics (Petrushov, "A Legal Expert's Opinion: When the Logic of the Political Struggle Is Placed Above the Law," September 10, 1991, p. 21). In spite of these warnings the *apparat* of the Communist Party was disbanded, property and archives were seized, symbols removed from government buildings, and activities suspended or declared illegal in almost every republic of the USSR ("Director's Review," Washington: *Kennan Institute for Advanced Russian Studies*, September 1991, pp. 5–12). As far as education was concerned, the aim was to strip the Communist Party of its power and prevent it from determining and implementing policies in public institutions, a role it had played for so long.

Summary assessments of Gorbachev's errors were made by Kornid Lybarsky in *New Times* ("Gorbachev," No. 52, December 31, 1991). He maintained that while "Gorbachev and his initial followers were incorrectly referred to as 'architects of *perestroika*,'" they actually were amateurs, since what they regarded as a design for reform had nothing to do with reality. They only had an instinctive understanding of the necessity of change and a feeling of shame for the disgrace that the senile system had brought to the USSR and the whole world. Indeed, almost two years after the reforms had begun, Alexandr Yakovlev admitted that when they started, "neither Gorbachev nor he had made any assessment of the scope of the problems facing them" (ibid.).

For seventy years, the leaders of the totalitarian state had no need to compete with their political opponents in terms of knowledge, competence, or flexibility of mind. The only "knowledge" required was the art of intrigue, and Gorbachev was a master of the art. To the degree that *perestroika* brought about reshuffles in the *apparat* and the phasing out of old generation cadres, Gorbachev's actions were on the mark, but he soon learned that he could not control the liberals, some of whom were still in the Party while others had left. Yeltsin, for example, changed the rules and acted in a manner to which the *apparat* was not accustomed. On the positive side, Gorbachev appointed two loyal liberals, Yagodin and Shadrikov, to leadership posts in the education sector to serve as tools of renewal. They knew what they had to do to reform the schools. Unfortunately, many of the others appointed by Gorbachev had no idea of democracy or how a free-market economy should work.

It is generally agreed that one of Gorbachev's major failings was in not moving quickly to introduce radical political and economic change. When, in 1991, he finally pushed for major reforms, his concessions came too late. "The ultimate expression of incompetence was his idea that *perestroika* would change what could not be reformed" (Lybarsky, op. cit.). Shevardnadze expressed a similar judgement in his speech, "Cry in the Wilderness": "I saw that he (Gorbachev) was still a prisoner of his own nature, his conceptions and his way of thinking and acting. . . . This is the enormous personal tragedy of Mikhail Gorbachev, and no matter how much I empathize with him, I cannot help but say that it almost led to a national tragedy." Lybarsky commented that "only a very convinced person could speak about the loyalty to the socialist choice and the necessity of a deeper reform of the Communist Party after the August coup" (Lybarsky, op. cit.). In the end, Gorbachev recognized the need to reject the system inherited from the Bolsheviks, but he still upheld the socialist choice.

The demolition of the system made it necessary to get rid not only of Gorbachev the general secretary turned president, but also Gorbachev the man. The initiator of revolution from above was scared of revolution from below. He was, according to knowledgeable commentators, indecisive. He vacillated, missed opportunities, and never declared that he would abolish the old bureaucratic communist system. Thus, many of those in power and representing the old regime sabotaged real reform. The success with which Matveyev's crusade for school reform was diverted into official channels is an example of the way the system continued to work under *perestroika*, namely, only the Party could be trusted to initiate and direct educational reform. The education reforms introduced by Yagodin and Shadrikov in 1988 were, perhaps, more cautious than those suggested by Dneprov and the pro-democracy colleagues who supported Matveyev; nevertheless, they were based on sound principles and carried out by many of the former educational *nomenklatura*.

Pre-Coup Politics

From his book, *My Final Hours* (*Time*, May 11, 1992, pp. 50–53), Gorbachev was quoted as saying that "between November 1990 and April 1991 there was an escalation of confrontation between conservatives and the forces of reform." Gorbachev failed to make clear why he abandoned radical economic and political reforms in the fall of 1990, and why he made common cause with the hard-liners. Even on August 18, 1991, the prime minister, Valentin Pavlov, expected Gorbachev to cooperate in supporting the coup. Gorbachev never seemed to sense that he was unpopular with the man in the street, that the Communist Party and the way it worked was under attack, and that opposition was mounting from within the leadership group.

Nor did Gorbachev understand the seriousness of the threats made by powerful republics to destroy the unity of the Soviet Union to which he was committed. For example, a declaration of sovereignty had been adopted by the Supreme Soviet of the Ukraine on July 16, 1990. In stating that the Ukrainian language should function in all spheres of public life, the Ukrainians demanded that Union arrangements should conform to their own constitutional provisions. On December 1, 1990, the referendum held in the Ukraine showed that an overwhelming majority of those who took part in it favored independence from Moscow. As for the Federation, Yeltsin refused to let Gorbachev know if he was planning to sign the new Union Treaty until the Ukraine announced that it had done so. Gorbachev believed that the decision taken by the Ukraine was being used by Yeltsin as an excuse for not committing Russia to a new Union Treaty.

Yeltsin's position in relation to the Party was clear. Russia's educational institutions were ordered by presidential decrees to cease involving students in Party matters and activities (Olga Bychkova, "Non-Party President Issues Decrees," *Moscow News*, No. 30, July 28, 1991). His orders were not unchallenged. Sergei Alekseev, chairman of the USSR Committee for Constitutional Oversight, asked Yeltsin to suspend the implementation of his decrees abolishing the Party until the committee had completed a review of their legality. But the central authorities no longer had the power to veto Yeltsin's decrees. In the end, the RSFSR Supreme Soviet ruled that Yeltsin's decree was fully in accordance with the USSR Constitution and the laws of the RSFSR (*Tass*, July 27, 1991).

Nikolai Andreyev ("Political Diary: Who Will Play the Game," *Izvestia*, July 3, 1991, p. 1) asserted that the CPSU was in crisis and that its unity no longer could be maintained. Andreyev concluded that the mutually exclusive trends and philosophies among Party members eventually would lead to a split in the Party. During the April 1991 plenary session of the Party's Central Committee, there was evidence of such a division. The *New Times* (August 6, 1991, pp. 6–7) reported that there were as many fundamentalist communist factions as there were pro-democracy movements. On the other hand, again according to Andreyev, many members of the Party found it difficult psychologically to give up their membership cards, even though they had distanced themselves from the militant orthodox Communists.

The USSR State Committee for Public Education and the Failed Coup

Under the above circumstances it is hardly surprising that each and every educational issue became highly personalized. Chairman of the State Committee for Education Yagodin, for example, became involved in disputes with Pavlov and officers of the armed forces. In a long article in *Uchitel'skaya gazeta* (July 23–30, 1991, p. 2), Pyotr Polozhevets reported that on July 18, 1991, the chairman of the State Committee on Education received an order signed by Prime Minister Pavlov demanding his resignation. The conflict between Pavlov and Yagodin was long standing. When Pavlov was Minister of Finance, Yagodin consistently pressed demands for increased financial support for higher education. The conflict escalated, until in April, 1991, Pavlov refused to recognize Yagodin as having ministerial standing and named Shadrikov, Yagodin's deputy, as acting chairman of the committee. Since Yagodin and his deputy for the most part agreed on policy, it might be inferred, according to Polozhevets, that Pavlov found Yagodin personally objectionable. It is also clear that Yagodin did not support the conspirators, of whom Pavlov was one, and had the support of Raisa Gorbachev.

If the source of the objection was a matter of policy, it may have been due to Yagodin's opposition to the USSR Defense Ministry's initiative to eliminate the draft deferment of university students. The issue had been simmering since 1987. On the evening of July 19, 1991, however, the Russian TV program *Vesti* announced that Yagodin had been dismissed at the behest of the USSR Defense Minister, Dimitri Yazov (another leader of the coup) (Stephen Foye, "Student Deferment and Military Manpower Shortages," *Report on the USSR*, Vol. 3, No. 31, August 2, 1991, pp. 5–9).

Yagodin had received support in the press, the All-Union Council of Rectors, and the ministers of education in the republics. Yagodin and the students who supported him were on vacation when Pavlov called for his resignation. When Gorbachev returned from his visit to London on July 24, he immediately reinstated Yagodin as acting chairman of the USSR State Committee on Education (O. Chistenkova, "The President Corrects a Bad Move," *Komsomolskaya pravda*, July 25, 1991, p. 1).

Role of the Students in the Failed Coup

An article by Massey in the *Chronicle of Higher Education* (op. cit., p. 54) raised some questions concerning the role of the students in the failed coup. Massey observed that the absence of students in the crowds that assembled in front of the Russian Parliament could be explained by the fact that the universities were on summer vacation and not many students were in Moscow. It was mainly middle-aged men and *babushkas* (grandmothers) who confronted the tanks and called upon soldiers to disobey the orders of the plotters.

The issue of student deferments from the army had been high on the list of policies over which the conservatives and the reformers disagreed. On August 21 the defense minister issued a statement saying the students would not be drafted into the army during the forthcoming year. Massey wrote that according to Anatoly Ovsyannikov, chief sociologist of the Soviet Union Committee on Public Education, this action was an attempt by the conspirators to attract student sympathy and support for the attempted coup.

The Moscow students had, indeed, been active. A strike committee had been organized to oppose attempts to push through the law under which thousands of students would have been sent into the army. Leningrad students persuaded a local antiriot police squad to defend the City Council. Student unrest was reported in Kazan and Kiev.

The issue of student deferments had involved Yagodin in the pre-coup conflict between Party and army hard-liners and those who wished to see changes in the system. According to Massey, rumors were spread that the USSR State Committee on Education had ignored an appeal from Yeltsin to stage a general strike against the coup. A spokesman for the committee claimed, however, that it had not received such an appeal. Nevertheless, Alexander Tikhonov, first chairman of the Russian State Committee for Science and Higher Education, said that his committee did "not recognize the authority of the conspirators and had followed the orders of the Russian president and the Council of Ministers of the Russian Federation" (ibid.).

On the eve of the coup, therefore, the Communist Party was divided into factions and rapidly losing its monopolistic power. Pro-democracy movements had gained strength, the Baltic republics and the Ukraine had announced their independence, and under Yeltsin the RSFSR was acting against the wishes of USSR agencies as though it were an independent sovereign state. It must have appeared to the conspirators that both the Party and Union which they supported were about to disintegrate. It must have been clear to them that, in spite of Gorbachev's support for the symbols of the old regime, he was not in a position to enforce his will on those who were pressing for radical political and economic change. The failure of the conspirators in their attempted coup hastened the end of the Communist Party and made it impossible for the Union Treaty, which would have preserved the Soviet Union, to be signed.

The Party

Even prior to the coup, many within the Party agreed that it had to change. At a plenary session of the Central Committee of the CPSU on July 25, Gorbachev described the draft of the new CPSU program as constituting a decisive break with the obsolete ideological dogmas and stereotypes of the Party. The draft affirmed the right of Party members to express their views freely, to be atheists or believers, and to work for the goals of the Party as they thought fit. There was agreement that the free development of each individual was dependent upon a more liberal and open Party policy embracing a humane democratic socialism. Furthermore, it recommended that the Party should go to the people and persuade them to elect Party representatives to bodies of power (M. Gorbachev, "On the Draft of the New CPSU Program," Plenary Session, CPSU CC, *Izvestia*, July 26, 1991, pp. 1–2).

The reform movement came too late. It probably persuaded the hard-liners in the Party who opposed reform to take action, but it reflected growing dissatisfaction among many distinguished members of the Party who had publicly announced their resignation or denounced its ideology. Even before the coup, Foreign Minister Shevardnadze, when interviewed by D. Sabov (*Komsomolskaya pravda*, August 3, 1991, p. 3), made it known that some members of the Party leadership had considered it necessary to create an effective and constructive opposition. The failure of the Party to reform itself convinced him to resign and to leave the Party. The *New Times* reported ("No Time to Lose," *New Times*, No. 27, July 9, 1991, p. 7) that, although some Communists were traditionalists, hard-liners, and Marxist-Leninists à la Andreeva, others stood for progressive reforms. A. Rutskoi, the Afghan war hero, considered himself to be a true Communist who was committed to reform and vowed not to leave the Russian Federation's Communist Party unless expelled (Olga Bychkov, "A Colonel Without Fear or Doubt," *Moscow News*, No. 22, p. 7). Rutskoi's parliamentary group found itself to be one of the three or four parties inside the CPSU. However, the so-called healthy forces in the Party were coming to understand the impossibility of an *apparat*-based method of building a Communist Party with a human face.

This latter view was stated by A. N. Yakovlev (T. Zamyatina, "I Have Decided to Reject Marxism," *Sovetskaya Rossia*, August 3, 1991, p. 1) when he confessed that during the early period of *perestroika* he had believed in the possibility of improving society and in the renewal of the Party. "Although decisions of the 28th Congress were encouraging," he came to realize that "things would continue as they were since the Party's troubles stemmed from the dogmas of Marxism." Some time later when asked why he had left the post of Gorbachev's senior adviser, Yakovlev asserted that the conservative forces were unwilling to cooperate with democratic-minded people. In spite of this, Gorbachev continued to believe a transformation of the Party was possible.

Many alternatives emerged to replace the Party. In Leningrad, arch conservative and university lecturer Nina Andreeva led a movement to establish the All-Russian Communist Party of Bolsheviks. Meanwhile, in an article in *Izvestia* ("The Number of Heirs to the CPSU Is Growing," *Izvestia*, October 28, 1991, p. 2), I. Prelovskaya maintained that the Democratic Party of Russian Communists had no desire to build a new society patterned after some sort of ideological model, but it would deal with life's specific problems. A. Rutskoi was elected chairman of this Party and socialist V. Lipitsky was made chairman of its board. Many delegates from sixty-eight republics, territories, and provinces in Russia met in Moscow to affirm their goal of moving towards a socialism which would include rule by the people, social justice, and a fight for the well-being of people. Rutskoi, however, declared in June 1991 that he was still a Communist, condemned the Party administrative system that ran the whole show, and asserted that society was becoming more democratic faster than the Party (Alexandr Rutskoi, "Out of the Trenches and into the Roundtable," interview conducted by I. Prelovskaya, *Izvestia*, June 14, 1991, p. 3).

Many senior members of the Party resigned; great numbers of junior members had already left. Many more were about to do so. Yet there remained many former members of the *apparat* who looked forward to regaining power. The attempted coup was about the future of the Party, but it only hastened the demise of it. However, it did not decisively resolve the position and power of erstwhile Communists.

A growing number of republics banned the All-Union Communist Party. After the coup collapsed, the Ukraine Supreme Soviet adopted an act of independence and abolished party cells in all state structures. Between August 24 and 25 the Byelorussian (Belarus) parliament adopted a resolution that eliminated the Communist Party, suspended its operations, and unanimously adopted a decision on independence. On August 27 the republic of Moldova was proclaimed independent, the Communist Party was proscribed, and its property nationalized. On the other hand, the president of Uzbekistan warned that suddenly stopping the activity of the Communist Party would plunge the economy into chaos. A Georgian commented that the new nationalistic ideology was more dangerous than the communist one. In Azerbaijan the Party was a powerful force and its members were an overwhelming majority in the Supreme Soviet. On the other hand, in Armenia the communist candidates for office suffered total defeat in the elections to the Supreme Soviet and by 1991 no longer had any say in governing (Mikhail

Shevelyov, "Azerbaijan-Armenian Conflict," *Moscow News*, No. 20, 1991, p. 4).

An article in *Time* ("The Most Amazing Show Trial Ever," *Time*, Vol. 139, No. 23, June 8, 1992, p. 10) revealed the lengths to which new Russian government, seeking to take over from the old Soviet Center a leadership role, was prepared in 1992 to go to discredit the Communist Party. It announced that the Russian government would argue before the courts that the CPSU was a criminal organization. Sergei Shakhrai, leader of Yeltsin's legal team, claimed that the hearing would be the second Nuremberg trial of the century. The proposed trial was intended to prevent the Party from reestablishing itself as an effective political force, at least in Russia. Soloveichik ("The Barking Monster Is Ugly, Huge and Loud-Mouthed," *Socium*, No. 5, May 1991, pp. 60–67) hoped that Russia would never return to the years when the USSR Minister of Education was supervised by a corresponding member of the Central Committee whose name was known only to a narrow circle but whose power was unlimited. He stated that no one had ever heard the name Yevgeny Kozhenikov, but this person had for years exercised unlimited power over the Ministry. All important educational decisions were published under the auspices of the CPSU Central Committee of the Party and the USSR Council of Ministers. Local school principals were most fearful of the members of the regional Party committee.

A New Bureaucracy

The victory of Yeltsin as the first democratically elected president did not of itself remove the *apparatchiks*. As Valery Vyzhutovich pointed out ("Events and Commentary: We Support Yeltsin Conditionally," *Izvestia*, October 7, 1992, p. 2), the roots still remained. In the provinces, power remained in the hands of the former *nomenklatura*. After the failed coup, in the absence of the Communist Party, the task remained of reconstructing a bureaucracy staffed with qualified people. Yeltsin turned to many of his old Communist Party colleagues from Sverdlovsk as well as to a small group of young politicians known as the "Young Turks." They urged Yeltsin to ban the

Communist Party (Alexander Rahr, "Russia's Young Turks in Power," *Report on the USSR*, Vol. 3, No. 27, November 22, 1991, pp. 20–23). Gennadii Burbulis, Yegor Gaidar, Sergei Stankevich, Andrei Kozyrev, Alexandr Shokhin, Nikolai Fedorov, Yevgeny Baburov, and Mikhail Poltoranin were members of this group. Many of these men were serving as RSFSR ministers when Yeltsin decreed on November 6, 1991, that a Council of Ministers would form the Russian Federation government, with himself as its chairman. With this innovation the balance of power shifted away from the old Communist Party bureaucracy. The "Young Turks" supported Yeltsin's strong authoritarian style of presidential leadership.

The Soviet Union could never have remotely satisfied the requirements that had to be fulfilled if it was to become a stable entity. Its inhabitants spoke many different languages, held many different religious beliefs, came from so many different ethnic backgrounds, and occupied a vast and varied land mass. Over the years, stability had been maintained through a powerful federal government and a Party structure held together by determined and ruthless, bureaucratic and Party *apparatchiks*. An internal passport system prevented the free movement of population. Educational policies were designed to create loyal men and women, firmly committed as patriotic citizens of the Soviet Union. The integration of an ethnic political elite and ethnic educated middle classes into a common All-Union regime, in fact, helped to suppress individuals by tying them to their nationality groups. Policies were legislated to placate these groups. Territorially based nationalities received preferential treatment, and the occupational interests of the educated ethnic middle classes were protected.

On the other hand, the KGB was ruthless in suppressing the activists of dissenting nationality groups. For example, even in the 1960s, Latvians in Riga engaged in secret political discussions, in spite of the threat of exposure hanging over them. Local leaders who tried overtly to develop indigenous power bases for national reasons were either demoted or punished. Nevertheless, some territorially based nationalists who preserved a degree of autonomous existence manipulated Soviet nationality policy to their own ends and were ready under *glasnost* to promote nationalism. The attacks made by the multinational democratic forces in Moscow, Leningrad, and a number of other large cities against the state-Party monopoly of power made it possible for parochial minorities to press their claims for independence and sovereignty. Paradoxically, the leaders of autonomous regions, which were dominated by the Russians, supported the attempted coup. While happy to see the end of centralized Soviet power, they did not wish to see republics that had declared their independence under the USSR Constitution break up into squabbling ethnic groups. This danger had by no means been averted in the summer of 1991.

Clearly, Gorbachev's call for reforms set in motion forces which went way beyond what he had intended. When the Baltic republics demanded independence against his wishes Gorbachev supported the hard-line *apparat*. During the early months of 1991 he supported the use of troops to prevent the Baltic republics from seceding from the USSR. Saulius Girnius ("Lithuania's National Salvation Committee," *Report on the USSR,* Vol. 3, No. 4, January 25, 1991, pp. 6–7) and Vladimir V. Kusin ("Patterns of Intervention," *Report on the USSR* (op. cit., pp. 3–6) compared the reaction of the Soviet authorities at that time to the way in which the Soviet government and local Communist Parties had suppressed opposition in Hungary in 1956 and Czechoslovakia in 1968. The Baltic states were not alone in proclaiming their desire to leave the Union. The Armenian leader Ter-Petrosyan predicted several months before the coup that the Soviet Empire was disintegrating, and he proposed that Armenia should secede. Consequently, only nine republics participated in the Novo-Olgarevo new Union Treaty process, known as the 9+1 meeting led by Gorbachev and Yeltsin.

Old and deeply held commitments of the kind Lenin had to face when creating the Soviet Union had surfaced under *glasnost* and *perestroika*. The rhetoric of the reform movement encouraged old-fashioned nationalism. Each of the Union republics longed for the fullest possible independence. The ethnic minorities faced a dilemma. Ethno-nationalism created demands for autonomous states for each of the minority groups. While self-determination included a desire for power and the end of unequal status, many small groups realized that their rights could best be protected by a strong central government. However, the movements towards sovereignty and independence, regardless of the consequences, proved to be irresistible.

Doubtless the failed coup accelerated the disintegration of the Soviet Union, but it did not immediately result in its demise. For several months Gorbachev remained president of the USSR and continued to act as though he were still in control of events. Gorbachev had always wanted to hold the Union together. He truly believed that the spiritual development of the Soviet people would suffer if there was no coordinating All-Union entity to further the advances in science and culture, maintain the Russian language as a means of communication between the nationalities, and preserve the monuments, museums, theaters, libraries, archives, and educational institutions. The desirability of maintaining some kind of Union between some of the former republics was debated up to, and after, the point at which the USSR was formally dissolved.

In this debate Yeltsin opposed Gorbachev's view. His decree banning the Communist Party from public institutions was against Gorbachev's known wishes. Moreover he made it clear that the power and authority of the central authorities of the Soviet Union should be reduced. He advised autonomous republics to seize whatever independence they could. In an address to the USSR Congress of People's Deputies on September 3, 1991, he anticipated the fears many had that the Soviet Empire might be replaced by a revived Russian Empire: "The Russian state having chosen democracy and freedom, will never be an empire, will never be an older or a younger brother. It will be an equal among equals" ("Nationalism and Self-Determination in the Republics: The Russian Revival," *Report on the USSR,* (Vol. 3, No. 41, 1991, October 11, 1991, p. 1–3). Gorbachev, however, criticized the view expressed by some members of the RSFSR leadership that Russia was the legal successor to the Soviet Union ("Gorbachev Gives Television Interview," *Report on the USSR,* Vol. 3, No. 43, October 25, 1991, p. 26). Alexandr Tsipko warned that actions based on political expediency frequently give rise to unanticipated consequences ("The Drama of Russia's Choice," *Izvestia*, October 1, 1991, p. 5).

Once Russia was freed from the Center, the disintegration of the Soviet Union progressed rapidly. In virtually all of the republics that had gained independence divisions on national or ethnic grounds surfaced. The position of Russia within the larger Union as an equal among equals and the position of the many nationalities within the Russian Federation and other republics posed many challenging problems and issues that would have to be confronted in the years ahead.

For example Yeltsin, according to RSFSR State Secretary Gennadii Burbulis, expressed doubts about the need for a new Union Treaty ("Yeltsin Doubtful about Need for New Union Treaty," *Report on the USSR*, October 15, 1991, Vol. 3, No. 42, p. 31). Burbulis, apparently seeing no future for the old Union, wanted Russia to replace the Soviet Union as the world's second superpower.

However, the complete breakup of the Union presented many problems for the Russian leaders. As many as twenty-five million Russians lived outside the former Russian republic. A majority of them would probably stay where they were, especially those non-Asians living in the Central Asia regions who were born and raised there. Others who had not learned the native language had an incentive for leaving. The cost of independence for certain Union republics was bound to be unacceptably high. Yeltsin said he might make territorial claims on neighboring independent republics where there were high concentrations of Russians facing interethnic conflict. On the other hand there was bound to be pressure for self-determination among non-Russian nationalities within Russia. The Ukraine with more than a hundred nationalities, Lithuania with its Polish population, Azerbaijan with its Armenians, and Moldavia (Moldova) with its Ukrainian, Russian, and Gagauz minorities were just a few examples of newly independent states with heterogeneous populations that could face similar costs. Indeed, only Armenia, with 93 percent of its population ethnic Armenians, could claim to have an ethnically homogeneous population.

The Russian Federation hesitated to declare itself independent because of its multiethnic composition (Vera Kuznetsova, "The USSR Shaping Up as an Asian-Russian Union," *Nezavisimaya gazeta*, October 1991, p. 13). Such Russian Federation republics as Tatarstan, Chuvashia, Bashkortostan, and Buryatia spoke out in favor of independent statehood. On October 15, 1991, the Tatarstan National Movement demanded that its deputies proclaim the withdrawal of the republic from the RSFSR and the Soviet Union ("From Hot Spots: Tatarstan—Freedom Seethes," *Pravda*, October 17, 1991, p. 1). Reluctantly Yeltsin agreed that the only way to keep the Russian Federation whole and indivisible was for her to join in any available alliance with other fully independent republics. He argued that if the Ukraine signed a treaty with Russia, the borders would stay as they were. If not, Russia would seek to reclaim the Crimea (given to the Ukraine by Khrushchev's decree) and the Donbass coal fields.

Difficulties also arose in the case of small minorities. The Khakass people were a case in point. They were on the verge of extinction; the move to create an ethnic Khakass autonomous entity was designed to protect themselves (A. Tarasov, "Khakassia: A People Under the Sky, but with No Place on Earth," *Izvestia*, December 20, 1991, p. 3). Unfortunately in that geographic region the Khakass people represented only 11 percent of the population and Russians some 79 percent. Another example is found in the Kalmyk people, who had been deported from their native land in 1943 but regained some of their former territory in 1958 as an autonomous entity. The Kalmyk Council of Ministers demanded a return of its former boundaries. Similar claims were being made by other groups. The Karachai, who had lost statehood and were deported in 1943, sought a return of land and independence. When the Cossacks proclaimed two Cossack republics within the Karachai territory (Lyudmilla Leontyeva, "Drawn Swords," *Moscow News*, No. 48, 1991, p. 5), the Cherkess people asserted a historical claim to some of the same land. Still another example of interethnic conflict was the Chechen-Ingush republic where the Chechen people challenged the constitutionality of this entity and wished to have it declared a secular Chechen republic, independent of the RSFSR and the Ingush people. The latter wanted it divided so that they could have a republic of their own ("The Chechen Jigsaw Puzzle," *Moscow News*, No. 48, 1991, p. 11). At the same time, North Ossetia was most vocal in registering its claim to part of the Chechen-Ingush territory.

The implications for the educational arrangements in these territories were profound. In the northern Caucasus, the earlier displacement by Stalin of ethnic groups speaking one of a dozen or more different languages had come home to roost. The roots of ethnicity, language, and cultural heritage now overwhelmed the Russian authorities. Tsipko made the point that few people realized how far the process of the USSR's disintegration had progressed ("The Drama of Russia's Choice," *Izvestia*, October 1, 1991). The preservation of an integral Union, he claimed, was necessary if Central Asia and the Caucasus were to be democratized. Only Russia could provide the basis of a Commonwealth of Independent States (CIS). Yeltsin, therefore, bore the burden of responsibility for the inevitable outburst of separatism within Russia and the former Soviet Union. And educators were left to face the enormous diversity in terms of nationality, ethnicity, language, cultural heritage, and political preference. The possibility that any kind of a unified educational system would survive in the CIS was very doubtful. In fact, any unity in view of this diversity would require statesmanship and perseverance in the years ahead. Gavriil Popov stated the issue of Union in a different way ("What I Have Read, Heard or Seen," *Moscow News*, No. 51, 1991, p. 3): "I have the impression that hatred of the Center and the desire to destroy it have outweighed all other considerations, even though the old Center is no more."

In spite of widespread opposition, an agreement on establishing a Commonwealth of Independent States was signed near Brest towards the end of 1991. Three geopolitical centers appeared—Russia and its republics and autonomous territories, the Ukraine and Byelorussia (Belarus), and Kazakhstan and the Central Asian republics (Leonid Ionin, "Requiem for the Union," *New Times*, No. 52, 1991, pp. 14–17). Hence the Protocol to the Agreement on a Commonwealth of Independent States was signed in Minsk on December 8, 1991. Then, on December 21 the

Alma-Ata Declaration announced the Commonwealth of Eleven Independent States.

On December 17, *Tass* reported that the Soviet Union would cease to exist on January 1, 1992. Yeltsin issued decrees asserting Russian control over all Soviet structures on Russian territories except those of the USSR Ministry of Defense and the Ministry of Nuclear Energy. The question of the status of the Soviet Army and Navy had yet to be negotiated. The breakup of the Soviet Empire brought an end to the Soviet educational system. It had been held together for over seventy years by policies formulated by the Central Committee of the Soviet Communist Party. Beginning in 1992, each independent state assumed responsibility for its own educational system. In turn, many of the constituent republics, autonomous entities, and territories in these newly independent republics staked their right to educate their own people in their own way.

PART TWO

Into the Future

CHAPTER 11

Sovereign and Independent Russian Federation

The argument advanced in this book is that in spite of determined efforts by the leadership of the Communist Party to change the Soviet educational system, after more than seventy years the schools were, except in some important respects, still very traditional. The replacement of a religious ethos with scientific materialism was one visible example of the attempt by the Soviet authorities to transform the ideological foundations of the old Russian school system. Another was a consistent refusal of the authorities to adapt the school system to meet the manifestly different talents and needs of children. Under *perestroika*, equality of provision came under attack. Policies were proposed to take into account individual differences by introducing differentiated school types and curriculums. Also there was a return to a religious ethos.

After the bloody October 1917 Revolution, three prolonged and devastating wars, and seventy years as one of the fifteen autonomous republics in the Union of Soviet Republics, the Russian Federation in August 1991 shook off the stranglehold of the Party and the yoke of the centralized Union. Preceded by months of acrimonious disagreements between Gorbachev and Yeltsin, the latter was dismissed in November 1987 from his Party leadership post in Moscow and membership on the Politburo. Much later, in March 1990, guided by the slogan "All Power to the Soviets," Russia held its first free and democratic election of deputies to the Parliament, with Yeltsin winning a seat as a deputy. Two months later, Yeltsin became the chairman of the Supreme Soviet and was in a position to place many of his democratic supporters in high public office. When on June 12,

1990, Russia declared its sovereignty and assumed control of its own economy, educational system, political administration, and cultural development, indirect control of the Federation government by the Party ended. A year later, Yeltsin was declared the first popularly elected president of Russia, thereby forcing USSR President Gorbachev to propose a new Union Treaty. With the failed coup of August 1991, the stage was set for the dissolution of the Soviet Union, and in December of that year Russia became a truly free, sovereign, and independent state.

The Russian Federation Administrative Structure

Of the 148 million people living in the Russian Federation, more than 130 million are Russians; 18 million represent some 130 ethnic groups. Over 109 million live in urban areas, and the 78.6 million females outnumber 69.4 million males. In some respects, Russia is a country homogeneous in nationality inasmuch as some 81 percent of its population are Russians and 86 percent consider Russian to be their native language. They inhabit all of the republics and regional entities, and they are the dominant group in the Federation from the standpoint of access to political power (Igor Shafarevich, "Russia Alone with Itself," *Pravda*, November 2, 1991, p. 1).

The Russian Federation, spanning eleven time zones from Vladivostok on the Pacific to Kaliningrad in Western Europe, embraces twenty-one national and autonomous republics, six territories, forty-nine provinces, two federal cities, one autonomous province, and ten autonomous regions. If Chechnya's declaration of independence from the Russian Federation stands, the number of republics will be reduced to twenty, with a total of eighty-eight republics and regional entities making up the Federation.

The Russian federal structure is made up of six types of member entities. The autonomous republics of the Russian Federation, as they were known under Soviet rule, became national republics. As sovereign states, these national republics had greater rights than the territories, provinces, and the cities of St. Petersburg and Moscow. They had their own constitutions, not charters; their own presidents, not executive administrators; and their own Supreme Soviets that enacted laws, not simply Soviets of People's Deputies that passed resolutions. Their people had their own citizenship and national languages; they could choose to remain within the Federation or negotiate special relationships. They had the right of ownership of their subsoil resources and everything that was erected on their lands. As for the territories and provinces, all of their resources were under federal control. In fact, an autocratic chain of command extended over all of the nonrepublic entities. Unlike the republics, all territories, provinces and cities were accountable directly to the president and the government of the Russian Federation. However, with the acceptance by referendum of the new Constitution on December 12, 1993, no mention was made as to the sovereignty of the republics. The territories, provinces, and federal cities now have equal status with the other federal entities. Local self-governments are independent, and their budgets are not part of the system of federal state power. Everyone has the right to determine and indicate his or her own nationality and to study and develop one's own language.

The twenty-one national republics:

Adygeya	Kabardino-Balkaria	Karelia	Tatarstan
Bashkortostan	Kalmykia-Khalmg Tangch	Khakassia	Buryatia
Chechnya	Karachai-Cherkessia	Komi	Tuva
Chuvashia		Mari-El	Udmurtia
Dagestan		Mordvinia	Yakutia-Sakha
Gorno-Altai		North Ossetia	
Ingushetia			

The six territories:

Altai	Khabarovsk	Maritime
Krasnodar	Krasnoyarsk	Stavropol

The forty-nine provinces:

Amur	Kaluga	Moscow Provinces	Pskov	Tula
Arkhangelsk	Kamchatka	Murmansk	Rostov	Tver
Astrakhan	Kemerovo	Nizhni Novgorod	Ryazan	Tyumen

Belgorod	Kirov	Novgorod	Sakhalin	Ulyanovsk Bryansk
Bryansk	Kostroma	Novosibirsk	Samara	Vladimir
Chelyabinsk	Kurgan	Orel	Saratov	Volgograd
Chita	Kursk	Orenburg	Smolensk	Vologda
Irkursk	Leningrad	Ormsk	Sverdlovsk	Vorenzh
Ivanovo	Lipetsk	Penza	Tambov	Yaroslavl
Kaliningrad	Magadan	Perm	Tomsk	

The one autonomous province: Jewish

The ten autonomous regions:

Aga Buryat	Komi-Permyak	Taimyr (Dolgano-Nenets)	Ust-Orda Buryat
Chukchi	Koryak		Yamal-Nenets
Evenki	Nenets		
Khanty-Mansi			

The two federal cities: Moscow and St. Petersburg

Republics still retain their constitutions and legislative bodies, but the territories, provinces, and regions now are permitted to have their own charters and legislative bodies. The Federation authorities may not encroach on the spiritual and cultural distinctiveness of nationalities. No one can be compelled to determine or indicate his or her nationality, and everyone has the right to use his or her native language and to freely choose his or her own language of communication, upbringing, instruction, and creative work.

Within the Russian Federation, Moscow and St. Petersburg have historically dominated all political and cultural life. But times are changing. Pyotr Gladkov ("Where's the Key to Success," *Moscow News*, Nos. 2–3, 1993, p. 3) offers a reminder: "Outside this arena lies a vast country, traditionally defined as 'the provinces' where people live by their own rules and laws. In the provinces, they watch the Moscow circus show with a bewilderment bordering on disgust. It is in the provinces that the most important things are happening today. Whoever understands this will wield real power in this country in five or seven years' time." Hence under the 1993 Constitution, territories, provinces, and autonomous entities now share unconditional equality with all Federation members.

Yeltsin was well aware that the wave of the future was moving toward regionalization of the Federation, with the real power located not in Moscow but in each separate republic and region. Little wonder then that Yeltsin issued a threat in March 1993: "At the center and at the local level a good many instances have been brought to light in which the executive branch officials are impeding the implementation of political and economic reforms. I am warning them that they are personally responsible for those actions and that I will remove the guilty persons" (Speech by Boris Yeltsin, *Rossiikie vesti*, March 23, 1993, pp. 1–2). Hence the December 1993 Constitution was designed to reign in the republic, territorial, and regional authorities who had tended to carry out orders from Moscow that corresponded to their own interests and to ignore most of the rest.

Nationalist Movements

As in the former USSR, Russian policy continued to promote a uniform nationality process which in effect built barriers between the different nationalities and minorities by tying individuals to their ethnic groups. In developing their own political administrations and bureaucracies, nationalities were firmly linked to their own national republics, elites, cultural traditions, and languages. By nurturing and strengthening these ethnic bonds, nationalities united themselves into meaningful political groups to assert their rights, demand the redrawing of boundaries, and push for national republic status. The December 1993 Constitution was designed to lessen these pressures on Moscow.

The presence of a large number of Russian and Russian-speaking people in all of the national republics and other entities of the Federation has been one important factor maintaining links and international bonds. Now, however, many of the Russians are under pressure to emigrate from some of the national republics and regions of the Federation, thereby eroding these links. Belligerent nationalism already has forced more than

100,000 Russians to depart Chechnya in 1992–93, leaving behind some 700,000 Chechens. Most Russians understand that they bear a special responsibility to see to it that the cultural and spiritual life of titular and nontitular minorities develop fully and freely. At the same time, Russia is having to cultivate its own identity, interests, and national traditions, while serving as the unifying force of a vast multinational nation.

In response to the growing nationalist movements, the Russian government prepared a draft "concept for a nationalities policy in the Russian Federation" (Vladimir Yemelyanenko, "A Nation Is the Same Thing as a Tribe," *Moscow News*, September 27, 1992, pp. 6–7). Professor V. Tishkov explained that the government is confronted with two concepts of a sovereign community of fellow citizens. One is based on the notion of ethnonationalism, namely, an ethnic community in the form of a nation built around the dominance of one single nationality. Special privileges usually are granted to the people who give their name to the national entity, while limitations are placed on the minority people who live there. The other concept is that of a multiethnic community of citizens with rights of national-cultural autonomy guaranteed to all nationalities. For the present, the Russian Federation has had to accept the right of national territorial self-determination within the framework of a unified Russian Federated state guided by universal democratic principles. Sergei Shikhovtsev maintains that the main obstacle to the building of a new multiethnic Russia is separatism and militant nationalism (Sergei Shikhovtsev, "Opinion," *Rossiiskiye vesti*, July 22, 1993, p. 2). The Russian Minister of Education, Tkachenko, has laid down a policy of developing national self-awareness and culture, but not a narrow nationality-based education.

In the past several years the wealth and money supply has shifted from the European regions to the Urals and the Eastern areas (Alexander Surinov, "Russia Has Split," *Izvestia*, February 13, 1993, p. 4). Although the Siberian region has enormous natural resources and potential wealth, over the years for the most part people there have lived like paupers. Now the average per capita income in these regions has increased markedly. In January 1993 people in the East had an annual income 4.9 times higher than those in the European areas of the Federation. The republics with the lowest income levels are Chechnya, Ingushetia, Mari-El, Dagestan, North Ossetia, Kabardino-Balkaria, and Mordvinia, as well as the farming provinces of Moscow and Penza.

A major issue arose in the renaming of the Russian Soviet Federated Socialist Republic. Yeltsin took the view that the name Russian Federation was sufficient. Deputies in the Russian Congress disagreed. In the voting, 871 voted for the name Russia, 30 voted against, and 30 abstained. Later the Congress returned to the issue because representatives of a number of the national republics and autonomous entities protested that the name Russia represented imperial thinking. They demanded that the name should reflect the federal nature of the new state. On April 17, 1992, Supreme Soviet Chairman Khasbulatov arranged a compromise by which the name was changed to "The Russian Federation-Russia, a Sovereign Federal State." But he also declared that "The Russian Federation" and "Russia" were equivalent in law. In the vote, the name "Russian Federation-Russia" was accepted by 759 votes to 77, with 30 abstentions (Olga Burkaleva, "In Search of a Compromise That Suits Everyone," *Rossiiskaya gazeta*, April 18, 1992, p. 1).

The New Russians

Because of internal conflicts and economic conditions in Central Asia, Georgia, Abkhazia, Azerbaijan, Armenia, the Baltic states, and some of the republics within the Russian Federation, Russia has had to absorb several millions of refugees, and the number is constantly growing. In 1993 some 300,000 Russians arrived from Tajikistan without money and possessions. To aggravate the situation still further, most of them wanted to settle in urban areas because they had lived in cities. Therefore Moscow authorities were enraged when, on June 25, 1993, the Russian Supreme Soviet abolished domicile registration. Mayor Luzhkov defiantly made it known that all Moscow municipal housing facilities would be assigned only to Muscovites who were officially recognized as residents, and no land would be allocated to refugees for the construction of housing. As a result of the cities refusing to absorb them, the refugees are being shunted to the Black Earth and rural regions and territories. The refugees have formed a "Migrant Society" to aid each other in adjusting to their new environment. They openly talk about the significant differences between their psychology and outlook on life and that of their fellow Russians. "We are Russians of a different sort. Over the past seventy years, a crazy selection process was carried on in Russia. Nonconformists were kicked out of the country, while drunkards and idlers were protected" (Igor Rotar, "Refugees: Russians of a Different Sort," *Nezavisimaya gazeta,* June 2, 1993, p. 3. *CDPSP,* Vol. XLV, No. 22, pp. 1–2).

Most of the refugees are hardworking and soon after arriving in a rural village locate construction materials to build their own houses, while the locals continue to live in their dilapidated living quarters. Jealousy and envy escalate between the local residents and the newcomers. Even though local schools exist, the refugees often prefer to establish their own schools for their children. The refugees express the hope that the "New Russians" will succeed in creating new rural communities to replace the dying villages from which young people have fled and in which old people are living in the past.

The Russian Federal Treaty and Equal Rights

The 1992 Russian Federal Treaty on "Demarcating Objects of Jurisdiction and Powers between the Federal Bodies of State Power of the Russian Federation and Bodies of Power of the Republics within the Russian Federation" was a first step in the process of returning some powers to the periphery. It was an attempt to define the relationships between the federal, national-republican, and other regional authorities.

The Federal Treaty guarantees the right of self-government at the territorial and national-state levels. It is supposed to protect the individuals' right to choose their own cultural identities and to have their interests and needs translated into reality. The opportunity is provided for all national communities and ethnic groups to exercise their political rights, maintain their social status, and meet their national-cultural needs. Article 1 covers those aspects of life over which the center claims power such as the Federation's cultural and national development. Under the joint jurisdiction of federal, republican, and regional agencies are physical training and sports, upbringing, education, and science. General principles of taxation in the republics are listed under joint jurisdiction because of the uneven economic and social development of constituent republics, regions, and territories within the Federation and because of the need for equalization subsidies.

In spite of the guarantees incorporated in the Federal Treaty, Tatarstan and Checheno-Ingushetia refused to sign. Bashkortostan only signed when an appendix was added giving it special territorial status. The Tatars and Bashkirs complained that their native language had been neglected and that their educational facilities were inferior to those provided in other republics of the Federation. However, any attempt at nation building in these two republics will be difficult because only a third of all Tatars and Bashkirs actually live in their native lands.

In 1992, Tatarstan produced 26 percent of Russia's oil, but 98 percent of its industry remained operationally under the jurisdiction of the Russian Federation government. In a referendum on March 21, 1992, in spite of Yeltsin's call for a "No" vote, over 62 percent of the voters favored independence. This came as a surprise because only 49 percent of the population are Tatars; Russians constitute some 43 percent of the population. Farid Mukhamedshin, chairman of the Supreme Soviet of Tatarstan (Viktor Radziyevksy, "Compromise Doesn't Suit Radicals," *New Times*, No. 48, 1992, p. 5), explained Tatarstan's concept of independence: "Tatarstan is not encroaching upon the integrity of Russia. It intends to enter into a union with Russia. New relations between us can become a structural model for Russia." Yet the "Fundamental Law of Tatarstan" actually has the effect of putting Tatarstan outside Russia and giving it its own independent budget, law-enforcement bodies, and system of education. When Russia declared its independence from the USSR in 1991, Yeltsin based his move on democratic rights but, when similar declarations were announced by Tatarstan and some other national peoples, Yeltsin and Supreme Soviet deputies refused to recognize their democratic rights.

The Taimyr autonomous region had hopes of becoming a national territorial unit within the Federation (Aleksei Tarasov, "Taimyr Intends to Leave Krasnoyarsk Territory," *Izvestia*, December 25, 1992, p. 1). The economic interests of the Norilsk industrial region is the primary reason behind the demand to opt out of the jurisdiction of the Krasnoyarsk territory in Siberia. Unfair redistribution of taxes has forced the authorities in Taimyr to seek special status under the Federal Treaty, along with the right to have its own separate budget and legal jurisdiction independent of the Krasnoyarsk territory. Changing its legal status, however, will necessitate the redrawing of Krasnoyarsk's territorial borders. This can only be done with the permission of the Krasnoyarsk Soviet, which is not willing to agree to the demand.

Likewise the Balkar people have hopes of becoming the Republic of Balkaria. In 1944 the Balkars were deported from Kabardino-Balkaria to Central Asia and Kazakhstan, which left the Kabardino people to inhabit the republic. Thirty-four years later the Balkars returned to their homeland to find that not one Kabardin village or town had been built on the Balkar land. Their goal is to declare two separate and independent republics of Balkaria and Kabardino, instead of the one autonomous republic of Kabardino-Balkaria.

The Arkhangelsk province soviet demanded that its provincial status be equivalent to that of a republic because, as a province, it was shortchanged (Ivan Bentsa, "Arkhangelsk Province Soviet," *Izvestia*, January 26, 1993, p. 2). As a republic it would be able to manage its own affairs without the limitations imposed on provinces.

An even more ambitious and troublesome undertaking was the attempt by the "Assembly of the Caucasian Mountain Peoples" to form a "Confederation of the Caucasian Mountain Peoples" made up of sixteen of Russia's North Caucasian republics, territories, and regions and Georgia's South Ossetia and Abkhazia. The inclusion of the latter two entities in the

Caucasian Assembly brought on a small-scale war between Abkhazia and Georgia.

In an extraordinary session of the territorial Council of People's Deputies of Stavropol in November 1992, an appeal was sent to the Supreme Soviet of Russia and President Yeltsin to grant all territories and regions the same powers as those given the national republics in the Russian Federation. Specifically the Stavropol Council wanted the status of a self-governing zone with the right to levy its own taxes and legislate its own laws independent by the Center (Lyudmila Leontyeva and Sergei Shelin, "Riot in the Province," *Moscow News*, No. 48, 1992, p. 1).

On July 1, 1993, the Sverdlovsk province soviet renamed itself as the Urals republic within the Russian Federation, but the Russian Congress of People's Deputies refused to confirm the change of status. Sverdlovsk, the largest of the Russian provinces in terms of population, did not proclaim its sovereignty, but asserted its right to be a "state within a state" with the freedom to make its own social and economic decisions (Lyubov Tsukanova, "The Urals Begins," *Rossiiskiye vesti*, July 3, 1993, p. 1. *CDPSP*, Vol. XLV, No. 27, 1993, p 1).

Then, on July 9 the Chelyabinsk province soviet requested that the Russian Congress of People's Deputies elevate the province's constitutional-law status to that of the South Urals republic, an independent member of the Federation. The Chelyabinsk province soviet vice-chairman maintained that this change was needed because "we are still receiving directives from Moscow in which everything is prescribed down to the last nut and bolt." The Russian Congress refused the request.

Many of the nationalists in the republics and regions have resisted the Russian Ministry of Education's imposition on their educational systems of a compulsory general education core curriculum; still others have accepted the principle of a core but demand a decrease in its scope. As for the Russian population in the national republics, the Russian Ministry of Education is especially concerned that their interests and traditions be protected and furthered.

It is clear that national languages of the republics will occupy a far more important place in the curriculum of the schools, in spite of the policy set by the Russian Ministry of

Education. Russian-speaking children and teachers will find themselves at a disadvantage in the educational systems of the national entities dominated politically by non-Russian-speaking leadership. Under such conditions, it may become more and more difficult to determine what the content of the Russian Federation core component in the school curricula is that will satisfy the various national entities.

Only in Dagestan, Chechnya, Chuvashia, Tuva, Karbardino-Balkaria, and North Ossetia do residents of "indigenous nationality" add up to more than half the total population. Hence the movement to establish national schools in the republics and regions raises many issues and sets the stage for present and future conflicts between national peoples. The Russian Federation Minister of Education, Yevgenii Tkachenko, illustrates the dilemma he faces by pointing to the fact that there are more than 1,000 Tatar schools in Bashkiria, and a similar number of Chuvash schools in Tatarstan. He states the problem in these words: "How many languages should be taught in a Chuvash school located in Tatarstan? Tatar, as the language of the republic where the school is located; Chuvash, as the pupil's native language; Russian, as the state language; and German, English or French as an election subject?" Tkachenko agrees that no pupil can cope with the study of so many languages. Choices will have to be made. Hence, each republic, territory, province, and city must be given the freedom to decide on its own which school types, curricula, and teaching methods are preferred, as long as a uniform and basic federal curriculum component is mandated. He believes that the right to have regional and local curriculum components protects the cultural and historic interests by providing for the study of the national languages and other specific local ethnic factors (Andrei Baiduzhy, "Reform," *Nezavisimaya gazeta*, August 31, 1993, p. 6. *CDPSP*, Vol. XLV, No. 35, 1993, p. 11).

Bashkortostan is an interesting case study of the many problems that confront Tkachenko in getting the republics to renounce the concept of national-territory rights and return to the purely territorial prerogatives that existed before the 1917 October Revolution. Bashkortostan is not a historically established republic but was established by Lenin and given the name of the Bashkir people. Now the Bashkirs as a minority are trying to assert their will over the majority of the non-Bashkir population. (Sergei Shikhovtsev, op. cit).

The Bashkortostan Minister of Education, R. Gardanov, issued an order in mid-1993 entitled "On the Curricula of General Education Institutions." The Bashkiri language and literature is made compulsory in all types of schools from the first through the ninth grade, even though Bashkir is not the state language. The time allotted to the Russian language and literature is reduced from seventy-six hours to fifty-four hours. Foreign languages are optional. "World Culture" will receive only one hour a week in order to provide time for four new subjects: "The History of Bashkortostan," "The Geography of Bashkortostan," "The Ecology of Bashkortostan," and "The Culture of Bashkortostan" (Sergei Kudryashov, "The Bashkirization of Bashkiria," *Izvestia*, July 20, 1993, p. 2. *CDPSP*, Vol. XLV, No. 29, 1993).

The Russians and Tatars, who make up the majority of the population, insist that the Ministry's order is unconstitutional. They are demanding that the Russians, Tatars, and Bashkirs all have equal state status with the right to determine the curricula of their own schools. Tkachenko is correct when he states: "To this day, the seeds of present and future conflicts between nationalities lie in the unresolved status of these national questions" (ibid.).

Moscow City Administrative Structure

The city of Moscow, surrounded by the province of Moscow, has its own autonomous government structure consisting of ten prefectures that are ruled over by prefects appointed by the mayor. Some of the prefects appointed by the mayor were not popular because they had held high positions in the Communist Party. The Moscow prefectures now have the right to elect their own executive committees and appoint their *apparat* (Natalya Davydova, "Moscow Municipality, Prefects Go to Work," *The Chronicle of Higher Education*, July 28, 1991, p. 3). Each prefecture is divided into residential districts of some 70,000 people. There are proposals to reduce in number the 120 residential districts in Moscow, each with its own education authority.

The city of Moscow is governed by a City Council made up of representatives from the 10 prefectures and the 120 residential districts. The City Council, headed by the mayor, serves as the policy-forming entity on a range of issues relating to life in the city. The mayor has the authority to issue decrees and to establish management bodies.

The Moscow City Council has a membership of 360 representatives, 3 from each of the 120 districts, under the leadership of a chairman and seven vice-chairmen, ten prefectural members, and a representative of the president of the Russian Federation. The Council has the authority to draw up development plans, determine the city tax rate, and oversee the executive administrative staff of the 120 districts. Each district has an executive committee of 30 deputies and a chairman and a vice-chairman to develop plans, maintain public order, provide consumer services, oversee the local schools, and supervise the cultural services. The mayor, advised by a consultative committee, rules over the government of the entire city. When Mayor Popov attempted to combine both culture and education into one administrative body, Mrs. Kezina, the very forceful director of Moscow schools and also Deputy Minister of Education of the Federation, blocked the move.

The ongoing political struggles in the Moscow city government continued after Gavriil Popov resigned as mayor and was replaced by his deputy, Yu. Luzhkov. Former Party first secretaries, *apparatchiks,* and *nomenklatura* continue to hold onto leadership roles on all levels of Moscow's government. In fact, the Communist Party "*Aktiv*" of the former Kalinin and Perovo borough Party Committees was revived. It reestablished its Party organizations, recruited members, held meetings at enterprises, research institutes, and district government bodies, and issued calls to work for the removal of Yeltsin ("Are Preparations Being Made?" *Vechernaya Moskva*, April 16, 1993, p. 1. *CDPSP*, Vol. XLV, No. 16, 1993, p. 7).

The Struggle for Political Power

Looking back upon the failed coup of August 1991, the former mayor of Moscow, Gavriil Popov ("August 21, 1991," *Izvestia,* August 21, 1992, p. 3) suggested that there might be four interpretations of that period in history. One view was that it was "a great revolution equal in significance to that of October 1917." Another pictured it as "a revolution of missed opportunities." A third was that it was "a revolution betrayed." And a fourth was that "there was no revolution at all." What is certain, however, is that the Russian Federation has suffered through three ongoing transformations which have had, and continue to have, a very disruptive impact on the educational system, namely, from totalitarianism to democracy, a command economy to a market system, and a multinational Soviet Empire to a multinational and multiethnic Russian Federation.

As president of the Russian Federation, Yeltsin took measures to overcome the totalitarian traditions in the political arena. He maintained that in the Russian Federation, the word "government" referred to the executive branch of power, namely, the president, prime minister, and Cabinet of Ministers, in contrast to the other two branches, the legislative and judicial. The Russian Federation Congress of People's Deputies had 1,033 members, whereas the Supreme Soviet was made up of 256 deputies elected by and from the Congress. By a simple majority of votes, the Congress had the power to veto decrees and orders issued by the president. The third branch was the Constitutional Court which acted as an independent arbiter of the law. Decisions of the Council of Ministers, decrees of the president, and any of the laws passed by the Supreme Soviet were referred to the Court to determine if they were in conformity with the legal norms contained in the Constitution of the Russian Federation.

At the opening session of the Russian Congress of People's Deputies in October 1991, Yeltsin was given the right to serve as prime minister. One month later the Russian Congress granted him the extraordinary power to rule by decree, with the Russian Supreme Soviet retaining the right to overturn any of his decrees within a week of being issued. Yeltsin then boldly declared that the government was accountable only to the president and not to the Parliament. Soon thereafter, the Congress challenged Yeltsin's rush toward an "Executive Presidency" modeled after that of the US. Yeltsin then found himself in an ongoing power struggle with the Congress of People's Deputies and the Supreme Soviet. Deputy Vladimir Isakov summarized the essence of the confrontation and prolonged struggle that took place in the closing months of 1993 (Ivan Rodin, "The Opposition Replies," *Nezavisimaya gazeta*, March 3, 1993, p. 2): "The main goal (of the Supreme Soviet) is to take away from the president his executive powers and give them to a Prime Minister named by the Parliament." The Supreme Soviet claimed the authority to vote no confidence in individual cabinet members as well as in the entire government. It demanded that all cabinet appointments be made by a prime minister, subject to confirmation of the Supreme Soviet, and that the president's authority be limited to serving as a ceremonial head of state.

The origin of this concept of legislative power is traced to the USSR constitutional reform introduced by Gorbachev and Lukyanov in December 1988. Gorbachev longed to be the president of the USSR, but he feared to stand for election. Consequently he created the post of president of the Supreme Soviet to bolster his leadership role and exploit fully the Bolshevik slogan "All Power to the Soviets." Later the Soviets on all levels of government asserted their authority to appoint executive and administrative officials without consulting the Party. Article 146 of the 1977 USSR Constitution stated that "the Soviets shall decide all matters of local significance." Hence "All Power to the Soviets" laid the basis of a law-governed state wherein the votes of the people and their elected representatives replaced the power held by the Party and its *apparat*. Likewise, Article 104 of the current Russian Federation's Constitution stated that the Russian Congress was the supreme body of state power and was authorized to deal with any question coming within the jurisdiction of the Russian Federation.

Ruslan Khasbulatov, as chairman of the Russian Supreme Soviet, insisted that the parliamentary concept of government found in many European countries was rooted in Russian parliamentary tradition. He maintained that the chairman had the authority to appoint the prime minister and members of the cabinet, making them collectively accountable to the Supreme Soviet.

The mayor of St. Petersburg, Anatoly Sobchak, gave his view of the ongoing struggle (Lyubov Tsukanova, "A New Design on an Old Canvas," *Rossiiskiye vesti*, September 17, 1992, p. 2). In his opinion, the deputies of the Russian Supreme Soviet claimed they were granted by the "RSFSR Law on Territorial and Provincial Soviets" the authority to control "anything and everything." Under the principle of "primacy," it was maintained, the legislative branch was given the right of control over the executive authority.

An article in *Rossiiskiye vesti* ("Boris Yeltsin Offers a Peaceful Solution," March 23, 1993, p. 1) took issue with Sobchak's view: "The root of our problem does not lie in the conflict between the executive and legislative branches nor in the conflict between Khasbulatov and Yeltsin. . . . It lies in the profound contradiction between the people and the former antipopular communist system, which still is not broken up and is again seeking to regain its lost power over the Federation. The former CPSU Central Committee officials have found easy jobs for themselves in the Supreme Soviet. It is they who are setting policy at the Congress and in the Supreme Soviet." Others were quick to point out that many former CPSU officials also held leadership roles in Yeltsin's executive branch of government.

Professor Yuri Afanasyev agreed that Russian political life was dominated by individuals whose one objective was to preserve all their perks and privileges of office ("Government and Society Must Unite," *Moscow News*, No. 11, 1992, pp. 10–11). Democracy for them was only a means to selfish ends. A noted political scientist, Igor Klyamkin, in an interview with Oleg Makarov, agreed with this assessment ("Though the Soviet Union Is No More, Soviet People Are Still Here," *New Times*, No. 13, 92, pp. 4–7): "In our political culture the status the leader's personality enjoys is incomparably higher than the status attributed to various parties, movements and state structures." Consequently, the factions and disagreements within the Russian government and its education sector are best examined in the light of the position and attitudes of individuals within the government.

Khasbulatov charged that Yeltsin's executive branch was so enmeshed in political struggles that the reform program was impeded. Although the president had been given more and more authority to issue decrees, the reforms were not implemented. In fact, Khasbulatov proclaimed that the scope of executive authority had seriously undermined the legislative functions of the deputies of the People's Congress and the Supreme Soviet.

Yeltsin, on the other hand, insisted that he had to be given more power because the Soviets on all levels of government encroached on the authority of the executive branches. Some regional and local soviets had taken out their own bank accounts, refused to approve budgets, issued their own executive directives, ignored the reform measures, and declared their sovereignty.

After the failed August 1991 coup, Yeltsin established a Presidential Consultative Council ("MN File," *Moscow News*, No. 4, January 21, 1993, p. 3.) as a kind of center for eighteen intellectuals to help the president draft and issue decrees. Its members worked on a voluntary and irregular basis. Independent of the council there was a group of presidential advisers who were salaried and met each Friday to discuss pressing issues and policies. Collective meetings with Yeltsin were held at least once every two months. In addition, advisers scheduled a personal hour-long meeting with the president each month and prepared memoranda of two or three pages on critical problems in the area of their expertise. When Dneprov was removed as Minister of Education in December 1992, he was named a presidential adviser on education.

The Council of Heads of Republics was formed in 1992 to protect the interests of the national republics. Under the former Russian Constitution the national republics had rights that were denied to autonomous republics, provinces, territories, and lesser governing formations. To counteract this inequity, Yeltsin in 1993 established the Council of Executive Heads made up of representatives of the autonomous republics, territories, provinces, and autonomous districts. This council served as a consultative body to facilitate relations between federal and regional executive administrators.

Although many members of the Council of Heads of Republics and Council of Executive Heads continued to pay lip service to a "centrist" policy on national issues, they warned Yeltsin that the power struggle in Moscow was undermining trust in central authority. In an effort to form a counterweight to the Russian Supreme Soviet, Yeltsin encouraged the formation of a Council of the Federation made up of the leading executive officer and chairman of the legislative branch of each of the eight-nine regional governing bodies of the Federation. Hence the Council of the Federation founded itself by a mutual agreement, claimed the right to formulate its own independent policies, and asserted its authority to implement the provisions of the Federal Treaty.

Early on Yeltsin had been given the authority by the Parliament to appoint personal envoys to monitor and speed up the reform program in the autonomous districts, provinces, and territories. As in the Tsarist's years, they were known as the "eyes and ears" of the sovereign to enforce the will of the central power. The envoys, in turn, dispatched their deputies to the lower-level executive entities, thereby forming a vertical system of presidential power. This concentration of power in Yeltsin's hands alienated many deputies of the Congress and Supreme Soviet and escalated opposition to Yeltsin as a person and to his reform program. Moreover, Yeltsin's practice of issuing decrees bypassing the Parliament and adding appendices "not for discussion" was especially irritating.

In March 1993 the Congress of People's Deputies refused to extend Yeltsin's right to appoint envoys to the provinces, territories, and autonomous entities. As a result, some of these regional areas elected their own chief administrators to break the hierarchical control from Moscow and at the same time to free the elected administrators from subservience not only to the president but also to the regional Soviets, which had in the past appointed these officials. As expected, many of the newly elected administrators were members of the former *nomenklatura,* but they came to be viewed as legitimate leaders of their regions and were given the authority to make decisions in the interest of their geographical areas.

On the other hand, the former mayor of Moscow, Popov, held the view that the democrats who seized power after the failed August coup were unprepared to govern the Russian Federation. The vacuum had to be filled by former Party *apparatchiks* and *nomenklatura* people who had shed their ideology and Party membership. Their expertise and administrative experience were needed to maintain the territorial integrity of Russia. For example, the former chief of the presidential staff, Yuri Petrov, served as Party first secretary in Sverdlovsk Province. Viktor Il'yushin, who heads the president's Secretariat, held a leadership role under Yeltsin in the Sverdlovsk *Komsomol*. The office of General Management of the Russian Government was still dominated by former members of the Central Committee of the Communist Party of the Soviet Union, along with former bureaucrats and executives from the military and industrial complex. Gennadii Burbulis, a former professor of Marxism-Leninism at Sverdlovsk University, for several years held the powerful post of first vice-premier responsible for political affairs. He sponsored the appointment of Yegor Gaidar as prime minister. These two men assembled a group of "Young Turks" to provide a liberal direction to Yeltsin's reform program. Sergei Shakhrai, legal councilor to Yeltsin, served as deputy prime minister; Sergei Stankevich, as state councilor to Yeltsin; Andrei Kozyrev, as Minister of Foreign Affairs; Mikhail Poltoranin, as Minister of Press and Media; Deputy Prime Minister Boris Saltykov, as chairman of the State Committee on Science, Higher Education, and Technology Policy; Minister of Labor Alexander Shokhin, as Deputy Prime Minister for Social Policy; Eduard Dneprov, as Minister of Education; and Vladimir Kinelev, as Minister of Higher Education. These "Young Turks" had contacts with Western thought and practice. Like those who turned out to protect the Russian "White House" in August 1991, they represented a generation shift.

In late 1992 the conservative leadership in the Russian Supreme Soviet demanded more expert and experienced leadership in the management of the economy and forced many of the liberals from office. With the appointment of Victor Chernomyrdin as prime minister (Irina Demchenko, "Chernomyrdin Remembers," *Izvestia*, April 3, 1993, p. 2), Yeltsin signalled a more conservative economic course in the Federation by permitting the prime minister to reestablish a State Planning Committee and a State Committee for Material and Technical Supply. These committees were given the responsibility of monitoring and regulating enterprises, factories, and agencies in the areas of (1) fuel and energy, (2) food, (3) military industrial conversion, (4) science, and (5) social needs. At the same time, Oleg Lobov resigned as chairman of the president's Expert Council to become First Deputy Prime Minister and Minister of Economics, with the mandate to revive certain features of the former planned economy and grant subsidies to needy enterprises.

Rebellion or Coup?

The ongoing struggle and gridlock between the Supreme Soviet and the government came to a showdown in September 1993, when Yeltsin and his advisers decided that only a clean break with the old Soviet-elected legislators could end the gridlock and bring about a democratic and workable government system. On September 1, Yeltsin issued a decree suspending Vice-President Aleksandr Rutskoi and First Vice-Chairman of the Russian Federation Council of Ministers V. F. Shumeiko from performance of their duties while under reciprocal accusations of corruption and legal claims against one another. Rutskoi protested that there was no constitutional basis for the suspension. Ruslan Khasbulatov declared Yeltsin's decree a flagrant violation of the Russian Federation's Constitution (Boris Pugachov, "Unconstitutional Boomerang," *Rossiiskaya gazeta*, p. 1. *CDPSP*, Vol. XLV, No. 35, 1993, p. 3). Khasbulatov also proposed calling into session the Congress of Russian Federation's People's Deputies to consider the question of removing Yeltsin from the presidency and asking the Russian Constitutional Court to rule on the constitutional status of the vice-president.

The Russian Supreme Soviet, meeting on September 3, suspended Yeltsin's decree and called for the removal of Yeltsin as president (Aleksei Lvov, *Rossiiskiye vesti*, September 4, 1993, p. 1. *CDPSP*, Vol. XLV, No. 35, 1993, p. 1). Vladimir Isakov reported the rumor that there were fears in Boris Yeltsin's inner circle that in the event of Yeltsin's illness or death, Aleksandr Rutskoi would come to power.

However, this was much more than a rivalry of the two branches of government and a personal conflict between Yeltsin and Khasbulatov. The real differences were brought into the open when a group of reformers in Yeltsin's government persuaded Prime Minister Viktor Chernomyrdin and Yeltsin to return the economic reformer Yegor Gaidar to his former post of First Deputy Prime Minister in place of the conservative Oleg Lobov. The moment Gaidar returned to the political scene was nothing less than a declaration of civil war. The Patriots and Communists in the Supreme Soviet declared that they would embark on the path of restoration of Soviet power. Ruslan Khasbulatov proclaimed that the "Soviets are precisely the people." Later he was charged with having initiated a civil war and for having issued the order: "You are at liberty to take any measures to defend the Soviet system" (Kronid Lyubarsky, "The Law of Executions," *New Times*, No. 29, 1993, pp. 6–7).

The confrontation reached the boiling point on September 21 when Yeltsin issued Decree No. 1400 discontinuing the legislative functions of the Congress of People's Deputies and the Supreme Soviet of the Russian Federation and calling for a new two-chamber "Federal Assembly of the Russian Federation" to replace it. In the interim, Yeltsin declared that the Federation would be guided by decrees of the president and resolutions of the government of the Russian Federation.

Members of the Supreme Soviet voted to ignore Yeltsin's decree, announced the dismissal of Yeltsin as president, named Rutskoi to replace him, and accepted the support of a coalition of die-hard Communists and nationalists operating under the name of the National Salvation Front.

Violence erupted on October 3 when Rutskoi incited his armed supporters to storm the mayor's headquarters and invade Ostankino TV Center. Yeltsin declared a state of emergency in

Moscow, cited Rutskoi and Khasbulatov as outlaws, removed Rutskoi as vice-president, and named Prime Minister Viktor Chernomyrdin to replace him. After the military assaulted the White House on the morning of October 4, Khasbulatov, Rutskoi, and some thirty of their followers were placed under arrest.

Eighteen months of political gridlock came to an end on October 4. The majority of Russians supported Yeltsin because they believed that a strong and powerful president was needed to restore stability, order, and direction to the country. Yeltsin's opposition in the Supreme Soviet charged that the use of two tank divisions and an airborne military force to overwhelm and subdue Parliament was actually a military "coup." Yeltsin's supporters, on the other hand, charged that the Chairman of the Supreme Soviet Khasbulatov and Vice-President Rutskoi had initiated a "rebellion" by inciting the paramilitary force, armed with automatic kalashnikovs, clubs, metal crowbars, and trucks to take over five floors of the mayor's office and invade the Ostankino TV Center.

The December 1993 Constitution

The termination of the dual power struggle in October paved the way on December 12 for the ratification by referendum of a new Constitution and the election of deputies to a new Federal Assembly.

Under the new Constitution, the Federal Assembly is the representative and legislative body of the Russian Federation and consists of two chambers. The Council of the Federation is made up of two representatives from each of the eighty-nine entities making up the Russian Federation; one will be elected from the legislative body of state power and the other from its executive body of state power. The Council of the Federation meets the demand for equalization of representation rights of all the geographical entities making up the Federation.

The State Duma consists of 450 deputies who are elected for a term of four years. They may not be active members of the civil service nor be engaged in paid activity, with the exceptions of teaching, research, or creative work.

This new Federal Assembly has little in common with the Russian Federation's former Supreme Soviet. According to Article 107 of the former Constitution, the Supreme Soviet was a legislative, managing, and supervisory body. As a result, its deputies spent much of their time and effort interfering in the day-to-day work of the government.

The major duty of the Federal Assembly is to make laws concerning taxation, budget, civil and criminal codes, pensions, and other such matters. The government is answerable only to the president. Since a member of Parliament can no longer call to account a member of the president's cabinet or executive branch, the principles of the separation of legislative, executive, and judicial powers are protected. Yeltsin cannot block the Federal Assembly from enacting a law if a majority of two-thirds approves it. The president appoints the prime minister and cabinet officers with the consent of the State Duma. He has the authority to issue decrees and directives that are binding throughout the Russian Federation. If the cabinet asks the Parliament for a vote of confidence and a vote of no confidence is given, the president has the right to ignore the vote or to call an election of the deputies.

No state or mandatory ideology may be invoked; political diversity and a multiparty system are legally recognized. As a secular state, no state or mandatory religion may be imposed. All religious associations are separate from the state and equal before the law. Basic human rights and liberties are inalienable and belong to everyone from birth.

Everyone who is legally on Russian territory has the right to exercise freedom of movement and to choose a place of sojourn and residence. Everyone is guaranteed freedom of conscience and freedom of religion, including the right to profess any religion or other convictions and to act in accordance with them. Everyone is guaranteed freedom of thought and speech. However, propaganda or agitation that implies social, racial, national, religious, or linguistic superiority is prohibited.

Everyone has the right to health care and medical assistance. Medical assistance at state and municipal health care institutions is provided to citizens free of charge, subsidized from the appropriate budget, insurance contributions, and other receipts. Everyone has the right to an education. Furthermore, everyone has the right, on a competitive basis, to obtain a free higher education. According to Article 43, "free preschool, basic general, and secondary vocational education is guaranteed at all state and municipal educational institutions and at enterprises." Basic general education is compulsory and parents or guardians are responsible for their children receiving this level of education. The Russian Federation will establish federal educational standards and maintain various alternative forms of education and self-education.

Inga Prelovskaya ("Protect the Schools," *Izvestia*, December 24, 1993, p. 4. *CDPSP*, Vol. XLV, No. 51, 1993, pp. 20–21) points out that the Constitution does not make it clear if the regular nonspecialized tenth and eleventh grades of the general secondary schools are free and open to all who wish to complete that level of education on a noncompetitive basis. Will basic vocational education be open and free to all who complete the basic general education school? Does it make sense to promise free preschooling, which has always been fee-paying for most parents, when secondary, vocational, and higher education is vastly underfunded?

Everyone is guaranteed freedom of literary, artistic, scientific, technical, and other forms of creativity and teaching. General questions of upbringing, education, science, culture, physical training, and sports fall under the joint jurisdiction of the Russian Federation's central government and the constituent entities of the Russian Federation. This joint jurisdiction applies equally to the republics, territories, provinces, federal cities, autonomous provinces, and autonomous regions.

The Russian language is the state language of the Russian Federation, but the republics still have the right to declare their own state languages. The latter may be used, along with the state language of the Russian Federation, in the republics' bodies of state power, bodies of local self-government, and state institutions. The Russian Federation guarantees to all its peoples the right to the preservation of their native language and the creation of conditions for studying and developing it.

An Enlightened Authoritarianism

A new Russian Federation era lies ahead for the Russian people. Many of the elderly, who fought for their country in World War II and helped to build a great Russian Empire, are still committed to the belief in the greatness of Russia and the social egalitarian ideals of communism. With the destruction of the Empire, economic collapse, political chaos, inflation, and widespread crime, many are cynical, disillusioned, and impoverished. It can truly be said that over the centuries the Russian people have experienced an unusually large number of hardships. During the election campaign many of the deputy candidates to the Federal Assembly joined with Vice-Premier Vladimir Shumeiko in calling for the creation of a new Russian ideology to recover the "image of Great Russia" and overcome "the image of a poor, disintegrating and unstable Russia that badly needs Western aid and leftovers of Western technology" ("Russian Politicians Stump with Nationalist Rhetoric," *The Christian Science Monitor*, November 29, 1993, p. 1).

Throughout most of their history the Russian people have been dominated by autocratic rule that stressed the need for stability, security, conformity, and fear of an open society. In spite of the restraints, however, great achievements have been recorded over the centuries in literature, music, ballet, architecture, mathematics, and theoretical science. Today, in theory, there is more freedom, but in day-to-day living there is widespread fear of inflation, poverty, and the uncertainty of the future. Little wonder that many Russians have lost faith in Yeltsin's political, educational, and economic reforms.

Having lived for so many years under totalitarian rule, some older Russians assert that they would be happy to return to those years of "stagnation" under Brezhnev, with a guaranteed income and minimal inflation. It is no surprise, then, that Vladimir Zhirinovsky's ultranationalist Liberal Democratic Party and Gennadii Zyuganov's Russian Federation Communist Party were the big winners in the December 12, 1993, election. In January, 1994, the opposition elected a diehard Communist Party official, Ivan Rybkin, as speaker of the State Duma. One of Yeltsin's advisers, Anranik Migranyan, accepted the fact that the people had voted "their support for Russian nationalism, order, stability, and authoritarianism. Now there is only a choice between different types of authoritarianism" (Daniel Sneider, "Russians Spurn Reformers, Embrace Authoritarianism," The *Christian Science Monitor*, December 14, 1993, p. 1).

Under the new Constitution, the State Duma's power is held to a minimum. Maximum authority is allocated to the president in a French model of a republic. Yeltsin has the right to disband the Parliament if it fails to accept for the third time his nominee for prime minister or if it attempts to force a vote of no confidence twice in three months.

Within weeks after the December election, Prime Minister Viktor Chernomyrdin and President Yeltsin signalled a turn toward a more conservative reform program that they hope will be more acceptable to the masses, collective farmers, and industrialists. Yeltsin dismissed many of his liberal aides and advisers, one of whom was the former Minister of Education Eduard Dneprov. The authoritarian spirit of the former communist *nomenklatura*, which continues to dominate the governing bureaucracy, is likely in the months ahead to blend in and reenforce the authoritarian structures of the executive branch of the government that are mandated by the new Constitution.

2

CHAPTER 12

The Politics of Russian Education

To be sure, the political uncertainty in Russia has had its effect on the control and administration of education. Clearly the political ambition for independence by some of the national republics, autonomous entities, provinces, and territories of the Russian Federation may outweigh their ability to provide a comprehensive and viable system of education.

It is sometimes too readily assumed that the way political power is distributed has an overwhelming impact on education. Perhaps the absence in the Russian Federation of legitimate and organized opposition parties and truly contested elections until December 1993 constituted a greater denial of democratic processes than had the power enjoyed by the central government. Although there were, and still are, far too few democratically oriented educators to implement successfully the needed reforms, Minister of Education Dneprov's strategy was to democratize the Russian educational system by means of decentralization, depoliticization, demonopolization, and deideologization. Many of his opponents, however, insist that his was a reform program of destabilization, degeneration, destruction, and degradation.

The radical departures from traditional Soviet practices in education and the decentralization of the centrally planned educational system that were introduced after 1988 served to arouse massive fears and resistance among many of the education bureaucrats who still wielded power, as well as among many of the teachers and principals who soldiered on in the schools day in and day out. For many decades the Russian Federation rigorously organized and controlled all schools, universities, hospitals and clinics, sports, and leisure activities to assure a level of equality and social justice for all of its people. It was generally agreed, however, that there could be no return to an all-powerful centralized Federation totalitarianism in government and education, even though there were frequent calls for some kind of authoritarian rule.

With the renaming of the Communist Party in Russia and the establishment of new versions of communist and socialist parties, it was predicted as late as December 1993 that few of them would ever again gain a position of authority. Although many individual members of the former Communist Party had continued to hold positions in the educational establishment, the Russian Congress of People's Deputies, and the Supreme Soviet, it was obvious that the Party's former educational aim of creating a "New Soviet Communist Man" was no longer accepted. Although socialists in other countries claimed that the aims of humane socialism were different from, and more acceptable than, those which were held by the Soviet Communist Party, few of the post-Soviet leaders in Russia were prepared to differentiate between the good and bad aspects of a Marxist ideology. Few educators were prepared to accept any kind of government-imposed ideology. Hence there was little or no interest in theoretical educational research designed to construct a model of what workers should know and what skills and attitudes they should possess.

Also it was obvious to most Russian educators after the February 1988 Plenum on Education and the December 1988 Congress of Education Workers that the traditional Soviet unified, standardized, and socialized common school for all Russian youth, with a common curriculum and uniform teaching methods, no longer could meet the needs of an individualized, diverse, privatized society. New concepts such as freedom of choice in the use of educational services, differentiation of school types and curriculum provision, diversity, privatization, democratization, and humanization were introduced as innovative educators identified with and responded to individual needs and cultural-ethnic group demands. Decentralization of the federal educational system was essential to meet the needs and demands of the national republics, territories, and provinces. Regardless of the system of administration and the educational goals imposed by governments, however, the outcomes of struggles between groups of teachers and educational administrators that take place probably determine on a microlevel what goes on in classrooms in the long run. It is clear that the fierce political infighting among educators in the Soviet and Russian education establishment over the past five years, was and still is, closely related to cliques with links to leading politicians. Therefore it was to be expected that Dneprov's appointment as Russian Minister of Education in 1990 would provoke outrage among many educators and politicians.

Since the conflicts between the "reformers" and the so-called "old guard" in the education sector were so highly personalized and entangled in struggles for power, policy decisions and reform programs were often accepted more on the basis of who formulated them rather than on their intrinsic merits. Most Russian educators agreed that some reforms were needed simply because of institutional stagnation and the alienation of so many of the students. But they disagreed as to the pace, scope, and kind of reform measures required. Most educators realized that the economic conditions greatly inhibited any comprehensive and radical reform of the schools. As the criticisms of Dneprov's leadership and reforms accumulated, however, many in the education establishment found common cause to unite and remove him, in order to be free to push ahead with their own agendas for reform and seizure of power.

Democratic Freedom and Religious Values

Dneprov's view that decentralization of policy formulation inevitably promoted democracy and democratic values was a simplistic belief. In an attempt to democratize the Russian educational system, local schools were given the freedom to define their own ideas of individualism, set their own goals, determine their own structures, and control their own finances. Under such conditions a national consensus was unlikely to be achieved, inasmuch as innumerable interest groups were free to participate in the formulation of aims. Ethnic diversity within

Russia and the turning to virtues associated with Islam, Orthodoxy, Protestantism, Catholicism, and many other religious and parareligious faiths had implications for the formulation of the aims and goals of the individual development of children. Therefore it became evident that if alternative secular aims were to be formulated and agreed upon, a much more refined conceptual analysis would have to be carried on in order to arrive at acceptable concepts of individual development and democracy. For example, Soloveichik, a pioneer in the educational reform movement, had explored the meaning of democracy and spirituality and its implications for education. It was clear, however, that his rather simplistic analysis offered little direction to teachers in the classrooms of the state schools.

The steady and marked increase in religiosity in the Federation is now forcing educators and cultural leaders to thoughtfully and critically reassess traditional and emerging value systems and their sanctions. Ever present are the traditional Russian values having their origin in peasant life, the enduring contributions of the Russian intelligentsia and Russian Orthodoxy, and totalitarian socialist values now severed from their Marxist-Leninist roots. Steadily growing in influence are the broadly-based traditional Protestant values based on the belief that God and Christ are the universal and everlasting source of the Truth, Good, and Right. Still more worrisome to some Russians is the widespread acceptance by youth of Western liberalism's premises that values are rooted in each person's interpretation of what is good for the individual and that the right of the individual to make private decisions as to what is true, good, and right is inalienable (Vadim Sazonov, "A New Symbiosis," *Nezavisimaya gazeta*, August 12, 1993, p. 5). The fear is that relativism, subjectivism, and individualism, in the form of absolute individual autonomy will be accepted in place of the rigid Russian Orthodox tradition that has viewed moral life as a slavish conformity to the laws and rules formulated by an external authority.

Under Communist Party control, Soviet educators were forced to eliminate Christian values from the educational system, in spite of the fact that most of these values were universally accepted. Historically, sharp distinctions were not drawn by most Russian educators between religious and secular universal human values. Some early educators found the source of their secular values in peasant life; on the other hand, Marx and Lenin sought them in urban and industrial societies. In fact, the Central Committee of the Party, on July 7, 1954, issued a resolution directing all schools to "saturate the teaching of history, literature, and natural sciences with atheistic content." Many teachers fanatically embraced atheism and sought to impose it by force on the students in their classrooms (V. Kalinen, "Fanatical Atheists and Freedom of Conscience," *Izvestia*, March 5, 1991, p. 4). Even as late as 1993, many teachers still possess this worldview. In spite of the negative Soviet stand relative to organized religion, Muslims, Baptists, Seventh-Day Adventists, Roman Catholics, Buddhists, and Russian Orthodox were permitted to operate their religious institutions openly during and after World War II, but only under severe restrictions and close supervision.

One of the first legal acts adopted by the Russian Supreme Soviet was the 1990 Law "On Freedom of Religion," which radically transformed church-state relations in the Federation. The law extended total freedom and independence to all churches and religious associations. This set the stage for a rapid revival of Russian religious life. By 1993 some 9,000 religious associations of various types and faiths had registered. The Russian Orthodox church now has over 5,000 active dioceses, monasteries, religious education schools, brotherhoods, and parishes. The number of Muslim associations has increased from 382 in 1990 to 2,600 today. Protestants have 1,150 places of worship; Old Believers, 114; Roman Catholics, 84; Buddhists, 56; Jews, 43; and Armenian Apostolics, 22. In addition, there are many minor sects and associations, such as Mormon, True Orthodox, Russian Orthodox Abroad, Jehovah's Witness, Unification Church, New Apostolic, Bahai, Hare Krishna, Dukhobor, Molokan, and Mennonite. More than 200 missions, brotherhoods, and sisterhoods are registered (Alexandr Kudryavtsev, "The State Cannot Be Neutral," *Nezavisimaya gazeta*, July 30, 1993, p. 5. *CDPSP*, Vol. XLV, No. 30, 1993, p. 19).

Young people especially are the targets of missionary efforts of many of the Protestant and minor faiths. The

International Christian Union for Youth and Family has branches all over the country. Religious radio and TV programs feature sermons and lessons on the life of Christ and on the church and its charitable activities. Billy Graham sponsors a religious television campaign called "Home Study." Most religious groups maintain Sunday schools (Oxana Antic, "Developments in Church Life," *RFE/RL Research Report*, Vol. 1, No. 1, January 3, 1992, p. 4).

A militant group in the Russian Orthodox faith contends that, as the traditional Russian religious faith, it should have a privileged status and be declared the state religion. Archimandrite Isoif takes this position (V. Mikheyev, "The Orthodox Didn't Go to Vatican," *Izvestia*, No. 30, 1991, p. 3). He says that he is not opposed to Roman Catholic parishes where they exist, but "they must not be to the detriment of the Russian Orthodox church. We object to the creation of a parallel missionary structure on our canonical territory. Only by fighting against heresies and evil can we protect the seen and unseen Holy Rus and Holy Russian Orthodox" (Yuri Ageschev, "Antiorthodoxy," *Literaturnaya Rossia*, August 21, 1992, p. 5). Andrei Kuraev, a deacon of the Russian Orthodox church ("Religion in the USSR," *Moskovskie novosti*, No. 23, 1991, p. 1), reports that the Patriarch has proposed to the Supreme Soviet that the Russian Orthodox church be granted the right to teach religion in state schools.

Sheikh Ravil Gainutdinl, who serves as Imam-Khatyb of the Moscow Mosque, rejects the notion of an established Orthodox state religion (G. Bilyalitdinova, "There Should Be No Privileged Religion," *Pravda*, December 3, 1991, p. 3): "Most regrettably, our country still retains the ideology of the Tsarist Empire which believes that the Orthodox Faith alone should be a privileged religion, that is, the state religion. . . . During the past 70 years of Soviet power, attempts were made to destroy Islam or reduce its role as much as possible. In European Russia and Siberia, where there used to be more than 14,300 mosques, only 80 have been preserved, and we lost over 30,000 clergymen." On the other hand, Alexandr Prokhanov, editor of *Den*, has suggested a "Eurasian Concept" which combines the traditions of Orthodoxy and Islam to combat that he calls the "insidious Zionism, Catholicism and Masonry of the West."

Much more disturbing to all of the traditional and canonical religious organizations is the growing number of parareligious, pseudoreligious, and noncanonical faiths and cults, such as "The Transfiguration of Mother of God," "Tantrists," "White Brotherhood," "The Mother of God Center," and "Hare Krishna." These groups aggressively and energetically recruit young people, many of them teenagers. Some are registered, but their charters rarely disclose the true nature of their purpose and role in society. The "White Brotherhood" is not registered as a religious organization, but aggressively engages in religious activity. An article in *Megapolis Express* (Anna Politkovskaya and Maria Meshchanova, "Human Beings: Victims of Psychological Violence," No. 29, July 28, 1993, p. 7. *CDPSP*, Vol. XLV, No. 30, 1993, p. 15) describes the heartaches and pains such cults inflict on many mothers and fathers:

> Lyudmila: My son is 20 years old; he studied at a machine-tool-building technicum. He attended the Mother of God Center. More than once I've heard him talking about me and his grandmother: "Death to those two vipers." The Mother of God Center urges the breakup of the family.
>
> Nina: My 19-year-old son recently joined the White Brotherhood cult. Before that he was a student at the Institute of Transportation Engineering. Then he left home. The White Brotherhood urges saving oneself from "demonic parents."
>
> Tamara: My 22-year-old daughter, Irina, a former student at the Moscow Construction Engineering Institute, declared: "You are not my mother, my mother is the Mother of God. There is no point in studying at the institute—the world is ending soon anyway!"

Argument i fakty (No. 28, July, p. 12. *CDPSP*, Vol. XLV, No. 30, 1993, p. 15) reports that a "Committee to Save Young People from Pseudoreligion" is demanding that the Federation authorities take action to protect their children. Members of the committee contend that their sons and daughters are drawn into cults which teach strict asceticism and abstinence, fasting, and renunciation of parents and ordinary joys of life. They forbid watching television and reading newspapers and journals. Students abandon their studies and their homes so as to have time to beg for donations for the support of the cults. The "White Brotherhood" preached that the "Judgment Day" would come in December of 1993.

In Arkhangelsk, opposing religious groups took to the streets. Fliers were posted announcing the "White Brothers" had declared war on Orthodoxy. The "brothers" broke into Orthodox churches and urged everyone to renounce Christianity and accept their deity "Maria Devi." They warned that only five days were left until the end of the world. In turn, many Orthodox youth of Arkhangelsk vowed their loyalty to Orthodoxy and pledged to defend tthe faith of their forefathers by physical force if necessary (Andrei Zamula, "Religious Wars Expected in Arkhangelsk," *CDPSP*, Vol. XLV, No. 30, 1993, p. 16).

On July 14, 1993, with pressure mounting to stop the proselytizing activities of these cults and the many foreign missionaries, the Russian Supreme Soviet (Yuri Vasilyev, "Religion: Freedom of Conscience in Russia," *Nezavisimaya gazeta*, July 23, 1993, pp. 1–3. *CDPSP* Vol. XLV, No. 30, 1993, p. 19) adopted an amendment: "On Making Changes in and Additions to the Russian Law of Freedom of Religion." Article 14 of the amendment restricted or forbade religious activity on Russian territory by foreign organizations, their representatives, and foreign citizens invited to the Federation as ministers. Section II of the 1990 Law, on "The Right to Religious Convictions and Religious Activity," was deleted, which indicated that the Supreme Soviet intended to resort to legal regulation of all activities of religious associations. Also, Article 10 of the 1990 law, on "The Equity of Religious Associations Before the Law" was declared invalid. In its place was a provision requiring "Religious Affiliation" to be recorded on passports, birth certificates, marriage certificates, marriage licenses, and military registrations. The right to hold atheistic convictions was deleted from the Law on "Freedom of Religion." Still to be decided was whether foreign religious associations, after state accreditation, could engage in charitable activities. It was clear that the aim of the new law was to put a stop to religious conversions of

Russians by foreign missionaries and to all activity of parareligious cults.

These amendments to the "Law on Freedom of Religion" received the backing of Patriarch Aleksei II of Moscow and "All Russ," who firmly believed that they provided "unshakable spiritual freedom for every Russian citizen and the right of a person to chose a religion and worldview." He affirmed: "We Orthodox Christians are simultaneously convinced that this choice must not be imposed from without, especially by taking advantage of our people's difficult material situation or through flagrant pressure on the individual that deprives him of his God-given freedom" (ibid.). On the other hand, Christian evangelical groups in Russia and the West protested that these restrictions were a serious barrier to religious liberty, a hindrance to the prospect for democratic development in Russia, and at variance with international agreements on human and civil rights and freedom.

Sergei Kurginyan, president of the Experimental Creative Center Corporation (Sergei Kurginyan, "Counteraction," *CDPSP*, No. 40, 1992), supported the ban on foreign religious missionaries: "The primary task is to defeat the forces that are deliberately and ruthlessly pursuing a program for the destruction of the Russian state and society." He opposed the movement in Russia to establish a "New World Order" founded on "Universal Human Values" and "Human Rights." He believed that these "Universal Values" prioritized extreme rationalism and positivism, while "Human Rights" proclaimed the absolute sovereignty of the individual. In his view, an alternative concept was that of an individual who was capable of incorporating the principles of his own historical ancestry, namely, the concept of personalistic *sobornost*. He believed that the general spirit of Russian community was capable of reconciling "unity with individual freedom" and creating a "lofty religious synthesis of the mystical and historical religions." This priority, he asserted, would bring to Russia real democracy and a "New Jerusalem."

Alexandr Kudryavtsev, head of the Russian Ministry of Justice's Department for the Registration of Religious Associations (op. cit., p. 19) agreed that the 1990 Law On Freedom of Religion was unrealistic under the prevailing unstable conditions: "One cannot agree to the state being 'neutral' in matters of freedom of religion and convictions. It cannot be neutral if the individual's rights are being flouted and the morals and health of the rising generation are being destroyed." Consequently, the Ministry of Justice must restrict uncontrolled missionary activity and proselytism while guaranteeing religious organizations the right to establish international contacts and invite fellow believers from abroad to serve or preach in the Federation on a permanent or temporary basis.

All of this raised some teasing questions for Alexandr Asmolov, the Russian Deputy Minister of Education, who believed that the state schools should teach children about religion and the "Universal Values" in an effort to return the country to God. To this end, he entered into a five-year contract with CoMission, an organization of some eighty American missionary and other evangelical societies, to teach Russian teachers Christian ethics, the values that Jesus taught, and how to live them in a secular society. But their instructors were warned to refrain from proselytizing and converting. Besides teaching values to Russian teachers in four-day seminars, they also agreed to demonstrate methods of teaching about religion without indoctrinating the students. This created some problems inasmuch as many of the CoMission instructors believed that "to act like Jesus and live his values, each person has first to accept and have faith in Him." They frequently showed the film "Campus Crusade for Christ," with its message of personal commitment to Jesus as Savior and Lord. Asmolov invited other religious groups to prepare teachers to teach the course "Christian Ethics and Morality: A Foundation for Society," but none accepted ("Iisus Khristos Loves You," *Newsweek*, January 4, 1993, p. 5).

Still to be interpreted and applied by the educational establishment and the government bureaucracy are the provisions of the December 1993 Constitution that state that "everyone is guaranteed freedom of conscience and freedom of religion, including the right to profess any religion as an individual or in conjunction with others or not to profess any with them. Everyone is guaranteed freedom of thought and speech." The new Constitution also states that "propaganda agitation that instigates social, racial, national, or religious hatred or enmity is not permitted. Propaganda of social, racial, national, religious, or linguistic superiority is prohibited."

Democratic Freedom and Westernization

Since great stress is placed on developing and nurturing democracy and democratic values in Russian society and in view of the trend in the Federation to interpret individualism in terms of nationality and ethnicity rather than in terms of democracy, the characteristics of a "good democrat" and the goal of forming the "Democratic Man" need to be endlessly debated. Given the present ethnic, nationalistic, and linguistic diversity, securing agreement upon a common set of new and all-embracing educational aims for the entire Federation may prove to be a very difficult and frustrating task.

Every effort is being made in the schools of many of the national republics and regions of the Federation to promote feelings and attitudes of national identity and patriotism. Instilling nationalism itself is a major aim in some of the schools. Moreover, the concern of many educators is that too much emphasis is being placed on the individual in the educational process, while the traditional communal spirit that can be traced back to the years before the October Revolution is being neglected. They are convinced that some common bonds and communal ties are best cultivated in childhood by the schools. Therefore, they maintain that Russian educators should identify and agree upon what these relationships should be and how they should be promoted by the schools.

Many conservative educators are concerned that Russia is seeking to acquire the end products of Western liberal political culture without experiencing the intervening processes of evolution and inner understanding. Rather than adopting Western ideas and institutions, A. Migrayan believes the Federation should envision social and political forms rooted in Russian traditions and those presently unforeseen ("The Long Road to the European Home," *Novy mir*, No. 7, July 1989, p. 166).

Still another concern is that Western educators are imposing their concepts and models of education upon Russia. This is the position taken by Sergei Kurganov ("Will Washington Teach Us Russian? Or What Makes Russia Different from Mozambique?" *Uchitel'skaya gazeta*, No. 41, 1991, translated by Ben Eklof): "I am profoundly disturbed by the intellectual level of the projects proposed by our Western Colleagues (with a few exceptions). . . . Time will pass and then our society will want to have its own schools." Kurganov firmly believes that "our scholarship and practice in education, concentrated in a small number of laboratory schools, is roughly a generation ahead of Western pedagogical thought." The schools to which he refers are those established in Moscow, Ufa, Krasnoyarsk, and Volgograd by one of Lev Vygotsky's pupils, Academician Vasily Davydov. Instructional materials in reading, writing, and arithmetic are being developed, not merely to promote skills and abilities, but to master the rudiments of theoretical reasoning and scientific understanding, as well as the capacity for independent, creative thinking. Furthermore, he maintains that "the Bakhtinian conception of twentieth century culture, developed by Bakhtin's Russian followers, has never been fully understood and applied in the West."

Kurganov believes that the Moscow philosopher V. Bibler, who treats dialogue as the core of contemporary thought, has created a model of dialogue education unique to Russia and that Western educators should take note of it. Moreover, he contends the authorial schools have no equivalent in the West: "Young, open-minded school directors have nurtured new educational approaches" in such institutions as the Davydov and Repkin Development School, the Shulesko School, the Tolstoyan School, the Zhedek School of Development Instruction, and the Tubelsky Self-Definition School. Finally, he cites the Isak Froumin School of Krasnoyarsk University in Siberia. Founded in 1987 as State School No. 106, it is a school laboratory with 1,700 students. Based on Lev Vygotsky's cultural-historical concept of psychic development, its educational program aims to socialize youth and develop children's ability to engage in critical thinking. Games are transformed into various cultural forms involving music, art, and acting, and a vast range of experimental teaching programs are under the direction of Academician V. Davydov of the Russian Academy of Education and Viktor Bolotov of the Russian Ministry of Education.

The Russian Academy of Education

It is true that under the totalitarian rule of the Communist Party most of the leading figures in the USSR Academy of Pedagogical Sciences and the USSR Ministry of Education were politically very conservative. Irene Khankasava ("Academic Theater or Pedagogical Drama," *Rossiiskaya gazeta*, January 11, 1992, p. 2) went so far as to assert that "they were true reactionaries." Nevertheless, it is true that in spite of the ideological restraints of those years some of the academicians and researchers did cooperate with progressive principals and teachers in introducing innovations in special and experimental schools.

An interesting example of the viciousness of post-Soviet education politics is found in the demise and transfer of the APS to the Russian Academy of Education. The sequence of events was precipitated by Yeltsin's decree of October 1991 declaring that All-Union organizations existing on the Russian Federation territory after December 1991 would no longer be financed by the Russian government. In November, the government proposed that the APS be transferred temporarily to the Russian Ministry of Education until its future status could be determined. The directors and representatives of the institutes in the APS and the three research institutes of the Russian Ministry of Education met to explore options for reconstruction. Each of the institutes held staff meetings to decide if they wished to move temporarily to the Ministry; sixteen of the twenty institutes agreed to move. For example, the Institute of Theory and History of Education agreed to make the move. Boris Gershunsky, director of the Center of Education for the Future, was elected chairman of the advisory committee representing the staff members of all the institutes of the APS.

The advisory committee recommended the establishment of an autonomous Russian Academy of Education. This led to Decree No. 58 on December 19, 1991, establishing the Russian

Academy of Education. *Uchitel'skaya gazeta* published part of the text of the decree, which was fully known only to a few educators. Later, Yeltsin's Decree No. 70 of December 26 placed the APS temporarily under the Russian Ministry of Education. Four directives were set forth: (1) to honor the request by the general assembly of staff members of the APS to become the Russian Academy of Education, supported financially by the Russian Federation; (2) to disband the APS and establish in its place the Russian Academy of Education, with its own structure, organization, and elected academicians; (3) to name an organizing committee of "founding academicians" who would determine the structure of the constituent institutes and departments; and (4) to appoint for life, without salary, sixty full "academicians" and ninety "corresponding members."

A. Petrovsky, a psychologist and APS academician, was named chairman of the organizing committee. In January of 1992 the names of the twenty-eight founding academicians were made known; among them were former APS academicians Petrovsky, V. Davydov, V. Kostomarov, and N. Nikandrov. Also named were a number of leading figures from institutions of higher learning and the Russian parliamentary education committee. The Russian Minister of Education Dneprov and B. Gershunsky were selected. Many of the others appointed were clearly regarded by the organizing committee as educational innovators worthy of such high honor. S. Soloveichik, who led the education media attack in 1987–88, and two school principals, Yambourg and Tubelsky, made the list. It appeared initially that the radical reformers had taken possession of the Russian Academy of Education.

The small number of former APS Academicians (six out of twenty-eight) named to the RAE was in sharp contrast to the transformation brought about at the USSR Academy of Sciences, as ordered by the January 24, 1990, Russian Supreme Soviet Decree "On the Creation of an Academy of Sciences of the Russian Federation and the Election of Its Membership." A year later, on January 15, the Russian Supreme Soviet established the Academy of Sciences and on March 25 announced the names of an organizing committee to draw up its rules and select its original members. The failed coup accelerated the process, and on August 23 Gorbachev granted the USSR Academy of Sciences full autonomy and ownership rights to state property under its control. In October the Academy abandoned its All-Union status and, by presidential decree, on November 21 became an entirely new Russian Academy of Sciences, with a large number of former academicians being elected. The chairman of the Russian Supreme Soviet, R. Khasbulatov, was elected a corresponding member and the chairman of the Supreme Soviet's Committee on Science and Education, V. Shorin, was made a full member.

The transformation process of the APS and the victory of the radical reformers did not go unchallenged. A very vocal and well-organized group of former academicians and staff members of the APS refused to accept the reconstructed RAE and appealed to Supreme Soviet Deputy Shorin to have the entire newly elected membership dismissed and its recommendations ignored. Shorin, as chairman of the Supreme Soviet's Committee on Science and Education, agreed that more rigorous criteria should be established as a basis for selecting the founding members of the RAE. An appeal was sent to First Vice-Premier Burbulis, a former professor, to investigate the matter. Those who were incensed by the arbitrary procedures used in appointing the founding academicians mounted a write-in campaign demanding that all founding academicians should meet the criteria of having the highest academic degrees and demonstrated research ability.

In January, Burbulis agreed to disband the original organizing committee, withdraw the names of the founding academicians, and delay the appointment of heads of institutes and departments until the RAE was in place. The thirteen members of the newly appointed organizing committee all held academically recognized degrees, were successful researchers, and represented a wide range of disciplines. They were officially recognized as the founding academicians of the Russian Academy of Education. Of the thirteen members, three were nominated by the Russian Ministry of Education (a notable omission was Dneprov), two by the Russian Committee for Science and Higher Education, one by the Russian Academy of Sciences, one by pedagogical universities and institutes, and two by general education schools. A significant presence on the committee were two nominees of the Russian Academy of Sciences who had not been on the first committee. Vladimir Shadrikov, a psychologist, former acting-president of the APS, USSR Minister of Education, and currently Deputy Minister of Higher Education of the Russian Federation and Victor Matrosov, rector of the Moscow Pedagogical University, were appointed to serve on the organizing committee of founding academicians. Notable omissions from the organizing committee were Soloveichik and the two school principals, suggesting that their appointment had been political.

Decree No. 225 of April 7, 1992, directed the founding academicians to determine the structure, budget, and mission of the RAE. The Academy was granted complete independence from the Ministry of Education. Academicians of the APS, who lived in the Russian Federation were given the option of continuing with the title of Honorary Academician of the APS, with a salary of 350 rubles for life, or they could become Honorary Academicians of the RAE for life, but without salary, as was the true of all RAE academicians.

The decree of April 10, 1992, provided for the election of twenty-seven additional academicians and seventy corresponding members. Councils of each of the Academy's institutes and those of the Ministry of Education were directed to submit the names of their nominees for academicians, together with their qualifications. To be elected by the committee of founding academicians, nominees had to receive at least a majority of the votes and, of these, the twenty-seven receiving the highest number of votes cast were elected academicians. If not elected as academicians, the nominees would be eligible for election as corresponding members.

On February 24, a number of militant academicians of the APS, headed by its vice-president, Razumovsky, who had not been named on either of the organizing committees, challenged the authority of the founding academicians to establish the RAE. Ignoring their protests, President Petrovsky appointed N. Nikandrov, former secretary of the APS, and V. Davydov, a noted psychologist, as vice-presidents. N. Nechayev, who had served as head of the Department of General Education of the USSR State Committee for Public Education under Shadrikov, was appointed Secretary. At this point, Razumovsky resigned as vice-president of APS and became a senior researcher in one of the institutes.

The decree of April 28, 1992, set forth details for holding further elections of academicians. On June 4, the thirteen founding academicians met and agreed on the structure of the RAE, its institutes, their directors, and departments. The first round of elections took place on June 12 for the twenty-seven academicians and fifty-three corresponding members. The RRAE was officially recognized as an autonomous institution in July 1992.

Over the years, leading figures in the APS like Kairov, Khvostov, Goncharov, Markushevich, Kostamarov, and Zubov had international reputations. They were elected for their academic achievements and not merely as a reward for their loyalty to the Party. With the new structure and election of academicians to the RAE, however, Shadrikov for one feared that the RAE had become more of a club, somewhat like the US Academy of Education. Shadrikov preferred a traditional Academy similar to the Russian Academy of Science.

The newly elected founding academicians of the RAE met in July 1992 to decide upon the composition of the governing Presidium. Four executive officers and sixteen members were elected. The Presidium then announced its central administrative structure and the institutes that would constitute the RAE. Appointments of the directors and the acting directors of the institutes were approved.

Officers: President—Arthur V. Petrovsky, psychologist

Vice-President—Vasili V. Davydov, psychologist
Vice-President—Nikolai D. Nikandrov, educational historian
Secretary—Nikolai N. Nechayev, psychologist
Members: Levon O. Badalyan—Russian University of Medicine
Igor V. Bestuzhev-Lada—Institute of Social Forecasting
Genadii A. Bordovski—Russian Herzen Pedagogical University
Andrei V. Brushlinski—RAS Institute of Psychology
Rolan A. Bykov—Center for Children's Cinema and TV

Boris S. Gershunsky—Institute of Theoretical Pedagogy
Vitaly I. Goldansky—Institute of Chemical Physics
Eduard D. Dneprov—Russian Ministry of Education
Victor L. Matrosov—Moscow Pedagogical University
Nikolai D. Podufalov -Krasnoyarsk State University
Vladimir D. Shadrikov—State Committee on Higher Education
Michail P. Schetinin—Krasnodar Center for Child Personality

Five divisions of the RAE were responsible for research activities.

Division of Philosophy of Education and Theoretical Pedagogy
Division of Psychology and Development Physiology
Division of Education and Culture
Division of Vocational Education and Professional Education
Division of Research for Primary, Secondary, and Higher Schools.

Most of the research institutes are located in Moscow; others are in Kazan, St. Petersburg, Tomsk, Novosibirsk, and Krasnoyarsk.

The RAE institutes and research library are listed as follows.

1. Institute of Theoretical Pedagogy and International Research in Education
2. Psychological Institute
3. Institute of Developmental Physiology
4. Institute of Development of Personality with four Research Centers of Preschool Education, Aesthetics Education, Social Education, and Family and Children Education
5. Institute of Educational Innovations
6. Institute of Correctional Pedagogy
7. Institute of General Education
8. Institute of Vocational Education
9. Institute of Teaching Aids
10. Institute of Secondary Specialized Education in Kazan
11. Institute of Higher Education
12. Institute of University Teacher Training
13. Institute of Administration and Economics of Education
14. Institute of Adult Education in St. Petersburg

15. Institute of Development of Schools in Siberia, Far North, and Far East located in Tomsk
16. Institute of Informatics located in Novosibirsk
17. Institute of Development of Higher Education and Retraining of Workers located in Krasnoyarsk
18. Institute of Applied Psychology located in Novosibirsk
19. Institute of Vocational-Technical Education in St. Petersburg
20. Ushinski State Education Library

Structurally the Russian Academy of Education resembles the former APS. The Institutes of Preschool Education, Aesthetic Education, and Upbringing of Children have been merged into an Institute of Development of Personality with the four Research Centers of Preschool, Social, Aesthetics, and Family and Children Education. The Institute of Defectology is now the Institute of Correctional Pedagogy. The Institutes of Curriculum and Methods, Labor Training, and National and Bilingual Education have been absorbed by the Institute of General Education. The Academy no longer sponsors the fourteen experimental schools with over 11,000 students. Boris Gershunsky serves as the director of the reorganized Institute of Theoretical Pedagogy and International Research in Education, which has been downsized to four departments.

1. Department of Philosophy of Methodology of Pedagogics—Laboratory of Philosophy and Educational Forecasting
   - Laboratory of Methodology of Pedagogy and Interdisciplinary Research
   - Laboratory of Theoretical Problems of Didactics—Laboratory of Theoretical Problems of Upbringing
   - Laboratory of Theoretical Problems of Educational Theory and Practice
2. Department of Comparative and International Research in Education
   - Laboratory of Innovative Processes in Education in the States of the Former USSR
   - Laboratory of the Study of World Experiences in Education and Pedagogical Sciences
   - Section of International Projects in Education

3. Department of History of Education
   - International Center for Methodology of Historical Research
   - Laboratory of History of Education in Russia
   - Laboratory of the History of Education and Pedagogical Sciences Abroad
4. Department of Theory and Practice of Educational Informatics
   - Laboratory of Educational Informatics
   - Office of Publications

The monopoly of the All-Union Ministry of Education and the All-Union Academy of Education over the schools and educational research activities came to an end with the demise of the APS in December 1991. The institutes with greatly reduced budgets are forced to supplement their revenue by competing in the open market with other private research bodies for grants and research projects proposed by federal, republic, regional, and local educational authorities. This is a first step in introducing market competition into the education arena. Many of the research reports of the institutes of the RAE are not published due to the lack of demand for them as well as the shortage and high cost of paper. Unfortunately, far too many teachers continue to have a low opinion of RAE research activities and believe that all too often they are irrelevant to the problems and concerns of classroom teachers.

A great number of nonstate research centers have been established which are staffed by energetic, enterprising, and professional young people, to name just a few: the Academy for the Development of Education, which is sponsored by the Moscow City Department of Education; the Research and Development Center of Creative Pedagogy; the Research Center "New School"; the Independent Institute of Child Upbringing; the International Academy of Self-Improvement; and many others. Their directors anticipate and respond very quickly to the demands and needs of the education establishment. When research proposals are announced these entrepreneurs immediately form small temporary groups made up of teachers, principals, professors, researchers, and other experts in the hope of being awarded research contracts. They operate with a high degree of flexibility in management and organization, which enables them to focus on urgent and pressing theoretical and practical problems in education. Their workshops, seminars, and simulations attract many teachers and principals; they provide a vast array of professional materials, tapes, and visual aids. Since the RAE and the research laboratories in higher pedagogical institutions do not possess the flexibility and staff resources with the needed expertise, they frequently lose out in the competition for research projects.

Still another innovation is the number of international academies that undertake research related to the problems and needs of Russian teachers in the former republics of the Soviet Union (CIS). With the disintegration of the Soviet Empire, many of the nonnational as well as the national educators in these republics wish to continue links with Russian educators with whom they previously had professional relations. The International Academy of Pedagogy in Moscow, for example, reaches out to serve young Russians in the CIS who wish to pursue higher education courses taught in the Russian language. This Academy has affiliations with many of the national institutions of higher education located in the CIS and offers on-site and correspondence courses qualifying their students for academic degrees. In March 1993, *Uchitel'skaya gazeta* published the charter of a proposed nonstate International Academy of Pedagogical Sciences established by some of the academicians of the former USSR Academy of Pedagogical Sciences, Russian teachers, and professors residing in the CIS.

Prelude to the Law on Education in the Russian Federation

Minister of Education Dneprov believed that educational systems in all civil societies should be guided by a basic and comprehensive education law. Therefore he took the initiative in developing a legal framework for the decentralized, differentiated, and open-ended system that had evolved in the Federation over some three years of sovereignty. He was quite frank in admitting that the points of departure in the process of legislating the "Law of the Russian Federation on Education" were: the February 1988 Plenum on Education called by the Central Committee of the Communist Party of the Soviet Union; the pioneering work of the USSR State Committee for Public Education; the recommendations of the 1988 Congress of Education Workers; the Declaration on the State Sovereignty of the Russian Federation; and the Declaration of Russian Independence. While Yeltsin wrestled with the need to dismantle the old Soviet economic and political system, Dneprov pressed vigorously ahead to secure legislation dismantling the old Soviet educational system.

In order to overcome the many contradictions and respond to the needs of the diverse geographic regions, an analysis was made of the previous USSR education decrees and statutes, the Federal Treaty of Russia, the Russian Constitution, the basic laws of the national republics of the Federation, and the orders issued by the autonomous entities, provinces, territories, and the federal cities of St. Petersburg and Moscow. Furthermore, it was proposed that the law should take into account the major changes that had occurred in the social, economic, spiritual, and political spheres of society, as well as the new role of the individual in an emerging democratic and free-market environment.

In drafting the proposed law, Dneprov held many consultations, conferences, and meetings with various interest groups, government bodies, and the Supreme Soviet's Committee on Science and Education chaired by Vladimir Shorin. When the Ministry's draft law was submitted to the Supreme Soviet's Committee on Science and Education, it was expected that the committee would approve it with minor revisions. Instead, the ensuing legislative process took a nasty and acrimonious turn. Shorin asserted that his committee had the constitutional right and duty to write the final version of the law. Furthermore, Shorin challenged Dneprov's authority to issue educational decrees without processing them through his committee.

Dneprov, as Minister of Education, was equally insistent that the staff members of the Ministry were best qualified to draft education decrees and the proposed law, allowing, of course, for minor revisions by the Supreme Soviet's Committee on Science and Education. Dneprov's position was buttressed by Yeltsin's concept of presidential rule, which had been approved by the Russian Supreme Soviet in the spring of 1991 soon after the declaration of the Russian Federation's independence. Yeltsin's concept of the separation of the legislative, executive, and judicial branches greatly expanded and strengthened the power and authority of the president of the Federation and his ministers.

When Dneprov joined Yeltsin on his return flight from Washington to Moscow in May 1991, he convinced the newly elected President Yeltsin to issue Decree No. 1, "On Priority Measures to Promote Education" (*Uchitel'skaya gazeta,* June 11, 1991, p. 1). Decree No. 1 acknowledged "the exceptional significance of education in promoting Russian cultural, intellectual, and economic potential" and accorded "priority status to education." The decree directed the Russian Ministry of Education to submit to the Russian Supreme Soviet by the end of 1991 a state program for the development of education in the Federation. It also called for the establishment of an education fund to provide the financial support for nonstate educational institutions. The decree specifically stated that in the "structure of executive power in the RSFSR, provision should be made for direct subordination of the official structure of educational governance to the office of the President of the RSFSR" (p. 1). By subordinating the structure of educational governance to the Office of the President, the stage was set for an ongoing power struggle between Shorin and Dneprov.

In rejecting the proposal for a purge of the *apparatchiks* and *nomenklatura* from the educational establishment, Yeltsin agreed to preserve the national territorial integrity of the Federation and to orchestrate a peaceful transition to a democratic form of government and education. When power was transferred from the Communist Party to a loose coalition of democrats and reformist *apparatchiks* in the Russian Federation, Dneprov assumed that he had the authority and power to introduce radical reforms. However, power in the education establishment is a complex mechanism that calls for binding together in tightly knit interaction the rank-and-file of teachers, school administrators, and interest groups on the national republic, regional, and local levels. Unfortunately Dneprov was never successful in effecting this kind of power to complete what he termed "The Fourth Reform of Education."

To his credit, however, Dneprov put together a well-intentioned educational reform program and a draft of the law that was committed to achieving the larger goals of decommunization, deideologization, decentralization, destatization, demonopolization, democratization, differentiation, humanization, and freedom. But within the education establishment, there existed a division of power between the "old guard," "opportunists," "reformist *apparatchiks*," and "democrats," all competing for authority and power. Dneprov's strategy in striving for a democratic system of education was to isolate, as much as possible, those who stood in the way of overcoming the remnants of totalitarian structures and practices. However, the longer he remained as Minister of Education and the more criticism of his reform efforts mounted, the more time the opposition had to unite in preparation for his removal as the driving force behind the radical reforms and author of the draft law. To make matters even worse, Yeltsin was unable to hold together his radical reformist supporters to provide a united front for innovation and change in the education establishment. In the final months leading up to the enactment of the "Law of the Russian Federation on Education," the feud between Shorin and Dneprov became increasingly heated, with Shorin calling for Dneprov's removal as Minister of Education and demanding that Academician V. V. Davydov, a leading reformer and world authority on psychology, be removed as one of the founders and as vice-president of the Russian Academy of Education.

The Law of the Russian Federation on Education

After many revisions and amendments, the law was finally approved by the Russian Supreme Soviet on May 22, 1992, and signed into law by Yeltsin in July. Dneprov had hoped for a law which would regulate only the most general aspects of policy and administration. What he received was an extremely detailed and legalistic document. The new law invalidates all of the decrees, laws, and orders of the national republics and regional entities that run counter to its provisions.

The adoption of the law has the effect of inhibiting the forces of centralization and encouraging regionalization and localization in education by mandating three curriculum components: federal, regional, and local. The federal general education component is compulsory for all schools in the Federation, and its successful completion is required to receive a diploma. The rest of the curriculum content is delegated to republic, territorial, provincial, and local education authorities. No longer do regional and local elites have to fight the federal ministry for rights to determine their curriculum content. This principle of designating three curriculum components was established in 1990 by the USSR State Committee for Public Education but was never implemented because of the disintegration of the Russian Empire. By laying down the boundaries of responsibility, the law protects the educational system from being adrift as the political tensions between the executive and legislative branches and the Center and regions escalate.

Transforming a totalitarian educational system into a democratic one that is in keeping with a market system and the noncommunist conditions of an independent state striving to become a democracy has been an extremely difficult task.

The monopoly of the state educational system had to be destroyed by establishing the right of independent, private, and religious schools to exist, as well as the right of students and parents to choose among the many different schools. Moreover, with the decolonization of the Soviet Empire, Russia had to develop its own national identity and institutions and at the same time protect the rights of its minority peoples. Hence the law had to be drafted to make certain that, in the future, political organizations, ideology, and other forms of "explicit socialism" could not capture the schools and educational administrative structures. The problem of "implicit socialism," on the other hand, presented a much more difficult challenge. Habits, traditions, attitudes, values, outlooks, and human behavior patterns implanted over a period of seventy years in an educational system are not easily legislated out of existence. It will take several generations before they can be eradicated.

The law declares education to be a fundamental, guaranteed, and inalienable right and recognizes that education has three different meanings in the Russian language. *Obrazovanie* refers to the formal teaching process, which in Western countries is called instruction or schooling. *Vospitanie* has to do with upbringing and the inculcation of moral and ethical values. *Prosveschenie* encompasses general enlightenment and personal cultural development. Traditionally the first two forms of education were the primary responsibility of the schools, whereas *prosveschenie* was primarily the responsibility of the community at large. In drafting the law, an attempt was made to bring the three together as an integrative process within the confines of the school.

Unlike previous Soviet educational practice, the law states that the first priority is teaching and upbringing—the "focused attention on personality, interests, and abilities of each individual learner—followed by a recognition of the needs of society and the state, in precisely that order." The law grants the state the right to define education in terms of a definite level of academic achievement and to confirm the attainment of defined learning goals with appropriate documentation. Hence the Russian Ministry of Education assumes responsibility for establishing educational, ethical, and cultural standards for all state and nonstate general, vocational, and professional educational institutions in all of the national republics and regions of the Federation.

The Russian Academy of Education and the Ministry of Education no longer hold a monopoly on the development of the Russian Federation's educational program. Instead, the law mandates that "the federal program for the development of education be worked out and modified on a competitive basis." Furthermore, once in every ten years the Ministry of Education must hold an open competition to redefine the state's educational standards. The latter is said to be necessary in order to preserve the integrity of Russia as a nation and the unity of the federal cultural and educational space. At the same time, the law recognizes the equality, independence, and self-determination of all titular and nontitular peoples and their right to further their own cultural, historical, educational, and ethnic traditions.

The humanitarian and humanistic goals of education in the Federation call for a curriculum that will reflect a concern for individual and community welfare, social reform, critical spirit, and cultural enlightenment. Reaching beyond knowledge-related goals, the school is to cultivate sensitive and democratic interpersonal relationships in the classroom and the entire life of the school. Democracy as a way of life in the sphere of education, as in all other domains of society, is deemed necessary. Excessive Russification and aggressive nationalism are discouraged.

The law provides for universal access to general education, but the age at which children are to be admitted is to be determined by each school's charter. A basic general education is made compulsory until the sixteenth birthday unless the requisite level of education is attained at an earlier age. Students fourteen years of age and over can be expelled for committing illegal acts or disruptive behavior. After the age of eighteen, a basic general education is pursued only by means of part-time study. Although vocational and professional education is free, first-time students must be admitted by competitive examinations. Families are given the right to choose among state and nonstate schools, and if they wish, they can opt for family, self-education, or external study. Education in the basic core subjects is free of charge whether in a state or nonstate school. But knowledge and skills taught beyond the required core are subject to payment by the parents. Grants to receive an education in nonstate general educational, vocational, and professional institutions are awarded by the state to individual students in proportion to the per student costs in state establishments. Political parties and religious associations are not to operate in public educational institutions or their administrative bodies. The USSR tradition of a secular education is to be preserved. General education schools are allowed to offer vocational and military training on an optional basis providing it is subsidized completely by outside agencies.

Each school's charter gives it the right to determine its own curriculum beyond the basic state-mandated general education core, its own testing program beyond the state requirement, and its own educational activities, teaching methods, textbooks, and internal assessment measures. Educational institutions may be established by federal, republic, regional, and local governments, native and foreign citizens, corporations, joint-enterprises, and voluntary and religious organizations registered on the territory of the Russian Federation. The law details the duties of national republics, territories, regions, and federal cities in carrying out the federal program in the sphere of education and their rights in defining and realizing their own educational programs that are not contradictory to the federal policies. Neither federal nor regional administrative authorities have the legal right to reach decisions independently as to which of the articles of the law to observe. The Ministry of Education is empowered to inspect any educational establishment and administrative office of education in connection with the fulfillment of the law.

Education authorities of local governments have the right to plan, organize, and manage all programs and activities that realize the federal plan of education. They are responsible for fixing the local budgets, constructing school buildings, and supplying equipment to the schools. The Russian Federation reserves the right to monitor the level of academic achievement by means of a state certification agency independent of the public school administration. And in an effort to make certain that state standards are met, the state has the right to bring suit against an educational institution if the state certification findings reveal that the graduates of a school are receiving inferior preparation. In such cases, the school can be subject to paying the cost of reeducating the graduates in other schools and possibly be subject to foreclosure.

The tradition of social protection is continued for those families requiring financial assistance during the period of compulsory education. Special education provisions are provided by the state for children with learning disabilities and outstanding talents. The latter can be granted special state scholarships for study abroad. The traditional right to receive a general basic education in the native language is guaranteed. In this case, however, all such accredited educational establishments, other than preschool, have to provide for the teaching of Russian as the second language. A range of other foreign languages may be taught if finances permit.

The federal government guarantees an annual budget allocation of not less than 10 percent of the national revenues in the support of education. It also guarantees that it will safeguard a corresponding amount in the budgets at all levels of government. These allocations are subject to indexation in accordance with the real rate of inflation. Various special tax concessions may be granted to encourage the further development of the Russian educational system.

All educational institutions have the right to conduct the income-generating activities stipulated in their charters. These may be: loans of basic funds earned by the school; leases and rents of properties; business operations in saleable goods and services; joint enterprises with other organizations; shares of stock in companies and promissory notes; and small factories to manufacture articles for sale. Various special tax concessions may be granted to businesses if they contribute to the further development of the Russian educational system.

Rights are guaranteed in specific sections of the law relative to social protection and upbringing of students, health care, responsibilities of parents, and working conditions of educational employees. The level of the average salary of education workers is set by the law. For professors and instructors in higher education the average salary must be twice the average earnings of industrial workers. For teachers it must not be lower than the average salaries of workers in industry. Additional allowances, rewards, and other incentives may be determined by each educational institution.

The law suffers from some major shortcomings. It is extremely legalistic and detailed. There is an abundance of slogans, concepts, and principles in need of clarification and definition. Deputy Minister of Higher Education Vladimir Shadrikov remarked: "Now that the Law has been legislated and signed by Yeltsin the difficult process lies ahead in interpreting and implementing its provisions." Moreover, there are some obvious contradictions in the Law. For example, Article 2 states, "Freedom and pluralism in education is to be guaranteed," and yet nonstate educational institutions, as alternative choices, are subject to severe regulations not applicable to state establishments. Nor does the law recognize that in the case of some of the national republics, having declared themselves sovereign states, their reentry into the Russian Federation will be on their own terms. Tatarstan, Chechnya, and Bashkortostan have established special relationships. Tuva's Parliament has asserted its right of self-determination up to and including separation from Russia. Chechnya has declared its independence. Many of the provinces and territories are demanding the same rights as the national republics of the Federation, and some are even declaring their sovereignty and independence from the jurisdiction of the Federal government. The Soviet of Vologoda Province, for example, has proclaimed itself a state within the Russian Federation. Once the new Constitution of Russia is adopted, no doubt the law will have to undergo an extended amendment process.

With general education now compulsory only until the sixteenth birthday, and the right of the school to expel students fourteen years of age and older for committing illegal acts or disruptive behavior, the number of school dropouts and criminal acts by minors is escalating (O. Karmaza, "Murderous Age," *Komsomolskaya pravda*, April 13, 1993, p. 8, *CDPSP*, Vol. XLV, No. 18, 1993, pp. 18–19). "Right now one of every three participants in a group crime is a minor, and one in every four extortionists is a teenager. . . . The number of criminals aged fourteen and fifteen has increased by more than 50 percent in the past five years." Compounding the problem is the drastic increase in the number of mentally ill teenage criminals. The director of the Mozhaisk Upbringing Labor Colony for youngsters aged fourteen through eighteen admits that almost 70 percent of them are mentally ill. "To this day, Russia does not have a single specialized treatment and rehabilitation institution for teenage law breakers who are mentally ill" (ibid).

Most juvenile criminals are sent to two types of special educational institutions, depending on their age (Andrei Baiduzhy, "Children Behind Bars," *Nezavisimaya gazeta*, March

31, 1993, p. 6. *CDPSP*, Vol. XLV, No. 18, 1993, p. 19). In Russia children eleven to fourteen years of age are placed in forty special upbringing-and-education institutions for boys and six for girls, while those youth fourteen and older are sent to special vocational-technical schools. Mostly they are retarded children who are not able to cope with the course offerings and are victimized by their peers. Adding to the problem, the economic crisis has forced the government to close some one-fourth of the special education institutions, with the result that there are not enough facilities to house juveniles who commit crimes. Without facilities of their own for juvenile criminals, the city and province of Moscow send their children who commit serious crimes to special schools in other regions of the country. However, the majority are lectured and warned to avoid similar offenses in the future and released to fend for themselves.

Under Soviet rule, there were local commissions on juvenile cases that had the authority to assign juveniles under the age of fourteen to special education institutions and regular vocational schools. These commissions were judged to have violated the "Rights of the Child" and no longer exist. Juvenile delinquents now come under the jurisdiction of courts of law. In September 1993 Yeltsin signed a decree "On Measures to Prevent Child Neglect and Juvenile Delinquency and on Protection of Minors' Rights" (Aleksei Chelnokov, "Problems of Teenagers," *Izvestia*, Sept. 10, 1993, p. 4). Unfortunately, there is a steady increase in the number of juveniles committing crimes, and at the same time, there is a shortage of special schools and special vocational-technical schools to care for them.

Deputy Minister of Education Asmolov admits that the crime rate for vocational-technical school students and dropouts especially has turned sharply upward since the schools are able to dismiss students for poor academic performance and misbehavior (Grigory Gleizer, "Crime Won't Go Down," *Izvestia*, August 20, 1993, p. 4. *CDPSP*, Vol. XLV, No. 33, 1993, p. 25). During the 1992–93 school year, over 80,000 pupils dropped out or were expelled from Moscow city schools. Asmalov maintains that these are not necessarily youth who are intellectually incapable of learning. In most cases, he says, they are victims of an educational system that is pedagogically incapable of teaching all children. Forty-five percent cited conflicts with teachers as the reason for dropping out of school; 38 percent said that they had been expelled; 24 percent left because they were doing poorly in their studies; and 23 percent left because they had taken jobs to supplement the family income. Although the schools now feel free to dismiss children for poor academic performance, behavioral problems, and mental and physical disabilities, the intellectual capacities of these students are adequate for the most part to perform school assignments. It is estimated that each year over 200,000 Moscow students fail to pass the competitive examinations to permit them to continue their general education upon completing the ninth grade. In the past, some of the dropouts from general education schools would enter vocational-technical schools, specialized secondary schools, and trade schools; but many of these institutions are now closed because enterprises refuse to support them. Most of those that still exist now select their students by competitive examinations. A few students enroll in night schools, but the majority take temporary jobs, roam the streets, or become involved in criminal activities. The number of street kids and homeless children increases each year. The Ministry reports that, of the some 400,000 pupils held in the same grade at the end of the 1991–92 school year, about one-third did not resume school the next year. Even more worrisome is the large number of students, although enrolled in classes, who skip classes to carry on outside business activities. "Low paid and harassed teachers are responsible for tracking down the truants" (Nick Holdsworth, "Fast Food, Hard Cash," *Times Educational Supplement*, August 13, 1993, p. 9).

Asmolov is convinced that a state program of psychological rehabilitation is needed for children and adolescents who have left school or are performing poorly in school. "We must not permit state schools (even the most elite) to limit the acceptance of children from their own microborough schools on any pretext. We must accept the fact that all children cannot be taught in the same way." Although Russian schools are being transformed into democratic, self-regulating, flexible educational institutions, Asmolov is convinced that "they must not allow the specialization or diversity of schools to reduce the opportunity for even a small proportion of our young people to complete their secondary education" (Gleizer, op. cit.).

Under Soviet rule the Young Communist League, Pioneers, and Octobrists were directly responsible for the leisure-time activities of teenagers. Unfortunately, most of the summer camps for city youngsters, hobby and sports groups, and pioneer palaces and clubs have been closed. Those that remain are private institutions; their fees are so high that most parents cannot afford to send their children to them. Unfortunately, the All-Russian Orthodox Youth Movement and the Union of Orthodox Fraternities do not have activity programs to take care of the out-of-school needs of children and youth. The primary concern of the Union of Orthodox Fraternities is one of identifying heretics, who are viewed as the "Servants of Anti-Christ," and propagandizing the "Grandeur of Russia" (Andrei Kurayev, "Why Did Not Orthodoxy Become 'Youth Religion?'" *Moscow News*, July 2, 1993, p. 15).

Supplementary Decrees and Laws on Education

In May of 1992 Yeltsin signed two decrees relating to education: "Additional Measures to Provide Social Protection and Incentives for Education Workers" and "Urgent Measures for the Economic and Social Protection of the Educational System." These decrees were in response to the demands of teachers that Yeltsin uphold the provisions of Decree No. 1, which mandated that priority be guaranteed in the education sector and pay raises be given to bring teachers to the average level in industry. Teacher committees in May 1991 threatened to strike and stage various collective actions in their demand that Decree No. 1 be implemented without delay (Inga Prelovskaya, "Teachers and Government on the Way to Compromise," *Izvestia*, May 16, 1992, p. 2).

Another draft law relating to education was legislated by the Russian Supreme Soviet in May 1992: "Protection of the Family, Mother, Father, and Child." This law restored on paper the priority of the family in the upbringing of children. It granted paid leaves to any member of the family to stay at home and care for one's child or children until the age of three. It proposed to pay a state benefit in an amount no lower than the minimum wage to a nonworking parent who was raising three children or a disabled child. The state was committed thereby to encouraging families to have children by providing social and financial support through state programs that were approved on the basis of the demographic situation at any particular time and place.

In April 1993 Yeltsin signed a decree: "On the Amounts of Social Benefits and Compensation Payments for Families with Children and Other Categories of Citizens" (Tatyana Khudyakova, "Benefits for Families and Children Increased," *Izvestia*, April 22, 1993, p. 1). The allowance of five times the monthly minimum wage is now paid upon the birth of every child. The social benefits and quarterly compensation payments to families with children have been constantly increased. And 1.5 percent of the monthly minimum wage is granted per day to each child enrolled at state general education and vocational schools.

All of these measures were in response to a drastic decline in the birthrate. In November and December of 1991 some 265,000 people were born in Russia, while 281,000 died. One year previously the figures were 309,000 and 269,000. In the city of Moscow in 1991 the number of deaths was one-third higher than the number of births (A. Frolov, "A Demonstration of Insight," *Sovetskaya Rossia*, February 11, 1992, p. 1).

The number of children with disabilities is on the increase and many school children have serious health problems. Many children do not have sufficient food or the right kind of food to eat. Consequently the incidence of illness among children increases sharply when they enter preschool institutions. By the end of the first year in school, over 50 percent of all children develop asthenia, which shows up in frequent headaches and in sleep and emotional disorders ("State Reports on the Condition of the Environment and the Population's Health," *Nezavisimaya gazeta*, October 7, 1992, p. 7).

Still another draft law "On the Situation with Respect to the Conscription Pool and Manning of the Russian Federation Armed Forces" evoked the rage of university students.

Traditionally, upon receiving internal passports at the age of sixteen, students were required to register at the district military enlistment office and be assigned a conscription registration number. Upon reaching the age of eighteen, they were subject to call-up for service. Once a call was issued the conscript could not leave the Federation. However, an increasing number of conscripts failed to appear at their draft boards. In spite of this, the draft law proposed to cancel draft deferments for regular students in higher educational institutions and to eliminate military departments in institutions of higher education except for some thirteen elite establishments ("New Entry and Exit Law," *Izvestia*, September 1, 1993, p. 5. *CDPSP*, Vol. 35, 1993, p. 19). Dr. A. Petrovsky, president of the Russian Academy of Education, and many other educators were quick to submit protests that under the proposed law conscription of such a large number of students would drastically undermine the country's intellectual potential (Valery Vyzhutovich, "Academic Alarm," *Izvestia*, November 5, 1992, p. 3).

Rather than reforming the military life style of conscripts to make it more attractive, the Russian Federation military command decided to expand the professional sector. As a result some 100,000 professional male and female soldiers are now serving under contract with their military pay ranging from 40,000 to 50,000 rubles a month. Finally, the Supreme Soviet amended the Law on Military Service ("On Military Duty and Military Service," *Izvestia*, May 20, 1993, p. 6) stipulating that specialized secondary, technical, and general secondary school students (in evening institutions) at the age of twenty, would be conscripted into the armed forces even though they had not completed their courses. Students enrolled in institutions of higher education that lacked state accreditation would no longer be deferred and would be subject to conscription. It was hoped that this policy would end the practice of many youths avoiding military service by enrolling in schools that had very easy entrance requirements.

Russian Ministry of Education in Disarray

At a conference in December 1993, the former Russian Minister of Education Dneprov characterized 1992 as the "most difficult year in the history of Russian schools (Ben Eklof, "The Most Difficult Year," *ISSE Newsletter*, Vol. 2, No. 1, 1993, p. 1). He pointed to the constant reshuffling at the top of the Ministry of Education, a campaign against Minister Dneprov himself, led by a faction in the Supreme Soviet's Committee on Science and Education, demoralization and flight from the schools by teachers, and a catastrophic budgetary situation. He failed to mention the problems the Ministry experienced in its relations with the "Wardship and Guardianship Center."

In an effort to prevent abuses, the Russian Ministry of Education established an agency known as "Children's Rights" to impose orderly procedures on international adoptions of children in the Russian Federation (Andrei Baiduzhy, "Children for Export," *Nezavisimaya gazeta*, April 29, 1993, pp. 1, 6. *CDPSP*, Vol. XLV, No. 17, 1993, pp. 19–20). Deputy Education Minister Saval Radmayev entered into agreements with foreign organizations engaged in arranging international adoptions. The Ministry assumed responsibility for processing all adoptions through the "Wardship and Guardianship Center" located in Moscow. "Strictly monitored by the Ministry of Education and directly accountable to local bodies, this and other centers were supposed to process international adoptions." Supervision by the Ministry was designed to prevent the sending abroad of children who might otherwise be adopted by Russian citizens.

In mid-November 1992, officials at the Ministry of Public Health and the Ministry of Education uncovered violations of adoption laws and the use of false documents. It was asserted that youngsters in children's homes had been hidden from prospective Russian adoptive parents so they could be given to international agencies. The prosecutor general's office and the Ministry of Education found that the director of the Ministry of Education's "Chief Administration for Social Protection of Children" had used false documents to send children from Moscow's children's homes to other countries (ibid.).

When the prosecutor general's office discovered that the Ministry of Education had received office equipment, fax machines, computers, cameras, and medical equipment from the foreign agencies in exchange for the Ministry's cooperation in adopting Russian children, all thirteen agreements concluded by the Ministry's "Children's Rights" office were cancelled. Later it was revealed that the Russian side had received $1,000 for administrative expenses for each child adopted.

It was generally agreed that the "Children's Rights" office as well as the Moscow city and regional "Wardship and Guardianship Centers" had fulfilled their responsibilities honestly and professionally. However, the Russian prosecutor general's office declared that the Ministry of Education had been derelict in monitoring the adoptive procedures and seeing to it that the adoptive laws were being observed. Since all of this happened on Dneprov's watch, he was held responsible for the actions of his staff members. On December 4, 1992, Dneprov resigned as minister of education and was appointed education adviser to President Yeltsin.

New Leadership in the Ministry of Education

In an interview published in *Uchitel'skaya gazeta* ("I Have Come to . . . ," February 16, 1993, p. 6) the new Minister of Education Eugene Tkachenko revealed that Dneprov had come to Sverdlovsk in September 1992 to offer him the post of first deputy minister but he did not accept until early November just weeks before Dneprov resigned as minister.

Born in 1935 in Omsk, Siberia, Tkachenko received a doctorate in technical science with a major in chemistry. For many years he served as a professor of vocational and technical education at the University of Sverdlovsk and was secretary of the Party committee at the university. Later he was named rector of Sverdlovsk Engineering Pedagogical Institute, which prepared teachers for specialized secondary vocational schools. No doubt this Sverdlovsk connection with President Yeltsin was a factor in his being appointed minister.

Tkachenko approaches the task of education reform with more caution than was the case with Dneprov. Two of his immediate concerns are to lessen the politicalization of the educational system and to encourage the use of teaching processes that will cultivate the desire to learn and meet individual needs. He accepts the curriculum changes introduced originally by the USSR State Committee for Public Education which mandated a federal, regional, and local component. The federal component, identical throughout the Russian Federation, assures a single educational space and the award of a standard diploma throughout the country. Instead of the traditional program of fourteen mandatory subjects in both the tenth and eleventh grades of the general education schools, the new curriculum is composed of eight broad fields, such as mathematics, natural and social sciences, and Russian language and literature. Within each field are a variety of subjects of which twenty hours are required and twelve hours are elective. Beyond this, six hours are optional for those who are willing to pay a fee and remain in school for a longer day. A somewhat similar experimental program is now being tried in the junior school (Andrei Baiduzhy, "Reform," *Nezavisimaya gazeta*, August 31, 1993, p. 6. *CDPSP*, Vol. XLV, No. 35, 1993, pp. 10–11).

The majority of schools in the Russian Federation are traditional general education institutions with a minimum of elective subjects. In many cities, there are five other types of general education schools.

1. Schools with mandatory, elective, and optional subjects
2. Schools with specialized subject profiles
3. Gymnasia and lyceums preparing for higher education institutions
4. Innovative and experimental schools
5. Private and religious schools

Some Russian educators criticize the categorizing of state schools as "general" or "elite." Tkachenko, however, defends this distinction by referring to the basic principle of Russian education as being that of "choice," which permits students to pursue an education in accordance with their interests and abilities. Larisa Piyasheva teaches in a private educational institution that is able to set its own rules and regulations, and in addition, admit its students in accordance with their wealth. "While having a number of advantages, the commercialization of education also has its flaws. I teach half-wit children of well-heeled parents." But she has gifted students as well (Victor Litvinchuk, "What Are the Schools Attended by Our Children Like?" *Sputnik*, September 1993, p. 4–5).

In addition to the federal component in all general education schools, regional and individual school components are permitted to encourage a revival of local self-awareness and culture. Although diplomas may be awarded in any of three languages, for example, Russian, Tatar, and Bashkir, the intent is to move toward bilingualism.

Tkachenko describes his style of work as one of "combining collegiality with tough democracy." By this he means encouraging discussion, weighing alternative variants, reaching decisions, and then carrying them into practice. The test, he maintains, is in the results. "I shall work in my own way, compromising when necessary, relying on specialists and different opinions and outlooks as a basis for projecting a core of strategic directions" (ibid.).

Although he supports many of the ideas and reforms introduced by Gennadii Yagodin and Vladimir Shadrikov of the USSR State Committee for Public Education and Dneprov as director of VNIK and later Russian Minister of Education, and he says that he respects Dneprov as a researcher, Tkachenko is opposed to destroying many of the features of the former USSR system of education that have evolved over the last seventy years. "There is much that is good and must be preserved" (ibid.).

Another major concern is that of developing a set of national achievement standards and measuring the performance of students in the various educational institutions of the Federation by constructing instruments to measure learning results in the basic general education core curriculum. Still another major concern is the development of a set of criteria for proper child development as a guide to curriculum construction and school activities.

Tkachenko believes that, in the teaching of Russian children, private and religious schools should be permitted to compete with the state schools, but that all state schools must be separated from the church. The history of religion can be taught in state schools and religious discussions can be conducted with the assistance of visiting scholars and church representatives. "But nothing beyond this."

Another concern is the need to interpret the Articles of the Law of the Russian Federation on Education and to carefully craft Ministry orders to carry out their provisions. And, finally, he is committed to continuing the development of a wide variety of experimental schools geared to the Federation's pressing social and educational problems and to the needs of students.

CHAPTER 13

The Reformed Russian Educational System

Most of the unique aspects of the common Soviet school that are regarded by the Communist Party as crucial to the creation of a New Soviet Man have been eliminated in the Russian educational system. The Russian school is changing from a unified eleven-year school system to one of differentiated school types, differentiated curricula, and differentiated teaching methods. The Russian state has voluntarily delegated to regional and local authorities many of its powers to educate and protect children. Military education is still offered as an elective. Socialist realism and Marxism-Leninism as the foundations of intellectual and moral education have disappeared. Little attention is given to polytechnical education, which was central to Soviet curriculum theory but was never successfully applied. Prohibitions and restrictions on bourgeois knowledge have been lifted; draconian constraints placed on the dissemination of religious knowledge no longer exist.

The Komsomol was disbanded as a Soviet organization in September 1991 and its property divided among the various republics and regional organizations. It was revived in the Federation in 1992 as the Russian Young Communist League under the leadership of Igor Malyarov and Mikhail Grachev and publishes a newspaper, *Bumbarash*. Likewise, the Pioneers continue to exist in some regions but under different names. However, the vacuum created by the closing down of the Party's youth movements is now partially filled by many new organizations such as the Boy Scouts and Union of Youth. Many of the national republics, regions, and cities have formed their own youth movements as have some of the newly created political parties. A national Council of Russian Youth Organizations coordinates the activities of many of these groups.

The Changing Russian School

The economic and political turbulence unfolding in the Russian Federation is having repercussions on the 67,000 state and over 500 officially registered independent schools. As for kindergartens and early childhood care, many parents are having to pay partial or full costs. Not more than 25 percent of preschool age urban children are enrolled in nurseries and kindergartens, very few of which exist in small towns and rural areas. In the past, many of the vocational and technical schools were sponsored and subsidized by enterprises and other kinds of businesses. About 60 percent of the vocational schools were in this category in the former Soviet Union. Many of these vocational schools have ceased operation. Vladimir Shadrikov estimates that the number of vocational students in Russia has gone from 329,000 to 66,000. As in many countries of the world, the extent to which vocational and technical training should be the responsibility of industry and business is a subject of ongoing discussion. Certainly it is paradoxical that, while the state is attempting to reduce its financial responsibility for educational costs, it is being forced to take on and develop more and more of the vocational and technical education programs.

The economic situation has been a decisive factor in persuading the Federation authorities to abandon by law the compulsory eleven-year schooling and replace it with nine years of compulsory education. Alevtina Fedulova, chairman of the Women's League and a deputy of the Russian Duma, is very vocal in her criticism of this change ("Our Movement," interview by Tatyana Khudyakova with Fedulova, *Izvestia*, December 2, 1993, p. 4. *CDPSP*, Vol.XLV, No. 48, 1993, p. 9). "I don't know another country that, having already established mandatory secondary education, would then take a step backwards and set the goal of a mandatory eighth-grade education." She claims that "this year alone, one million children were unable to attend kindergartens and nursery schools because they have been closed and their buildings sold to commercial structures, or because the cost of their services has gone up 30 to 50 times."

Most Russian educators believe that free education should be available at least up to the level of higher education. However, debates continue as to whether guaranteed free and compulsory general secondary schooling for all Russian youth, after the age of fifteen, can be adequately financed by the impoverished federal and local governments of the Federation. The mayor of Moscow is on record as saying that as a poor society Russia can't afford ten and eleven years of free education. Most schools in the Soviet Union were never very well maintained or equipped. Now, however, there is widespread evidence that far too many school buildings are in urgent need of repair and that instructional materials are in very short supply. Although the nine-year compulsory phase of the eleven-year school continues to function throughout the Federation, in many of the schools little incentive exists to follow the proposals of the innovators for reforming the teaching methods.

Insofar as Russian curriculum theory and practice are concerned, the basic knowledge universally found in educational institutions throughout the world continues to dominate the content of Russian general education schools and higher educational institutions but no longer must it be interpreted within ideological constraints. In practice the basic curriculum, together with a few elective subjects in most of the nine-year compulsory general education schools, continues to be encyclopaedic and compulsory for all students. Although part of the curriculum is now a school-level decision, only about 8,000 of the 67,000 Russian schools have radically revised their curriculum models, adopting modernized subject syllabi, and restructured themselves. However, many new subjects such as ecology and economics are finding their way into the curriculum.

The trend is to give students more choice in differentiated curriculum offerings and in total class load (See chapter 12.). Schools will be free to choose their own elective and optional subjects. For example, a maximum permissible class load for the last two years of schooling will be thirty-eight hours each week; and the minimum, thirty-two hours. Of these, only twenty hours will be required subjects for all students, twelve are elective, and six additional hours are purely voluntary for those who opt to remain longer in school each day. Hence, in the traditional eleven-year general education school, where the majority of students are enrolled, out of this diversity students will be able to choose subjects in accordance with their interests and abilities (Andrei Baiduzhy, "This Will Be A Historic Year for Russian Schools," *Nezavisimaya gazeta*, August 31, 1993, p. 6. *CDPSP*, Vol. XLV, No. 35, 1993, p. 11).

Curriculum reform is a step forward but many students are still doomed to academic failure and may well drop out of school unless the learning environment is drastically altered to provide sensitive and understanding teachers who are able to relate the subject content to the needs of children. Economic, political, and personal stress is making families and local communities less able to raise normal children. More and more students are coming to their classes without adequate food, clothing, housing, and medical attention. The number of families living below the poverty level is increasing.

Another problem is that textbooks and qualified teachers for many of the subjects all too often are not available. In the past most of the Soviet textbooks, syllabi, teaching methods, and school structures were for all practical purposes identical. Tkachenko claims that in the past two years the Russian Federation has printed 227 million textbooks with 87 titles, and about 50 percent of all textbooks in use are of the new type. But, he admits, that "it is impossible for even the most highly developed state to print in the twinkling of an eye the 400 million textbooks that we need" (ibid).

The Cultural Heritage Foundation, established by George Soros and Boris Raushenbakh, sponsored a competition to find replacements for old and modified textbooks and study aids. Over 1,200 school textbook proposals were reviewed by a committee composed of representatives from the Russian Federation Ministry of Education, the Russian Committee on Higher Education, and a presidential adviser. Reviewers narrowed the number of proposals to 400 and the authors were given subsidies to complete their books. The finished textbooks were evaluated and the best were printed in trial editions to be tried out in selected schools. Those that are well received by the teachers and pupils will be mass printed and distributed in the Russian schools (Otto Latsis, "Capitalist Soros," *Izvestia,* August 5, 1993, p. 5. *CDPSP,* Vol. XLV, No. 31, 1993, pp. 22–23).

The University of Western Ontario in Canada for the past two years has been consulting with a small group of Russian teachers–authors on the writing of a civic education textbook to replace that of Marxism-Leninism formerly used in the last two years of schooling. The first draft of the textbook was used in selected schools of Moscow for the 1993–94 academic year. The authors, editors, and publishers of the textbook are Russian professors and teachers working under the sponsorship of the Office of External Affairs and International Trade of Canada. The co-directors of the project are Natalya Voskresenskaya of the Russian Academy of Education and Douglas Ray of the University of Western Ontario.

Russian school courses, for the most part, do not provide knowledge that pupils can use in meeting modern societal demands imposed by present-day conditions in Mother Russia. Earning a living, participating in civic activities, assuming family life responsibilities, and carrying on leisure-time activities are just a few of the needs of children and adolescents that are largely ignored in most of the newly differentiated school types and differentiated curricula. On the other hand, there has been a reduction in the total hours allocated to science content from more than half the total school curriculum to about one-third. Conversely, the humanities are allotted about 40 percent of the total curriculum content.

Many of the proposals made by the USSR State Committee for Public Education in 1988–91 continue to have relevance for Russian education. The All-Union general education core component of the curriculum designed by the USSR State Committee has been rethought and revised in terms of the requirements and needs of the Federation, its national republics, regional, and local entities. However, the Ministry has expressed the need for a much larger Federation core than most of the regional authorities will accept.

In moving away from uniformity and catering to regional and ethnic differences and diversity, the Russian Ministry of

Education is searching for a common general education core curriculum appropriate for all schools and all children in the Federation, a definition of national standards, testing instruments to assess academic achievement, and procedures for accrediting the nation's schools. Each school, beyond the mandated federal and regional general education cores, has the right to determine its own local curriculum core content, quality standards, and methods of teaching.

It is unlikely that a strong body of opinion among teachers and administrators will favor a move toward a radical reconstruction of the traditional curriculum. Perhaps in the twenty-first century some aspects of radical curriculum change will be achieved by forces similar to those which led to reforms introduced in many Western countries after World War II.

In the upper grades the schools are not rushing to adopt integrated syllabi that bring the related individual disciplines into one course, but the Cultural Heritage Foundation textbook project is presently developing such textbooks in the hope that more integrated courses will be introduced in the schools. In the natural sciences, for example, these courses draw together the subject matter of physics, chemistry, and biology and relate them to modern living. The USSR State Committee for Public Education and the USSR Ministry of Education developed such syllabi in early 1990. They required careful selection from the mass of historical and traditional data found in each specialized area. However, the criteria that determine the content for the new upper grade syllabi in the Russian schools continue to be found in the logic of the disciplines and the natural environment.

The curriculum debates unleashed under *perestroika* continue as to the role and function of specialized profiles in mathematics-physics, biology-chemistry, humanities, foreign languages, social sciences, and even pedagogy and medical science in the last two years of the eleven-year school. Tradition serves to perpetuate the status of profiles that are taught in preparation for higher degrees. University academics insist that the integrated courses do not prepare students adequately to study in an institution of higher learning. Moreover, many of the teachers in the senior classes do not possess a sufficiently broad level of knowledge in all of the separate subjects to successfully teach integrated courses. For these reasons integrated courses are most likely to be found in the lower grades.

In School No. 1201, due to student demand and interest, the principal and teachers agreed to add for the academic year 1991–92 an economics profile to the existing science and humanities profiles. One of the courses, "Junior Achievement," was imported from the United States. The principal announced that for the 1992–93 academic year, those students in this profile who did not want to pursue the last two years of the physics, chemistry, and biology cycle could opt out. But during the summer word was received that the universities would not admit these students, even if they applied to enter the humanities or social science faculties. So the proposal was abandoned.

Students are legally guaranteed the right to enroll in any state school that has free places available at any time during the academic year and in any class. Regular eleven-year schools may offer in-depth course profiles in various areas of academic specialization together with several foreign languages, music, and enrichment subjects. Pupils may compete to enter any of the profiles offered in a school, and once admitted, they may determine their own pace and time frame for the mastery of the compulsory level of education. Moreover, an additional examination in any subject may be taken if the student believes the final year-end grade given by the teacher is too low.

Parents may transfer their children from an ordinary state school to an alternative state lyceum or gymnasium, but competitive entrance must be passed and a monthly fee paid for the courses that are offered beyond the basic state-mandated core. For the 1992–93 school year the fees ranged from 800 to 1,000 rubles per course. Class size is usually small enough for teachers to care for the needs of individual students. Many of the state lyceums and gymnasia are co-sponsored by private enterprises, institutes, and universities. The teachers employed in the lyceums, gymnasia, and in-depth courses usually have professional qualifications higher than those teaching the regular courses. Many of these instructors also teach courses in institutes and universities. It appears that principals, given a choice, are more likely to prefer differentiated school types than in-depth differentiated and individualized curricula in regular eleven-year schools.

Traditionally, vocational and technical schools provide another type of alternative education in specialized skills. Boris Gershunsky is one of many educators who is of the opinion that Russian vocational and technical schools need to undergo drastic reform to improve the skills of their graduates. The modernization of Russian enterprises demands a much higher level of vocational, technical, and general education for students. Consequently, many vocational and technical schools are refusing to accept nine-year dropouts; frequently admission is based on competitive examinations. In the past a small percentage of vocational school enrollment places was reserved for problem children. Commissions for Youth Problems at the local level reviewed the cases of such children and granted them permission to leave the regular state school early to enter vocational schools. Now these students are left to fend for themselves.

Still another alternative for students with special needs is enrollment in independent and religious schools. Admission to many of these schools is based on competitive examinations and the ability of parents to pay for extra services and special academic subjects. Although the federal government pays for the teaching of the basic compulsory core courses, fees are charged for all additional subjects and activities just as they are in state schools. They may take the name of lyceum, gymnasium, or college and be sponsored by individuals, churches, religious organizations, or private enterprises. The Christian Lyceum for the Humanities in Moscow has clergy from five denominations on its teaching staff. Two certificates of graduation are awarded for successful completion of course work, one for religious studies and one for general education. For those who wish to prepare for the clergy, there are four parallel denominational seminaries. The latest and most fashionable schools are the Kuban and Novosibirsk Cossack Institutes offering unique and intensive military courses.

Eduard Dneprov reported that 40 percent of the alternative schools stressed the humanities; 30 percent, physics and mathematics; 20 percent, chemistry and biology; 5 percent, religious orientation; and 5 percent, national heritage. However, as the market economy continues to develop so have special schools highlighting courses in economics, marketing, and management. For example, the Moscow Education Center is sponsored by several banks to prepare students in foreign languages and banking operations. Moscow Institute of Economics and Statistics and the Institute of International Business Statistics have rigorous competitive entrance examinations and extremely high tuition fees. The Moscow School of Economics is sponsored by the Russian-American Institute of Pedagogical Systems. It enrolls students in four articulated divisions from pre-school to the business college, which are described below (Yuri Shamilov, *IPS*, Moscow, 1993).

The Moscow School of Economics ABC (Ages 5–6)

> Upon leaving this school a child will be able to listen to, understand, and speak, as well as write and read Russian and English as native languages.

Comprehensive School (Ages 7–15)

> Individual teaching technologies are used in all grades. Students work at their own speed and own goals. Russian and English bilingual teaching materials.

Economics School (Ages 15–17)

> Twelve to fifteen students are in each of the tenth and eleventh grade classes. Basic academic classes are given plus macro- and micro-economics, marketing, finance, business principles, psychology of communication, etiquette, business ethics, business law, English, another foreign language, general and social psychology, and internship. Further studies in the US and Britain are encouraged.

Business College

> A three-year course leads to an International Certificate and a Bachelor's Degree. Students are encouraged to continue education at other institutions of higher education in economics, business administration, and law.

A major deterrent to the establishment of even more of the alternative independent and religious schools is the coexistence of hyperinflation. Tuition fees must be constantly increased and, even then, the income received may be insufficient to cover the mounting costs of operating the school. Another deterrent is the tradition of free education that continues to be deeply imbedded in the public psyche. For example, Tatyana Markulova (Jo Kearney, "Private Success," *Times Educational Supplement,* April 23, 1993, p. 21), a former member of the CPSU, established a private school in Novorossysk. She was denounced by her former colleagues as a traitor to Lenin's socialist cause, but local enterprises and patrons helped her by furnishing classrooms that were leased from the state for 100,000 rubles a year.

There are about 500 registered independent schools in the Russian Federation, enrolling some 25,000 out of a total of 20 million school children, less than 1 percent (A. Baiduzhy, op. cit.). Tkachenko affirms that the Ministry of Education will provide special help to those independent schools that are "unique test sites and new teaching methods are being worked out. . . . In the foreseeable future the share of private schools in Russia is hardly likely to exceed 2 percent to 3 percent."

While the recourse to market forces is enhancing quality in education and leading to greater diversity, divisiveness, distrust, and escalation of expectations, it is also furthering inequality in access to education. Schools opting for differentiation and individualization have been able to reduce the number of students enrolled in their classes, introduce competitive entrance examinations, add subjects which have status appeal to an elite group of students, and employ professors from higher educational institutions to add prestige to their institutions. On the other hand, some of the critics of alternative schools maintain that many of them, state and nonstate, have introduced little in the way of innovation except for a change in name. In fact, they contend that very few of the schools in the Federation have departed from traditional practices.

In order to attain legal status as a school and to administer state examinations, the nonstate schools must be officially recognized and certified by the Ministry of Education. Today many of the independent schools are not registered and do not have the right to issue graduation certificates to students. Some principals have made arrangements for their students to take examinations in other state schools or private ones that have been registered. The Ministry's Director for the Preparation of Innovative and Nonstate Programs, Aleksandr Kuzyakin, observes that, in contrast to the elite state schools, many of the nonstate schools offer a below-average level of education. On the other hand, the flight of some of the best teachers and administrators from regular public schools to elite gymnasiums and lyceums or to private schools and business enterprises has contributed to a further decline in the prestige of some of the regular public schools.

Natalya Gara, director of the Russian Ministry's Department of Curriculum, believes that definite progress can be achieved in diversifying and individualizing teaching and the school curriculum in all schools if the teachers and principals are willing to take the initiative (Pista Monks, "Princess Diana Signals a Revolution," *Times Educational Supplement*, January 29, 1993, p. 13). "Teachers are free to draw up their own approved programs of teaching . . . 20 percent of teaching time is free so the school or teacher can choose what to teach during this set-aside time." True as this may be, freedom and variety in the curriculum will have to be backed with money and new teacher education courses before the innovative programs have any real impact on most Russian schools and teachers.

Sadly, there is very little money available and dynamic, creative, and self-directive Russian teachers know there is little relationship between the effort they put into their classroom activities and the reward they receive. As one teacher put it: "Why should I go through the stress of developing new teaching methods, enriching the content, and upsetting conservative colleagues and parents?"

Far too many Russian teachers still rely on "commands and orders." Such traditional teaching routines no longer work in many schools but neither do some of the more democratic methods. School government is successful in a few schools but a disaster in others. The complaint is frequently heard that pupils have too many rights without obligations. Many students are refusing to volunteer to clean classrooms, serve as monitors, and assist in maintaining school order.

Eduard Dneprov hoped to transform state schools into public institutions with greater citizen and parent participation.

He soon discovered that all too often the democratic goals and procedures were not fully understood and participatory activities haphazardly undertaken. On the other hand, pedagogical councils that were restricted to school personnel and elected as members of a collective had limited success in determining school policies.

In times of financial crisis, as exists in Russia today, the switch from schools that meet communal needs to those that cater to individual and local demands in a diverse society is likely to impose costs that may become prohibitive. The one hope is that by giving entrepreneurship free reign, the economy will recover and the public purse will be sufficiently replenished to pay for all the innovative educational programs. On the other hand, any decisions to transfer public school property to cooperatives or into private hands is likely to arouse widespread opposition.

Higher Education

The extremely high admission standards set by a growing number of higher education institutions, so high in fact that most graduates from regular state schools are turned away, are creating problems for many families. Even students receiving private tutoring experience difficulty in gaining admission and often are forced to enroll in preparatory faculties of higher education institutions with very high tuition fees. All this is happening despite the shortage of applicants at many of the universities and institutes. It is said that such practices raise the prestige image of the higher education institutions and justify the charging of high fees. In spite of this, many parents at great personal sacrifice pay to have their children tutored, and in some cases, enroll them in preparatory courses at higher education institutions.

Inga Prelovskaya maintains that rumors about the declining prestige of higher education are exaggerated. In contrast to 210 applications for every 100 spots in higher education institutions in that year, there were 195 applicants in 1993–94. Law, psychology, and foreign language faculties still have five applicants for each place but this is not true for other departments of the universities. Higher education administrators are certain that an over-all enrollment shortfall will take place in their institutions for the 1994–95 academic year in view of the continuing decline in the secondary school enrollment. They contend that this will force them to accept inadequately prepared students to fill enrollment quotas as a means of avoiding staff reductions and a shortfall in institutional financing. Unfortunately, the greatest decline in enrollment continues to occur in the technical institutes mainly because there is a lack of employment of their graduates (Inga Prelovskaya, "Rumors," *Izvestia,* September 30, 1993. *CDPSP*, Vol. XLV, No. 39, 1993, p. 24).

Traditionally, a university was considered to be much stronger and more prestigious than an academy, and both were considered more prestigious than an institute. It was taken for granted that only those higher education institutions that conducted basic research and offered graduate training in the basic disciplines could carry the name university. All of this is no longer true.

Of the 250 higher education institutions of the Federation in 1992, only 41 were officially recognized as universities. One year later the number calling themselves universities had increased to 92. There was a huge backlog of applications from academies and institutes documenting why the State Committee on Higher Education should recognize them as universities.

The Polygraphic Institute and the Gnesin Institute of Music are now academies, and the Moscow Institute of Aviation Technology, the Moscow Forestry Institute, the Bauman Higher Institute, and the Lenin Pedagogical Institute are just a few of the institutes which have become universities. Moreover, many are adding the name "State" to distinguish themselves from private institutions and hoping that they will thereby be given increased financial support in developing Russian sciences.

The procedure for petitioning for a change in name requires an institution to prepare a thick file of documents describing the activities of the institution, its curriculum, and its scientific and research accomplishments, together with the approval of the institution's academic associations and the local political executive authority. Once accepted by the State Committee, the petition is submitted to the appropriate scientific councils for approval. Beginning in 1994, however, the State Committee has announced that official state approval will no longer be needed for a change of name. At the present rate of name changing, soon there will be no institutes left in the Federation (Vyacheslav Baskov, "A Light Potion," *New Times*, No. 245, 1993, pp. 26–27).

The declining value of the ruble has had a serious effect on academic life. The flow of foreign newspapers, literature, and journals into Russian libraries and research institutes has diminished and in many cases ceased entirely. It is increasingly difficult for academic institutions to finance domestic and foreign travel for their own and foreign scholars (Aleksei Vasilyev, "The Russian Intelligentsia Must Be Saved Now," *Izvestia*, April 24, 1992, p. 7).

Far from Moscow, in Siberia, a real catastrophe is unfolding. Not far from Novosibirsk lies the famous Akademgorodok, noted for its liberal spirit, scientific research accomplishments, and the first mathematics-physics secondary schools and Olympiads, which were founded in the Khrushchev era. The status and educational accomplishments of the professors were higher than in any other part of the Federation except Moscow. Now it is in dire straits. The personnel are paid extremely low wages and its scientists are completely demoralized. Isolated in Siberia, they have few opportunities to supplement their incomes with additional research work. The scientific town only has its institutes. Unless financial resources are provided soon, the university's scientific center will completely disintegrate.

A similar fate may befall the Moscow Physical-Technical Institute (PTI) and the Moscow State Technical University (MSTU), which were until recent years restricted academic and research institutions. Once lavishly subsidized by the military as a defense research center, the PTI is hoping to survive by increasing the number of fee-paying students from former Soviet republics and other nations. On the other hand, MSTU has developed a program for educating deaf and hearing-impaired students and is also recruiting foreign students. Unfortunately, the number of foreign students in Russia is decreasing now that state subsidized scholarships are no longer available. In the 1980s there were over 120,000 foreign students in Russia; now there are some 16,000, with about 350 of them from the US. Tuition for foreign students in 1992 ranged from $1,500 to $6,000 for short-term courses. Unless there is a more generous transfusion of government money to these and Russia's other higher education institutions, many will have to close their doors. In an effort to survive, some may have to lower their entrance requirements and raise their quota for fee-paying students.

The economic crisis is also taking its toll in that fewer young and talented students are pursuing undergraduate and graduate study in the traditional disciplines of the natural sciences, mathematics, engineering, and technical specialties since there are greater manpower needs in many other new and emerging fields. Even more worrisome, 30 percent of the members of the faculties of Moscow higher education establishments have left their positions to take appointments abroad or enter the business world. Many of the higher education institutions have opened departments of economics, business management, accounting, and jurisprudence to attract students ("What a School-Leaver Should Know," *New Times*, No. 27, 1991, p. 15).

On the other hand, Patrice Lumumba People's Friendship University (PFU), founded in the 1960s to educate students from the Third World countries, appears not only to have survived but to be flourishing. Prior to 1991, Russian students were admitted solely on recommendations from regional Party committees, and Third World students by approval of the Central Committee of the Party. When Professor Vladimir Filipov became rector in 1992 there were ten times fewer first-year students from foreign countries than in the 1980s.

He is quoted as saying: "When my predecessor, Rector Stanis, went to the Ministry of Higher Education in the 1970s to request more money to improve the science programs, he was bluntly told: 'Teach Marxism-Leninism to your Africans and you will need no other science'" ("New Rector's Concerns," *Moscow News*, No. 35, 1993, p. 12).

As the dean of the Department of Physics and Mathematics of PFU prior to becoming rector, Filipov had set such rigid standards that his department graduated only 40 percent of the entering freshmen. In fact, graduates had to qualify for two diplomas, one in a major discipline and the other in a foreign language. For the 1933 academic year, 800 Russian and 300 foreign students were admitted, in contrast to former years when 70 percent of the student body was from Third World countries. The present policy is to recruit as many students as possible from the republics and regions of the Russian Federation and others from the West. The Russian State Committee on Higher Education in 1993 officially recognized forty-one higher education institutions as universities. The PFU was ranked third after Moscow State University and St. Petersburg University.

The Novgorod Polytechnical Institute is a new and unique higher education institution. Conceived as a multilevel and multispecialized establishment, it is made up of a polytechnical institute, a vocational college, a pedagogical institute, a specialized polytechnical school, a teacher lyceum, and a gymnasium. It is now opening branches in Borovichi and Staraya Russa ("People," *New Times*, No. 49, 1993, p. 29).

A bombshell was aimed at the higher education establishment in September 1993 with a proposal to revolutionize the organization and finance of Russia's system of higher education. The Russian Ministry of Finance and the State Committee on Higher Education objected to Russia's state-run higher education institutions, most of which are highly specialized, being under the jurisdiction of some twenty-one different state ministries and financed by the central budget (Andrei Baiduzhy, "The Collapse of the Schools," *Nezavisimaya gazeta*, December 14, 1993, p. 6. *CDPSP*, Vol. XLV, No. 50, 1993, p. 17).

One of the proposals is to transfer the majority of the higher pedagogical institutions out of the structure of the Russian Ministry of Education and into the jurisdiction of the republic, territorial, and regional Departments of Education and Budgets. The proposal also calls for most of the other higher educational institutions to be taken away from the many federal ministries and transferred to the government structures of regional and local authorities. However, the Russian Federation State Committee on Higher Education would retain under its control, and within the state budget, those higher education institutions which serve Russian needs. Moreover, the federal government would continue to allocate federal monies to higher educational institutions for the training of a specific number of specialists that are in short supply and greatly needed by the state. These institutions would have to compete for grants to train the needed specialists. By no longer financing higher education schools based on student enrollment, pressures would be reduced on the federal budget.

With the disintegration of the centralized economy, it is evident that Moscow no longer is able to determine the personnel needs of industrial, commercial, educational, and other government and social services. The reformers maintain that regional and local authorities know best the educational needs for their own specialists and teachers and the amount of financing required for training programs.

Viktor Bolotov, Russia's Deputy Minister of Education, fears that transferring the higher pedagogical institutions out of the Ministry of Education will undermine the coordination of teacher training and school reform and have an adverse effect on the entire system of education. The rectors of these institutions believe that once the transfers are made to the regions and the institutions are no longer under the Ministry of Education, many of them will become comprehensive universities in which teacher education will be downgraded. They point out that of the more than 100 Russian higher education institutions that have been transformed into universities and academies, more than half were teacher training institutions. Since the regions need a vast array of specialized personnel, the temptation is ever present to transform teacher education establishments into comprehensive universities. When this is done, teacher education departments are likely to lose out to other departments in the struggle for financing. In fact, after pedagogical institutes were transformed into universities in Tver, Kaliningrad, Yakutia, and Kalmykia, the Russian Ministry of Education tried to establish new teacher training institutes.

is proposed transition in teacher education, if it is ented in the Russian Federation, may come to resemble a ment which took place in the United States in the late nii... teenth and early twentieth centuries. The normal schools that were training elementary school teachers were transformed into state teachers colleges and then into state universities. The newly established midwestern state universities offered professional education departments to train secondary school teachers, and many of the liberal arts colleges appointed professors of education to the established academic departments of philosophy and psychology. This evolving diversity in teacher training programs in the United States was in response to the dynamic changes taking place in society and signalled a willingness to experiment with alternative patterns of teacher education.

The Russian Budget

One of the most pressing problems facing the Federation is inflation, which is largely due to subsidizing inefficient farms and enterprises, satisfying populist demands for social protection, contriving to finance many of the former republics of the Soviet Union, and supporting the poorer regions of the Federation. Minister of Finance Boris Fyodorov placed the blame for the deficit on the government itself. Increasingly every minister acts as a lobbyist for his branch of the economy. A government program is approved, then a few weeks later each minister goes to parliament and starts lobbying for additional rubles. Battles are waged constantly over budgetary appropriations between government blocs, the executive branch, and the Supreme Soviet; Moscow, St. Petersburg, and the provinces; the national republics and the other regions of the Federation; and the many interest groups. These battles grow more intense and fierce each year.

The Russian Minister of Finance repeatedly chastised the Russian Supreme Soviet for appropriating large sums of rubles for its own socially oriented programs. Many of the members had failed to shed their socialist mentality and were committed to guaranteeing social protection to the masses. Although the Supreme Soviet had mandated that the deficit should not exceed 5 percent of the national product, it continued to approve huge appropriations to uphold the ideal of social justice. Consequently, social welfare expenditures presently account for roughly 45 percent of the federal budget. On the other hand, by law 10 percent of the country's budget is supposed to be allocated to the schools. The actual amount allocated in 1993 was 5.7 percent. In August of 1993 the Ministry of Finance admitted that it had failed to provide some 50 percent of the budgeted rubles needed for salaries of teachers and even less for repair and construction of school buildings.

The Russian Minister of Finance submitted a proposal to the Supreme Soviet to reduce the size of the deficit by curbing payments into the pension and social insurance funds and increasing the VAT tax by 7 percent. The Central Bank made matters worse by issuing a flood of new rubles to cover underfunded credits. As a result, the 1993 third quarter budget showed a deficit of 8.6 trillion rubles. This was four times more than the budget shortfall for the previous two quarters. Subventions, credits, and subsidies exceeded one trillion rubles.

More than a dozen of the territories and provinces of Russia contributed over one-half of their total revenues to the federal budget, but received in return barely one-fourth of what they had transferred. On the other hand, fourteen of the Russian national republics received more than they contributed. To overcome these disparities, starting in 1994 the federal and regional budgets will be completely separated. This indeed will be a revolutionary change. The federal parliament will establish its own independent federal taxes and the republic and regional parliaments will establish theirs. This will end the traditional unitary budget system under which taxes were paid first to the republic and regional governments, which then passed the revenue collected on to the central government. Little wonder that the governor of Nizhni Novgorod, Boris Nemtsov (Vladimir Ionov, "Money for the Lazy," *Moscow News*, Nos. 2–3, 1993, p. 12), was unhappy with Yeltsin's 1993 budget for giving a shot in the arm to those regions that lagged behind in privatization and still refused to open free business zones. "They keep half the tax revenue while those that are committed to reform keep only 5 percent." As a result, Nizhni Novgorod faced a thirty billion ruble deficit at a time when the Federation had delegated to the province fiscal responsibility for general education and vocation schools, pedagogical and agricultural colleges, the construction of housing and roads, and the maintenance of communal transport.

Yekaterinburg, Samara, Vladimir, and Moscow faced similar financial problems. Consequently, the more prosperous regions advocated greater decentralization. Stavropol territory, for example, demanded the status of a self-governing zone with the right to fix its own tax rates. Even more worrisome, more and more republics and regions refused to transfer certain of their revenues to the central treasury.

The estimated revenues for the 1994 budget are twenty-two trillion rubles, with expenditures targeted at forty-six trillion. Russia's First Deputy Minister of Finance S. Dubinin warned: "If we don't receive any new revenues, inflation will take on such proportions that million ruble notes will actually be required to keep up with it" (Vladimir Gurevich, "In Budget Ecstasy," *Moskoviskye nvosti*, No. 30, 1993, p. A 13. *CDPSP*, Vol. 29, 1993, p. 9). In spite of this warning, the Central Bank has continued to extend credits of billions of rubles to enterprises even though some 70 percent is never recovered (I. Savvatsyva "If You Want to be a Minister of Finance," *Komsomolskaya pravda*, April 13, 1993, p. 7).

In late August 1993, the Russian Supreme Soviet overrode President Yeltsin's veto of the budget, which would have resulted in what Russia's Minister of Finance Fyodorov called a "catastrophic" budget deficit of 218 trillion rubles (1,200 rubles to $1 US). Consequently, Fyodorov declared a state of financial emergency after having to approve payment of wage and salary arrears for all employees of budget-financed bodies, which included those in the education sector. He stated that the only hope of improving the financial situation would have to come from rescinding many of the promises for additional social entitlements and expanding the tax base for additional revenue. With the defeat of the reformers in the December 1993 parliamentary election, however, it is unlikely that Yeltsin will opt for fiscal restraint.

Unfortunately, the "leftover" principle of financing social welfare, health, and education still prevails in the Russian Federation. Many factories and enterprises continue to be responsible for the social welfare of their employees, including housing and schools. Hence the pressure continues to have regional and local governments levy taxes to finance social welfare programs. Most government officials, however, are in no mood to take on these added burdens. For example, the Petrodvorets Watch Company is now a private corporation (Anita Raghavan, "Profits? No, Please!" *Wall Street Journal*, November 10, 1993, p. A 1), but it continues to finance a sports program, kindergarten, medical clinic, and housing. About 25 percent of the factory profits pay for social services. Now the factory is proposing that the workers contribute toward the cost of housing and that the kindergarten and sports programs be self-financed. Or, better still, that the local government finance these social services.

A still greater problem is the very precarious financial straits in which the military now finds itself. Some 60 percent of the service personnel of the military did not receive their pay in July 1993; some still had not received the June payment. Over 77,000 discharged officers were without apartments and more than 125,000 military families lacked housing. The Ministry of Finance revealed in August 1993 that it owed the army's budget two trillion rubles.

All hospitals and medical centers are operating on drastically reduced budgets. The Kashirka Cancer Center, the Herzen Clinic, and the Institute of Medical Radiology have closed their doors. Many centers were not only unable to buy medicine in February 1993 but also had not paid their personnel for many months.

Michel Hester describes the impact of the financial crisis on towns in the Arctic regions ("Moscow's Budget Cuts," *Moscow Times*, March 27, 1993, p. 6). Kosisty, located 2,100 kilometers north of the Arctic Circle, is one of a dozen outposts being closed. "For those who remain, there are no doctors, no teachers." Khatanga, another fishing and hunting outpost of some 5,000 people, lost its school and hospital. About 50,000 people have left the North region over the past three years.

There are reports of an estimated 10,000 homeless children in St. Petersburg alone. Other cities are facing similar numbers. Many of these children are placed in children's homes, boarding houses, and special boarding schools. In many cases they are abandoned by their parents in railroad and metro stations and are too young to know their names. Another large number are children deprived of parental care due to alcoholism or imprisonment. Infant homes are swamped with abandoned babies. Today families are defending themselves from economic hardship by postponing and, in some cases, deciding against having children. This, in the long run, will have many implications for the education sector.

In September 1993 Yeltsin signed a decree "On Measures to Prevent Child Neglect and Juvenile Delinquency and on the Protection of Minors' Rights." Leonid Kurant of the Russian Ministry of Internal Affairs' Department for Prevention of Juvenile Crime reported that about 20,000 youth are in education and labor colonies. The decree mandates the establishment of special institutions for teenagers requiring special rehabilitation and the reorganization of holding and placement centers into temporary detention centers for juvenile criminals within the structure of the Ministry of Education. Left unsaid is the financial inability of the Ministry to fund all of its present commitments to education (Aleksei Chelnokov, "Problem Teenagers," *Izvestia*, September 10, p. 4. *CDPSP*, Vol. XLV, No. 36, 1993, p. 24).

With the dire needs of some families to consider, the Russian Council of Ministers has continued the entitlement of a lump sum allowance in the amount of five times the monthly minimum wage paid to each family upon the birth of a child. Moreover, 1.5 percent of the monthly minimum wage per day is granted to each child enrolled in vocational and general education schools. In higher education institutions, undergraduate students receive a monthly stipend of 4,500 rubles and graduates 9,000.

Professional people and pensioners on fixed incomes cannot exist without taking other jobs. The fields in which the largest number of people hold additional employment are reported to be public health, education, culture, and science (Maria Matskevich and Leonid Kosselman, "Adapting to Circumstances," *Nezavisimaya gazeta,* Issue 2–3, May 1993, p. 8).

Russian Education at a Critical Point

Yeltsin has never been able to deliver on his promise to make education a priority, in order to develop Russia's intellectual, cultural, and economic potential ("Decree No. 1 of the President of the Russian Federation: On Priority Measures to Promote Education," *Uchitel'skaya gazeta*, June 11, 1991. Translated by Ben Eklof).

> Article II. Beginning January 1, 1992, to institute a salary increase for employees in education; increase the average wage or salary in education. . . . For instructors at institutions of higher education, twice the level of industrial workers. . . . For teachers and other employees in pedagogy, not lower than the average salary in industry in the RSFSR. For instructional support and other personnel in education the average salary pertaining to comparable work in the industrial sector in order to maintain the above wage and salary equivalencies until January 1, 1995.

Local authorities pay for the cost of building new schools and maintaining existing ones, while the central government pays the salaries of the teachers. It is estimated that of the budgetary expenditure on education, about 80 percent goes for teachers' salaries. If any increases in teachers' salaries are granted beyond those contracted by the Ministry, the national republics and regions must draw upon their own resources to pay them. Although the consolidated budget in 1993 allocates 176.4 billion rubles to the support of general, vocational, technical, and higher education, representing 10.6 percent of the total budget of the Russian Federation, Tkachenko claims that only 5.7 percent is actually being received. Things are even worse with the repair and construction of schools (Andrei Baiduzhy, op. cit.).

The Minister of Education fully understands that the schools will never be adequately funded unless the massive subsidies granted to inefficient farms and enterprises, the poorer republics and regions, and pet projects of government ministers are either eliminated or greatly reduced.

The erosion of salaries in the education sector brought about by inflation and the differentiation in wages among various categories of workers is well documented in the Russian press. In March 1992, the earnings of the highest-paid 10 percent of employees grew to eleven times, and by September to sixteen times, the lowest paid workers. The extent of true salary differentials was revealed by the chairwoman of the Donetsk Province trade union of medical personnel when she pointed out that, in 1992, the pay of a highly qualified surgeon with the rank of professor was only one quarter of that of a cleaning woman working in a mine. Prominent scholars who conducted organized research in 1991 received between 3,000 and 3,300 rubles a month, while the salary of the Russian Minister of Education was slightly more than 5,000 rubles.

On April 20, 1993, a cost-of-living adjustment of salaries in the education sector was legislated, along with the indexation of salaries, and 200 criteria to determine salary adjustments (Ben Eklof, "The Most Difficult Year in the History of Our Schools," *ISSR Newsletter*, Vol. 2, No. 1, 1993, p. 3). However, revenue to finance the increases in salaries still must come in part from the budgets of the local governments. Unfortunately, not all local governments are able to meet the federally mandated targets.

Knovolov ("Government to Pay Part of Expenditures," *Izvestia*, January 28, 1993, p. 1) points to the fact that as state and collective farms are being reorganized, responsibility for school facilities and their upkeep are transferred to the budgets of local governments, along with the burden of supporting hospitals, apartments, and preschools. Many local governments are insisting that the federal budget must accept responsibility for at least half of the maintenance costs of the schools since the local tax revenue is not sufficient to cover these costs.

Some schools are engaging in various kinds of business enterprises in order to make a profit and give students experience as entrepreneurs. Yambourg, a progressive Moscow school principal, sponsors a school-based business that publishes textbooks and innovative teacher materials. The earned profits enable the school to provide services to students that are not funded by the state. Also there is a suggestion that schools having financial problems should be allowed to go bankrupt and reorganize. It is even suggested that perhaps financially ailing schools should be sold to private individuals or converted into cooperatives. The movement to a free market has many implications for education unheard of in the history of Russia.

As the number of alternative school programs and the variety and kinds of schools continue to grow, the Ministry is taking steps to establish national standards and accreditation procedures. To many Russians it is disturbing to know that children in the Federation do not have a level playing field with equal opportunity to master the basic core curriculum. The controversial "equal school delivery standards" are now the responsibility of each republic and regional educational authority to maintain. Fair opportunity to achieve the required learning outcomes that will be assessed nationally implies that all schools will accept and teach the common core curriculum that is mandated by the state standards; teachers will be professionally competent and able to teach the core; instructional materials and teaching aids will be available to promote mastery; administrations will be supportive and committed to attaining high standards; and resources will be adequate to finance the entire program. In the absence of any of these conditions, the desired high standards in all schools in the Federation will not be attained.

It is quite clear that the current education reform has resulted in winners and losers. The winners are the academically talented students in cities who have the innate ability to compete in entrance examinations to elitist gymnasia, lyceums, and in-depth profiles and the money to pay extra fees for additional courses or enter the growing number of independent and experimental schools. The losers are the students at "risk" who are not able to cope with the traditional knowledge-based, compulsory nine-year curriculum, in spite of the curriculum reform, and cannot hope to find a place in a vocational or trade school. Because of the economic crisis, those who drop out of school and take a job or "work the streets" to supplement the family's income are the real losers.

The major issue confronting Chairman Yagodin and his deputy, Shadrikov, of the former USSR State Committee for Public Education, and Eduard Dneprov, the Russian Minister of Education, continues to badger the current minister, E. Tkachenko. How rapidly and pervasively should educational reforms be pushed ahead? Under Gorbachev and Yeltsin this question divided the "liberals" from the "conservatives." The liberal leadership of the USSR State Committee for Public Education introduced and implemented educational reforms much faster than the conservative Party bureaucrats could digest. Although the reforms of the USSR State Committee for Public Education were more cautious than those advocated by Dneprov and the supporters of Matveyev and Soloveichik, they were based on sound principles and carried out in a professional manner by many of the *nomenklatura*. On the other hand, Dneprov's aggressive policy of educational reform alienated a great many of the teachers, principals, and bureaucrats.

As the power struggle continued to unfold in 1991–92, the orientations of the various interest groups became more and more obvious. The conservatives took a stand for gradual and evolutionary reform, retention of some central controls, and preservation of the best of the past achievements of the Soviet educational system. On the other hand, having nothing but contempt for the Communist traditions of Soviet education, its bureaucratic monopoly, and the research work of academician researchers of the APS, Dneprov believed that only radical and sweeping reforms could destroy the totalitarian thinking and practices of the past. The conservatives charged that Dneprov had no concern for the impact that such radical transformations were having on the teachers, administrators, students, and parents. They objected to the denigration of the educational achievements of the past and to the efforts being made to destroy them.

Certainly the appointment of E. Tkachenko as Minister of Education in December 1992 has signaled a slower and more cautious approach to reform, a time for critical analysis and evaluation of the best of the Soviet educational traditions as well as the recent reforms, and a rethinking of the unmet needs of children and society.

The Russian general education school is no longer the unified and articulated institution in which, in the past, students automatically moved from the first through the eleventh grade. Not every ninth grader will find the tenth grade accessible. Tkachenko defends the new promotion policy by saying that "a teenager must understand that knowledge is capital and must be fought for. . . . We are not going to forcibly drive anyone into the schools" (Baiduzhy, op. cit.). However, he does concede that, since a majority of students will be retained in the regular eleven-year general education school, differentiated teaching methods as well as optional and integrated subjects are basic to the reform. All students, therefore, will no longer be required to follow a uniform track and a common curriculum taught in a uniform way.

In the next phase of Russian education reform, the Ministry must face the challenge of improving the professional quality of Russian teachers. Differentiated school types and curricula demand a view of teaching as one of a personal relationship between teacher and student that is intimate, warm, and friendly in the process of mastering the curriculum content. This concept was well expressed in the manifesto, "Pedagogy of Cooperation," proclaimed by Matveyev and Soloveichik during the "1986–88 War of the Media." Reforming the curriculum and school structure alone will not suffice. Teachers with a firm conviction in the ability of students to learn, a dynamic personality that inspires students to study, and the capacity to create, choose, and use their own curriculum materials and teaching methods are essential to democratic teaching.

This will be only the first step toward establishing a federal professional education system in which accreditation, state licensure, advanced certification, and standards will be merged. Such an accreditation program will contribute to the endorsement of valid and reliable standards in Russian schools and be viewed as a tool to maintaining quality teacher preparation standards throughout the Federation.

The assumptions are that the teachers of Russia will teach the prescribed common core content and that all children will master it. The state-approved textbooks and state-mandated tests will impose a framework for the teaching of the core. Teachers in the classrooms in the various republics, territories, regions, and local areas may now actually make many of their own choices as to the emphasis and interpretation they wish to give to the curriculum content as well as to its presentation. Even teachers in the same school building may be teaching different versions of the federally mandated general education core. The taught curriculum very often differs from the official one. Moreover, there is collateral learning that goes far beyond what both the education authorities and the teacher intend. Students have a way of picking up traits of teachers, which in the past were all too often authoritarian and autocratic. How teachers teach is an intimate part of what they teach.

As a result of the reforms initiated by the USSR State Committee for Public Education in 1988–91 and those initiated under the leadership of Dneprov at VNIK and the Russian Ministry of Education, many of the general education schools of the Russian Federation are more democratic, self-regulating, flexible, and humane than their predecessors in the USSR were. On the other hand, some of them are extremely elitist, narrowly specialized, and selectively differentiated. Perhaps critics are justified in contending that the reform is primarily a restoration of the pre-Soviet and traditional models and is being carried on, for the most part, by former second echelon *nomenklatura* education officials rather than by the dissident "Democrats" of the *perestroika* period.

The deepening economic crisis and the instability of the political situation have marginalized the liberal reformist leadership and fueled a yearning on the part of many teachers to return to a more stable learning and teaching environment. Most certainly the appointment of E. Tkachenko as Minister of Education is a victory for the "centrists" in the education establishment and has brought a temporary stabilization to the Russian educational scene. His leadership may also have the consequence of elevating a new conservative orientation to a permanent power role in the Ministry. Continued educational reform in Russia and the scope of future innovative initiatives no doubt will depend upon the extent to which Yeltsin is able to retain popular support as a person and advance his political and economic reforms. The final shape that the Russian educational system will take and the goals to which it will be committed are far from certain in the soon-to-be twenty-first century.

Index

REFERENCE BOOKS IN INTERNATIONAL EDUCATION

EDWARD R. BEAUCHAMP
Series Editor

EDUCATION IN THE PEOPLE'S REPUBLIC OF CHINA, PAST AND PRESENT
An Annotated Bibliography
by Franklin Parker and Betty June Parker

EDUCATION IN SOUTH ASIA
A Select Annotated Bibliography
by Philip G. Altbach, Denzil Saldanha, and Jeanne Weiler

TEXTBOOKS IN THE THIRD WORLD
Policy, Content and Context
by Philip G. Altbach and Gail P. Kelly

EDUCATION IN JAPAN
A Source Book
by Edward R. Beauchamp and Richard Rubinger

WOMEN'S EDUCATION IN THE THIRD WORLD
by David H. Kelly and Gail P. Kelly

EDUCATION IN ISRAEL
A Source Book
by Yaacov Iram

MINORITY STATUS AND SCHOOLING
by Margaret A. Gibson and John V. Ogbu

TEACHERS AND TEACHING IN THE DEVELOPING WORLD
by Val D. Rust and Per Dalin

RUSSIAN AND SOVIET EDUCATION, 1731–1989
A Multilingual Annotated Bibliography
by William W. Brickman and John T. Zepper

EDUCATION IN SUB-SAHARAN AFRICA
A Source Book
by George E.F. Urch

ARAB EDUCATION IN TRANSITION
A Source Book
by Byron G. Massialas and Samir A. Jarrar

EDUCATION AND CULTURAL DIFFERENCES
New Perspectives
by Douglas Ray and Deo H. Poonwassie

CONTEMPORARY PERSPECTIVES IN COMPARATIVE EDUCATION
edited by Robin J. Burns and Anthony R. Welch

EDUCATION IN THE ARAB GULF STATES AND THE ARAB WORLD
An Annotated Bibliographic Guide
by Nagat El-Sanabary

INTERNATIONAL AND HISTORICAL ROOTS OF AMERICAN HIGHER EDUCATION
by W.H. Cowley and Don Williams

EDUCATION IN ENGLAND AND WALES
An Annotated Bibliography
by Franklin Parker and Betty June Parker

CHINESE EDUCATION
Problems, Policies, and Prospects
edited, with an introduction by Irving Epstein

EARLY CHILDHOOD EDUCATION IN ASIA AND THE PACIFIC
A Source Book
edited by Stephanie Feeney

UNDERSTANDING EDUCATIONAL REFORM IN GLOBAL CONTEXT
Economy, Ideology, and the State
edited by Mark B. Ginsburg

EDUCATION AND SOCIAL CHANGE IN KOREA
by Don Adams and Esther E. Gottlieb

EDUCATION AND DISABILITY IN CROSS-CULTURAL PERSPECTIVE
edited by Susan J. Peters

RUSSIAN EDUCATION
Tradition and Transition
by Brian Holmes, Gerald H. Read, and Natalya Voskresenskaya

THE UNIFICATION OF GERMAN EDUCATION
by Val D. Rust and Diane Rust

THREE DECADES OF PEACE EDUCATION AROUND THE WORLD
An Anthology
edited by Robin J. Burns
and Robert Aspeslagh

EDUCATION AND DEVELOPMENT IN EAST ASIA
edited by Paul Morris
and Anthony Sweeting

TEACHER EDUCATION IN INDUSTRIALIZED NATIONS
Issues in Changing Social Contexts
edited by Nobuo K. Shimahara
and Ivan Z. Holowinsky

LEARNING TO TEACH IN TWO CULTURES
Japan and the United States
by Nobuo K. Shimahara
and Akira Sakai